T0365253

GOD'S MARRIAGE AND MAN'S DIVORCE

Biblical Instructions for Contemporary Families

DAVID BOUDREAUX

WESTBOW
PRESS®
A DIVISION OF THOMAS NELSON
& ZONDERVAN

WestBow Press books may be ordered through booksellers or by contacting:

WestBow Press
A Division of Thomas Nelson & Zondervan
1663 Liberty Drive
Bloomington, IN 47403
www.westbowpress.com
844-714-3454

Scripture taken from the King James Version of the Bible.

ISBN: 978-1-6642-9851-4 (sc)
ISBN: 978-1-6642-9852-1 (hc)
ISBN: 978-1-6642-9850-7 (e)

Library of Congress Control Number: 2023907646

Print information available on the last page.

WestBow Press rev. date: 05/04/2023

CONTENTS

CONTENTS

DEDICATION

I would like to dedicate this book to all the successful marriages out there that have been able to overcome the trials and tribulations of this world and have stayed together through thick and thin, for better or for worse. As a young man the one thing that I wanted more than anything else was to find the perfect partner whom I could depend on to stay with me for life. I believe it is God's plan for every person who desires to serve God, and does not have the gift to do it alone, to find the perfect mate to share their life journey with. Too often we either don't find out what God's plan is for us until it is too late, or we just don't trust him enough to wait for it to come. I believe there is a perfect man for every woman who wants to share her life with a mate in the pursuit of pleasing God. My advice to this woman is to stay diligent in prayer and pure in body and soul while you wait for God to lead you to this man. Just like God created Eve for Adam He created you for your perfect mate as well. All that is necessary for your dreams to come true is for you to trust God and wait for the man of your dreams to come. I'm not suggesting that for every woman there is a man waiting, I am saying for every woman who trust God and has a desire to live a life that is pleasing to Him with her perfect man, he will come. In our society today, being a mother and a housewife is not considered anything special, but in God's eyes woman was created mainly for this purpose and fulfilling God's will is the highest calling there is. If you desire this role in your life as a godly woman, God will make it happen. If you are a godly man that desires to serve God with the perfect woman then God has already created her for you and is preparing her for you. Just keep serving God, keep praying for her arrival in your life, and keep yourself pure in body, soul and spirit. God will bring her to you just like He created Eve and prepared her for Adam and then brought her to him.

PREFACE

This book is a compilation of information intended to prepare those who are contemplating marriage, or are already married, how to have a successful marriage based on God's Words. The Lord has requested for me to make this information available to all those who desire to have a marriage that will last, "till death do us part", or until Jesus returns to take His followers home. I have cited hundreds of verses in this work, through the guidance of the Holy Spirit, in order to create a Biblical commentary on the subject of marriage. This is a work that started over twenty five years ago and has been in progress since that time. It includes numerous real life stories and illustrations for the purpose of clarification regarding God's instructions on these topics. Many of these illustrations are collections from different professionals in their specific fields of expertise and many are instructions derived from sermons that I have heard through the years and sermons and lessons that I have taught and preached through the years. Oftentimes I have heard people say, *Wives and husbands and children don't come with instructions.* Well now they can because God has inspired me to provide that for those who are interested in doing His will in their lives. I wish I could say that I have had the perfect marriage since day one, but unfortunately for many of us, we were not blessed enough to have had the benefit of knowing or understanding God's Words early in our lives and only began to understand God's will after we had already made many mistakes. Maybe the reason I went through these experiences is because God was preparing me to make this information available to the world. In this book you will find instructions concerning marriage, divorce, having children, mixed marriages, intimate relations, family finances, God's way of guiding the home, disciplining of children, church attendance, and the appropriate celebration of holidays and a host of other topics that families will face in their struggle to have a happy home and life that is pleasing to God. One out of every two marriages end in divorce in the United States of America and the family unit is being torn apart. I believe the reason for this destruction of the family unit today, is because marriage is entered into as an experiment rather than a lifelong commitment as God intended it. To God the marital relationship has immense significance in His plan for mankind as well as the spiritual implications that it represents. I think if most people had even the slightest comprehension of the importance of this God ordained institution that it would be entered into with much more caution and preparation than it is today. My prayer and my purpose for making this information available to all, is to prepare those who are considering entering into a marital relationship as to the obstacles that they will soon face and how to overcome them. To help those who are already in a marital relationship and are currently facing situations that they are not equipped with the Word of God to face successfully. To assist those who are considering having children and have perhaps given little thought as to how it will affect their marriage. This work is the most comprehensive piece that I have personally ever seen on these topics and I believe it is probably the most needed information in our nation today.

CHAPTER 1

Marriage in the Beginning

**The Three Most Important Decisions
You Will Make in Your Lifetime**

There are three major decisions each person will have to make during his or her lifetime that are more important than any other decisions the person will ever make.

1. What to do about his or her soul
2. What to do about his or her service
3. What to do about his or her spouse

In the following chapters, we are going to discuss each of these decisions in great detail.

What to Do about Your Soul

The first question, what to do about your soul, revolves around the decision to accept the gift of eternal life through Jesus Christ or reject it. The type of life you will live and the types of relationships you will have all depend on this decision. Because of the significance of this decision, we are going to cover this in the very first chapter.

What to Do about Your Service

Provided that you choose to accept Christ, the second question is whether you are the kind of person who has the ability or gift to spend your entire life serving God alone or if you need to have a lifetime mate with whom to share your life and serve God. To serve God, you must have a pure vessel or body to offer to God for His service. If you aren't able to keep yourself pure as a single man or woman (through celibacy), then the only other way to remain pure in God's eyes is through marriage. If you haven't chosen to accept Christ yet, then hopefully this book will help you to understand why this decision is so important.

What to Do about Your Spouse

This brings us to the third most important decision you will ever make, and that is what to do about your spouse. If you have concluded that being single is not an option for you as you strive to stay pure in the sight of God, then choosing the right person to marry will now be the most significant decision you will make in your life. The apostle Paul and Jesus both proclaimed that the best thing a single person can do to serve God is to stay single, but as I have pointed out, this isn't always possible. For a Christian, the only alternative to a life totally dedicated to God alone is to live a life dedicated to Him with a wife or husband.

God created us, and He knows most of us won't be able to live a life of celibacy. Because of this, He created a wife for Adam. God also knows all about you and your needs, and if you are the kind of person who doesn't do well alone, then God has probably already created a spouse for you too. Now let's look at these verses describing what God did to fulfill this need.

It Isn't Good for Man to Be Alone

"It is not good that man should be alone. I will make him an helpmeet for him" (Gen. 2:18).The word *helpmeet* comes from the Hebrew word *ezer*, which means a worthy helper or aide. The woman, created to help or aid man, was fashioned using one of Adam's ribs. "And the Lord God caused a deep sleep to fall upon Adam, and he slept: and He took one of his ribs, and closed up the flesh instead thereof" (Gen. 2:21).

The woman was created for the man and brought unto him. After I went through many trials and tribulations related to bad relationships in my personal life and then spent several years being alone, I was no longer looking for a wife. I had given up on the idea of ever having a happy marriage; that is when God brought the wife He had been preparing for me straight to my doorstep.

I used to tell people that they needed to go out if they were going to find someone, because God wasn't going to deliver the right person to their doorstep. But I was wrong. Just like God did for Adam, He created her for me, prepared her for me, and brought her to me. I would have saved myself a heaping helping of heartache if I had just been patient enough to wait for her from the start. Unfortunately, at the time I didn't know this was how it was supposed to work. "And the rib, which the Lord God had taken from man, made He a woman, and brought her unto the man" (Gen. 2:22).

The Woman Was Created for the Man

"Neither was the man created for the woman; but the woman for the man" (1Cor. 11:9). Adam called her *woman* (Hebrew, *ishshah*) because she came from the man (Hebrew, *ish*). She was taken out of the man. In other words, Adam gave her part of himself. "And Adam said, this is now bone of my bone, and flesh of my flesh: she shall be called Woman because she was taken out of Man" (Gen. 2:23).

This is why women are addressed by titles derived from men's titles. For example, *woman, ma'am, madam,* and *maiden* are derived from *man. Ms., Miss,* and *Mrs.* are derived from *Mr.* and so forth. The woman was given to the man to be his helper.

The Woman Is Equal to the Man

It has been said that God used a rib to create the woman because she came from Adam's side, not from his head or foot. She is to be by his side as an equal. Notice in the verse cited above that Adam proclaimed she was "bone of my bone and flesh of my flesh." This is because man is God's highest creation in His eyes, and for Him to create someone else to be just as significant (equal), He would have to create her from the man.

They Became One Flesh

The genders were also created to accommodate human needs and were partly intended to create a bond between the husband and wife that sealed the union, which made them one together. This is part of the process that ends the two of them being individuals and helps them to become a separate, complete person together. I believe the consummation of the marriage is the final part of the process because this is when the husband gives part of himself to his wife, and they become one (John 17:21).When God gives the born-again Christian part of Himself (the Holy Ghost), that is when the Christian becomes one with God. Because of this, I also believe that the sexual experience between the husband and wife is a picture of the union between God and humankind. This is also what Adam did; he gave part of himself to Eve. This is why the Word of God stresses the importance of sexual purity both before and after the wedding.

It is also worth mentioning here that this is the same process

God uses to create spiritual birth. When we receive the Holy Spirit, we are born of God, which is what Jesus called being born again or the second birth (John 3:7).When the husband gives part of himself to his wife (through his seed), God uses this process to create life in their children. It is also interesting that this is the same method God the Father used to allow His Son to be born through a physical birth. Mary, the mother of Jesus, was impregnated through the power of the Holy Spirit and brought forth the manifestation of God bodily in the person of Jesus Christ. To make sure I'm clear, this means Jesus was the only man who ever lived who had spiritual life before He had physical life. By the way, the name Jesus means "God is salvation" or "God our rescuer," and the name Christ means "the chosen one or the anointed one."

> And, behold, thou shalt conceive in thy womb, and bring forth a son, and shalt call his name JESUS. He shall be great, and shall be called the Son of the Highest: and the Lord God shall give unto him the throne of his father David: And he shall reign over the house of Jacob for ever; and of his kingdom there shall be no end. Then said Mary unto the angel, How shall this be, seeing I know not a man? And the angel answered and said unto her, The Holy Ghost shall come upon thee, and the power of the Highest shall overshadow thee: therefore also that holy thing which shall be born of thee shall be called the Son of God. (Luke 1:31–35)

> Beware lest any man spoil you through philosophy and vain deceit, after the tradition of men, after the rudiments of the world, and not after Christ. For in him dwelleth all the fulness of the Godhead bodily. And ye are complete in him, which is the head of all principality and power. (Col. 2:8–10)

Know ye not that your bodies are the members of
Christ? shall I then take the members of Christ,
and make them the members of an harlot? God
forbid.What? know ye not that he which is joined
to an harlot is one body? for two, saith he, shall
be one flesh. But he that is joined unto the Lord is
one spirit. Flee fornication. Every sin that a man
doeth is without the body; but he that committeth
fornication sinneth against his own body. What?
know ye not that your body is the temple of the
Holy Ghost which is in you, which ye have of God,
and ye are not your own? For ye are bought with
a price: therefore glorify God in your body, and in
your spirit, which are God's. (1 Cor. 6:15–20)

Marriage Is More than Just a Physical Bond

These verses make it clear not only that the physical part of a marriage
is part of the joining process of the couple to make them become one
but also that marriage is more than just a physical connection. If this
physical joining was all marriage consisted of, then this wouldn't be
called "fornication" when it happens outside of marriage; it would
be called "marriage."

The Perfect Wife

Now let's take a more specific look at what God says about a good
wife.

Who can find a virtuous woman? For her price is
far above rubies. (Prov. 31:10)

A virtuous woman is a crown to her husband: but she that maketh ashamed is a rottonness in his bones. (Prov. 12:4)

Whoso findeth a wife findeth a good thing, and obtaineth favour of the Lord. (Prov. 18:22)

House and riches are the inheritance of fathers: and a prudent wife is from the Lord. (Prov. 19:14)

Let thy fountain be blessed and rejoice with the wife of thy youth. Let her be as the loving hind and the pleasant roe, let her breast satisfy thee at all times and be thou ravished always with her love. (Prov. 5:18–19)

A gracious woman retaineth honour and strong men retain riches. (Prov. 11:16)

Every wise woman buildeth her house but the foolish plucketh it down with her hands. (Prov. 14:1)

A virtuous woman is hard to find, but she is worth more than anything money can buy. A virtuous woman is a woman with very high moral standards. A woman of virtue is a woman of strength and valor. She is a great force for good, being chaste and morally good. This is referring to a godly woman. A godly woman is a wonderful blessing to everyone around her but especially to her husband. She is not a brawler (fighter) or contentious (arguer), but only kind words proceed from her mouth. " Whoso findeth a wife findeth a good thing, and obtaineth favour of the LORD" (Prov. 18:22)

David Boudreaux

What Is the Purpose of a Wife?

This wife (helpmeet) God intended for a man to have alongside him prevents loneliness, shares good times and bad, hurts when her husband hurts, and laughs when he laughs. She can cheer him up when he is down and give him encouragement when he is discouraged. She will help him tackle all his endeavors and keep him from quitting when the battle gets tough. She will be there to comfort him and love him when it seems like the whole world has turned against him. She will care about him when no one else cares and support him when no one else will. She will trust him to be head over their family and lead them in the ways God would have them go. Even the strongest and most independent man would do better if he had a good woman. As Meryll Frost said in the Port Author News in1946, "Behind every great man is a great woman."

Mixed Marriages

In the beginning, before the fall of man, Adam and Eve were both considered God's children. This was before Satan tempted them and they allowed sin to corrupt them. "What fellowship hath light with darkness or righteousness with unrighteousness" (2 Cor. 6:14). After the fall of man, God started working on ways to reconcile man with his creator (Himself) right away, and the first method was a covenant God made with Abraham. The descendants of Abraham (Israelites) became God's chosen people, and the laws came, and marriages between God's chosen people were blessed by God. The Israelites were discouraged from marrying people who weren't part of their community. They were also forbidden to marry many different peoples and tribes. When these marriages took place anyhow, they were considered mixed marriages.

This label was not based on race but rather on the fact that these people worshipped false gods. In today's society among Christians,

8

a mixed marriage is between someone who is saved and someone who is not. This mixed marriage has nothing to do with race but rather with the fact that Christians shouldn't submit themselves to the temptations the world has to offer. This temptation would be unavoidable if they were married to someone who still serves Satan. For these reasons I believe it is most important that the first thing that should be considered when a Christian chooses a mate is whether that person is a child of God or not. There is only one way to become a Christian, and I'm going to cover that base right here and now.

We Need a Savior

The first step toward salvation from the destiny of eternal separation from God in a place called the "lake of fire" is to realize we need to be saved. We need a savior because we are all sinners and fall short of the glory of God.

> As it is written, There is none righteous, no, not one.
> (Rom. 3:10)

> They are all gone out of the way, they are together
> become unprofitable; there is none that doeth good,
> no, not one. (Rom. 3:12)

> Whose mouth is full of cursing and bitterness.
> (Rom. 3:14)

> Now we know that what things so-ever the law
> saith, it saith to them who are under the law: that
> every mouth may be stopped, and all the world may
> become guilty before God. Therefore by the deeds
> of the law there shall no flesh be justified in his

sight: for by the law is the knowledge of sin. (Rom. 3:19–20)

For all have sinned, and come short of the glory of God. (Rom. 3:23)

You may think you are a good person and that you aren't guilty of any sin bad enough to send you to hell. What you need to understand is that which sins you are guilty of is irrelevant. Sin is disobeying God's laws, and everyone is guilty of doing that. This fact makes sins without degree because they are all equal in the fact that we have all disobeyed God in one way or another. Because of this, no one is innocent; we are all guilty before God. Allow me to illustrate.

How many lies do people have to tell before they are guilty of being liars? How many sins must they commit before they are guilty of being sinners? I think we all know the answer. So how many sins must we commit before we are guilty before God of breaking His laws? We need to realize that we were already guilty. Jesus didn't come to make us guilty of sin; we did that on our own.

You Cannot Be Saved by Being a Good Person

Some would tell you that you can earn your way to heaven by doing good works or, in other words, by keeping God's laws. If it were possible to keep all the laws, then that would be a true statement; but it isn't possible. The problem is that humans aren't capable of keeping God's laws, and that is why God gave us the law, so we would be able to see our guilt. If we could keep all the laws, we wouldn't need a savior. We would find salvation by good works, but the Bible tells us that isn't possible. "For by grace are ye saved through faith; and that not of yourselves: it is the gift of God. Not of works, lest any man should boast" (Eph. 2:8–9).

The Bible also teaches us that the wages (payment we deserve) for being sinners is death. This refers to spiritual death. "For the wages of sin is death; but the gift of God is eternal life through Jesus Christ our Lord" (Rom. 6:23).

The word *death* here means "to separate" or "to snatch away." In this case, it refers to the separation of your spirit from the presence of God for all eternity. The laws of God were given to humankind to make us realize we needed to be saved from ourselves because of what we have done. This same verse, however, also declares that there remains a glimmer of hope for humankind. That is because God is willing to give us a gift. This gift He offers to humans is eternal life through His Son, Jesus Christ. People aren't able to save themselves, but God has a plan for their salvation. This salvation is a gift from God and cannot be earned by any man or woman.

Don't try to blame God for the human condition. He has done everything possible and everything that is needed to save us. "For God sent not his Son into the world to condemn the world; but that the world through him might be saved. He that believeth on him is not condemned: but he that believeth not is condemned already, because he hath not believed in the name of the only begotten Son of God" (John 3:17–18).

To Be Saved You Must Repent

After you realize you are a sinner and stand guilty before God, you must feel remorseful for your sins or sorry that you are unable to be sinless. This is repentance; without repentance, there is no remission of sins (without repentance sins cannot be forgiven). Another way to look at repentance is as a change of mind. It is a decision you make to turn from sin and living a life for the devil toward righteousness and living a life for God.

> For godly sorrow worketh repentance to salvation not to be repented of: but the sorrow of the world worketh death. (2Cor. 7:10)

> The Lord is not slack concerning his promise, as some men count slackness; but is longsuffering to us-ward, not willing that any should perish, but that all should come to repentance. (2Peter 3:9)

> Repent ye therefore, and be converted, that your sins may be blotted out, when the times of refreshing shall come from the presence of the Lord. (Acts 3:19)

Believe Jesus Is God

After you have repented, now you are prepared to receive the gift of eternal life. This is accomplished by believing Jesus is the Son of God and that He came here to earth from heaven to die on the cross to pay the price for your sins. This is obviously not the same as just believing there is a God. It is believing that Jesus Christ is God and that He came here to save you. The devil believes in God and trembles with fear in God's presence. "Thou believest that there is one God; thou doest well: the devils also believe, and tremble" (James 2:19).

You Must Ask God for Salvation

Believing is faith—that is, believing Jesus is who He claims to be and that He can do what He says He can do for you. When you repent of your sins and believe in Christ, all that remains is for you to ask Him to save you. "That if thou shalt confess with thy mouth the Lord Jesus, and shalt believe in thine heart that God hath raised him from the dead, thou shalt be saved. For with the heart man believeth unto righteousness; and with the mouth confession is made unto salvation. For the scripture saith, Whosoever believeth on him shall not be ashamed. For there is no difference between the Jew and the Greek: for the same Lord over all is rich unto all that call upon him. For whosoever shall call upon the name of the Lord shall be saved" (Rom. 10:9–13).

You Must Exercise Your Faith

Faith must be exercised to mean anything. If I say I believe my old Firebird will get me to the store, some may believe me, and some may not. I may not even believe it myself; faith without action is empty. However, if I drive it to the store, then I have proved that I have enough faith, and I'm willing to trust it. Then faith means something. I can stand on the side of the road, believing I can go to the store all day, but unless I get in the car and go, I'm not going to get to eat that candy bar and drink that soda.

If you call on Jesus to save you, then you must exercise your faith and believe in your heart that He did what you asked Him to do. Just believing in God doesn't do it. Even believing Jesus can save you if you ask Him won't do it. You must ask Him to save you and believe He did what you asked Him to do. When you put your faith in Christ, there is no more condemnation (you are no longer guilty of being a sinner). "But God commendeth his love toward us, in that, while we were yet sinners, Christ died for us" (Rom. 5:8).

After you become a child of God through our Lord Jesus Christ, there is no power in heaven, in hell, or on earth that can change that. "For I am persuaded, that neither death, nor life, nor angels, nor principalities, nor powers, nor things present, nor things to come, Nor height, nor depth, nor any other creature, shall be able to separate us from the love of God, which is in Christ Jesus our Lord" (Rom. 8:38–39).

Ask God to Forgive You for Being a Sinner

You should understand that you aren't asking God to forgive you for every individual sin you have ever committed in your lifetime. You are asking Him to forgive you for being a sinner.

> Two men went up into the temple to pray; the one a Pharisee, and the other a publican. The Pharisee stood and prayed thus with himself, God, I thank thee, that I am not as other men are, extortioners, unjust, adulterers, or even as this publican. I fast twice in the week, I give tithes of all that I possess. And the publican, standing afar off, would not lift up so much as his eyes unto heaven, but smote upon his breast, saying, God be merciful to me a sinner. I tell you, this man went down to his house justified rather than the other: for every one that exalteth himself shall be abased; and he that humbleth himself shall be exalted. (Luke 18:10–14)

Jesus Forgave Me for All My Sins

When you ask Him to forgive you for being a sinner, Jesus forgives you for all your sins—past, present, and future. Since you hadn't committed any sins at the time Jesus died for your sins, that means He died for your future sins. If all your sins—past, present, and future—are forgiven when you are saved, then how can you lose your salvation because of sin?

Salvation Cannot Be Lost

Unfortunately, some would tell you that you can lose your salvation by not following or keeping God's laws. This doesn't make any sense to me. If there is no good work I can do that is good enough to save me in the first place, how are good works going to keep me saved? I personally thank God that my salvation doesn't depend on my ability to keep God's laws. I think I would lose my salvation in the first ten minutes of every day. Good works can't save you or keep you saved. As long as you have doubts about whether Jesus actually saved you like He said He would or doubt that you may be able to stay saved, you limit God's ability to use you to do His work while you are here on earth. It is God's will for every Christian to become mature in his or her spiritual life and be a servant in His ministry.

I would like to encourage those who have read this plan of salvation and haven't already secured their place in heaven to do so right now. Even if you think you may have gone through all the motions or said all the words but didn't really understand what you were doing at the time, you should do so again. I don't believe you can get saved unless you understand what you are doing when you do it. I say it is better to know for sure. If you were saved the first time, then you are just reaffirming your position with God; and if you're not sure, this will give you the assurance you need to move forward in your Christian life. Just say this simple prayer.

If You Want to Be Saved, Just Believe and Ask

> Heavenly Father, I know I am a sinner, and I cannot go to heaven with my sin. I am sorry for being a sinner, and I am coming to You, asking for Your forgiveness. I believe Jesus Christ is Your Son, that He is God, and that You have the authority to forgive me. Lord, please forgive me for being a sinner and make me a born-again child of God. Lord, I believe You have done what I asked You to do, and from this day forward, I want to live a

life that is pleasing to You. In Jesus's name, I pray, Amen.

Now that we understand what a mixed marriage is and what being saved means, I think we should consider what God says a good wife should be like. Apparently, God thinks this is very important because He dedicated nearly an entire chapter in the book of Proverbs to describe the virtuous woman for us. She is probably not what most of you think.

The Perfect Wife According to God

Proverbs 31

Verse 10: Who can find a virtuous woman? for her price is far above rubies.

Verse 11: The heart of her husband doth safely trust in her, so that he shall have no need of spoil.

Verse 12: She will do him good and not evil all the days of her life.

Verse 13: She seeketh wool, and flax, and worketh willingly with her hands.

Verse 14: She is like the merchants' ships; she bringeth her food from afar.

Verse 15: She riseth also while it is yet night, and giveth meat to her household, and a portion to her maidens.

Verse 16: She considereth a field, and buyeth it: with the fruit of her hands she planteth a vineyard.

Verse 17: She girdeth her loins with strength, and strengtheneth her arms.

Verse 18: She perceiveth that her merchandise is good: her candle goeth not out by night.

Verse 19: She layeth her hands to the spindle, and her hands hold the distaff.

Verse 20: She stretcheth out her hand to the poor; yea, she reacheth forth her hands to the needy.

Verse 21: She is not afraid of the snow for her household: for all her household are clothed with scarlet.

Verse 22: She maketh herself coverings of tapestry; her clothing is silk and purple.

Verse 23: Her husband is known in the gates, when he sitteth among the elders of the land.

Verse 24: She maketh fine linen, and selleth it; and delivereth girdles unto the merchant.

Verse 25: Strength and honour are her clothing; and she shall rejoice in time to come.

Verse 26: She openeth her mouth with wisdom; and in her tongue is the law of kindness.

Verse 27: She looketh well to the ways of her household, and eateth not the bread of idleness.

Verse 28: Her children arise up, and call her blessed; her husband also, and he praiseth her.

Verse 29: Many daughters have done virtuously, but thou excellest them all.

Verse 30: Favour is deceitful, and beauty is vain: but a woman that feareth the LORD, she shall be praised.

Verse 31: Give her of the fruit of her hands; and let her own works praise her in the gates.

1. A virtuous woman (morally good) is worth far more than rubies.
2. Her husband trusts her with his whole heart, and in her he has all he will ever need.
3. She will do only good things for him and nothing bad as long as they live.
4. She goes out and finds the things she needs to make a good home for him, and she isn't afraid of working with her hands.
5. She goes out and gathers the food and other necessities she needs to feed her family.
6. She rises early in the morning if she needs to in order to prepare meals for her husband and children to make sure they have all they need.
7. She will go out and look at property she might need to provide for her family, and she will make the purchase and plant a garden to grow food. (Does this sound to you like a woman who isn't allowed to make decisions on her own?)
8. She keeps herself in shape so she can do anything she needs to so she can take care of her family.
9. She is able to judge whether what she has accomplished is good and what else she needs to do.
10. She will stay up late at night, if need be, to do the things she has to.

11. She will make clothes, blankets, coats, or whatever her family or other people need.
12. She always stretches her hand out to the poor and the needy. (Much of the work she does is intended to provide not only for her own family but also for others in need.)
13. She isn't afraid of the cold weather coming because she has made sure that everyone in her family has warm clothes and is prepared.
14. She makes nice clothes, tapestries, and things for her home and herself.
15. Her husband is known by all in the town because she has only good things to say about him.
16. She makes fine linens and girdles, sells them, and delivers her goods to the merchants. (There is nothing wrong with a wife having her own job, money, or even her own business.)
17. She is known for her strength and honor, and she shall rejoice in time.
18. She speaks with wisdom.
19. From her mouth proceed words of kindness.
20. She looks well to the needs of her household.
21. She will never be considered idle or lazy.
22. Her children call her "blessed."
23. Her husband calls her "blessed" and praises her.
24. She will have a reputation for being a good moral person.
25. She shall fear the Lord and be praised.
26. She will be rewarded for her hard work and will be known for her good works in the town.

God Gave Me the Perfect Wife, and He Can Give You One Too

I would like to put in a plug right here for my beautiful wife, Mona DeAnne Boudreaux. She has to be the closest person I have ever met to being this Proverbs 31 woman. She knows what her role is in our marriage, and she accepts the fact that God leads the family through her husband. That fact doesn't keep her from giving her input and opinion on all subject matters, and I have come to realize that her input is extremely valuable. She takes care of our home, the yard, the children, the grand children, and me. She does all the cooking, cleaning, and yard work. She is the best cook in the country, by the way. She sews, buys and sells, and shops for our clothes and shoes and coats; she always makes sure we all have everything we need. She takes care of me in every way I could imagine. She is a true believer, and she trusts me with everything we have. She would follow me to the ends of the earth. She loves me with unending love. She cares for me when I don't deserve it. She is very talented as well.

When we decided to start a church, we went all over the place, looking for a pulpit, because I told her I needed my hands to preach, so I sought something on which to lay my Bible and notes while preaching. After driving around all day, looking for an appropriate pulpit, we gave up and went home. I was tired and went up to my study to rest. About an hour later, she came to me and said, "I want you to come and look at something." She brought me downstairs and showed me the pulpit she had just finished building for me. She also makes blankets, hats, signs, and all sorts of things to sell; but mostly she gives them away. She makes most of the things we give to people for Christmas and birthdays.

She keeps the house organized and spotless. A couple of days ago, after I had just gotten home from work, she started telling me about her new adventure in the yard. She has been in charge of all the exterior decorating at the house, and you can ask anyone, but she does a beautiful job. She even built all of the fences and flower boxes herself.

Anyhow she told me that she was changing the yard again by taking out an old wooden sidewalk that ran behind the house. Half of the wood was rotten and needed to be replaced, but I just didn't have the time to deal with it right now. Anyhow, she started tearing out the sidewalk. At first, I was a bit disappointed because I liked the sidewalk there. Then I thought about all she had done in the past, and I told her I also was excited about what she was planning to do there because I had mistakenly questioned her before. I say "mistakenly" because even though I may not have agreed with what she was doing at first, when she is finished, what she does always looks better than I could have imagined. There is no question in my mind that God created her for me and brought her to me.

CHAPTER 2
Christian Marriage Guidelines

As I talk to Christians, it seems as though the most common question people have is this. With the majority of marriages ending in divorce nowadays, who is it okay to marry, and when is divorce allowed? Most people have already experienced problems in a marriage, and even though they desire to live a life pleasing to God, they don't see how that is possible because they have already been divorced, or they married someone who had already been divorced. Maybe they are in a marriage with an unbeliever and don't know what they should do.

We are going to cover these issues and many other Christian marriage scenarios. As we discuss some of the rules laid out concerning marital guidelines, some of you may be offended or discouraged and not understand why God said these things. If you will be patient and read all the way through, I will explain these things to you, and you will clearly understand the reasoning behind the instructions.

What Constitutes a Marriage in God's Eyes?

Before we start talking about specifics concerning proper marriages as opposed to improper ones, I should point out what constitutes a marriage. I believe if God is to recognize and bless a marriage, it needs to consist of at least these five elements:

1. **Moral:** For a marriage to be pure in God's eyes, it requires a commitment to a monogamous relationship between one man and one woman (no other partners allowed).
2. **Spiritual:** This commitment is obviously to one another, but there is also a commitment to God to keep this promise, because this is a sacred institution God ordained. He is the witness of the union.
3. **Physical:** This is a physical representation of the spiritual joining of two to make them one flesh, a commitment to be there to meet each other's needs physically and spiritually. This is a very serious commitment because it is for life, and it is a picture of our relationship with God.
4. **Legal:** There is a legal element because God tells us we are subject to the powers appointed over us. "Render unto Caesar that which is Caesar's" (Luke 20:25). If you're not married legally by the designated authorities, then you aren't married in God's eyes either.
5. **Testimonial:** This is the marriage ceremony. This is similar to the baptism in water being symbolic of the baptism of the Holy Spirit. It is an outward profession of an inward action. It is a profession to the world before God that the two of you have made a lifelong commitment to each other. This will hold you accountable to your commitment to one another before God and humankind.

Numerous scriptures deal with marriage because it is such an important issue, but perhaps the most instructional passage concerning marital responsibilities and privileges is 1 Corinthians 7:1–35. Due to the complexity of these instructions, I want to go through this passage of scripture one verse at a time. We will be examining scriptures on different topics throughout this entire book in this way. The scriptures are the source of all truth, knowledge, and wisdom (2Tim. 3:16).

It Is Best to Stay a Virgin

"Now concerning the things whereof ye wrote unto me: It is good for a man not to touch a woman" (1Cor. 7:1). The apostle Paul starts out by saying it is best if you can just not touch a woman at all. The main reason for this, according to him, is that it allows you the opportunity to give 100 percent of your time and devotion to serving God. This is true, but as Paul admits later in the chapter, not everyone can do that.

Marriage Is for the Purpose of Preventing Fornication

"Nevertheless, to avoid fornication, let every man have his own wife, and let every woman have her own husband" (1Cor. 7:2). Here Paul tells us the main reason to get married is to avoid fornication. Fornication in the Bible means sex outside of marriage. This is usually talking about sex with two unmarried people. Normally when one of the two is married and cheating on his or her spouse, it is called "adultery." Notice that Paul points out the fact that this can be a problem for both sexes. This is a glimpse of equality in the sexes, even though it may not be the way we want. The fact is, some people of both sexes have such a strong sex drive that they aren't able to live a life of celibacy, and this is normal. One other thing I will point out here is the fact that it says every man should have his own wife. Does that mean he owns her? If it does, then the next part of the verse says every woman should have her own husband, which means she owns him just as much.

"Let the husband render unto the wife due benevolence: and likewise also the wife unto the husband" (1Cor. 7:3). It stands to reason that since one of the main reasons to get married is to prevent fornication, the next point to be made is that these married couples should not hold out on each other concerning their marital responsibilities. *Benevolence* refers to a kind, charitable act for someone else. In this situation, Paul is clearly stating that they should be kind to one another by meeting each other's sexual needs whenever either of them desires it.

Since most people believe it is usually the wife who uses sex as a bargaining chip, I find it interesting that he first tells the husband not to do this. The man shouldn't hold out on his wife, and the woman shouldn't hold out on her husband. This will prevent fornication because they are married, and it will prevent adultery because sex in a marriage is undefiled and natural (Heb. 13:4). We will talk about this matter more later, but it is important to know that sex between married couples is what God intended (not to mention procreation).

"The wife hath not power of her own body, but the husband: and likewise also the husband hath not power of his own body, but the wife" (1Cor. 7:4). In this verse the word *power* simply means authority. The wife has authority over her husband's body when it comes to the bedroom, and the man has authority over his wife's body as well. Ladies and gentlemen, according to God's Word, you don't have the authority to tell your husband or wife no when it comes to meeting each other's marital needs; you are to be charitable to one another.

"Defraud ye not one the other, except it be with consent for a time, that ye may give yourselves to fasting and prayer; and come together again, that Satan tempt you not for your incontinency" (1Cor. 7:5). In this verse Paul is very blunt. He says you should never say no to your spouse unless it is with consent (that is, you both agree to it) so you separate yourselves for prayer and fasting. This marital relationship is trumped only by your relationship with God. God should always come first, even ahead of your spouse (Luke 10:38–42).

Since abstinence should be only with consent, I believe any other act in the bedroom between husband and wife should also be with consent. We will discuss that more later as well. Then he goes on to state the reason for this. If you don't keep each other satisfied in this area, it will open a door for Satan to tempt you through incontinency. This is referring to the sinful release of bodily fluids caused by the lust of the flesh. So it stands to reason that if your sexual needs are met at home, you will most likely not have a lust problem. Does that mean that if your husband or wife is cheating or considering cheating on you, it is because you aren't meeting his or her needs? Maybe! It may not be the reason your spouse is cheating, but if you aren't meeting his or her needs, you have opened the door for that temptation.

"But I speak this by permission, and not of commandment" (1 Cor. 7:6). No commandment from the Word of God clearly states this, but Paul is telling us what the Holy Spirit told him to say about the subject. They didn't have the New Testament at the time this epistle was written, and Jesus didn't give specifics about this topic in His sermons either, so there was nothing previously written in the Word of God concerning this issue. Today Paul's writings are part of the scriptures, and his advice is equal to any other scripture.

"For I would that all men were even as I myself. But every man hath his proper gift of God, one after this manner, and another after that" (1 Cor. 7:7). In this verse Paul expresses his own opinion here by emphasizing that personally, he thinks everyone would be better off if they all stayed single like him, but he also understands that God doesn't give everybody the ability to do that. "I say therefore to the unmarried and widows, It is good for them if they abide even as I am" (1 Cor. 7:8). To the unmarried, meaning anyone who is single for whatever reason, it is better to stay single if he or she can.

"But if they cannot contain, let them marry: for it is better to marry than to burn" (1 Cor. 7:9). If they cannot control their lusts for the opposite sex, man or woman, it is better to get married than to burn with lust in their hearts. This is talking about lust, not hellfire. Jesus said that if you lust after a woman, you have already committed adultery with her in your heart (Matt. 5:27–28). That rule goes for women too.

"And unto the married I command, yet not I, but the Lord, Let not the wife depart from her husband" (1 Cor. 7:10). Paul was just repeating what Jesus had said in (Mark 10:6–9). Jesus didn't explain it any further in Mark, but here Paul gives us more details on the topic. "But and if she depart, let her remain unmarried or be reconciled to her husband: and let not the husband put away his wife" (1 Cor. 7:11). Again, these are the same instructions Jesus gave in Mark.

A Saved Person Is Not Obligated to Stay Married to an Unsaved Person

"But to the rest speak I, not the Lord: If any brother hath a wife that believeth not, and she be pleased to dwell with him, let him not put her away" (1 Cor. 7:12). Paul is saying that now he is going to tell us more than Jesus did about the topic. This is not in contradiction to Jesus' teachings at all. It is giving more details on the topic. He was speaking through the inspiration of the Holy Spirit. I believe that when Jesus said the only acceptable reason to divorce was adultery, He was specifically talking about marriages between two saved people. We know saved people shouldn't marry unsaved people.

> Be ye not unequally yoked together with unbelievers: for what fellowship hath righteousness with unrighteousness? And what communion hath light with darkness? And what concord hath Christ with Belial? Or what part hath he that believeth with an infidel? And what agreement hath the temple of God with idols? For ye are the temple of the living God; as God hath said, I will dwell in them, and walk in them; and I will be their God, and

they shall be my people. Wherefore come out from
among them, and be ye separate, saith the Lord,
and touch not the unclean thing; and I will receive
you. And will be a Father unto you, and ye shall be
my sons and daughters, saith the Lord Almighty.
(2Cor. 6:14–18)

So, if a saved man has an unsaved wife and she chooses to stay
with him, even though he lives for God, which she probably doesn't
understand, he should stay with her. This is because she could end
up being saved because of his testimony. Ordinarily she would be
considered an unclean thing because she is not saved, but because
they are one through marriage, she is sanctified (cleansed) through
him. "And the woman which hath an husband that believeth not,
and if he be pleased to dwell with her, let her not leave him" (1 Cor.
7:13).

Let's say a saved woman is married to an unsaved husband, even
though he doesn't understand her. If he is happy staying with her,
then she shouldn't leave him. In this case, since the husband isn't
saved, the woman becomes the spiritual leader, and the husband is
sanctified by her. There is also a good chance he could end up being
saved because of her.

In a Mixed Marriage, the Saved Person
Sanctifies the Unsaved Person

"For the unbelieving husband is sanctified by the wife, and the
unbelieving wife is sanctified by the husband: else were your children
unclean; but now are they holy" (1 Cor. 7:14).This is because the
saved person in the relationship will bring God's blessings on the
family. It is also because it is the saved person's responsibility to
teach the sanctification of the body to the rest of the family. The
saved husband or wife, by his or her manner of living, will teach the

rest of the family to sanctify or separate themselves from ungodly people. This sanctification is applied only to the body. This doesn't mean the unsaved person is saved. *Sanctified* means separated or cleansed, not saved.

"But if the unbelieving depart, let him depart. A brother or a sister is not under bondage in such cases: but God hath called us to peace" (1 Cor. 7:15). However, if the unsaved person in the marriage doesn't want to stay in the marriage, then the saved person is not obligated to try to hold on to him or her. It takes two to keep a marriage together; it takes only one to tear it apart. Paul admits that if the unbeliever wants to leave, there is nothing the Christian can do to keep him or her from doing so. The Christian isn't held accountable for the divorce in this case. He doesn't say whether this releases the Christian to marry again, but in my opinion, if the believer is no longer bound, then he or she is free. One thing we know for certain; if the unbelieving spouse who left commits adultery (has sex with someone else or gets remarried), then the Christian is also certainly free to remarry. "God hath called us to peace" refers to the fact that if the unsaved partner wants to leave, the Christian can't stop him or her. It's difficult for there to be peace in a home where one serves God and one serves Satan.

"For what knowest thou, O wife, whether thou shalt save thy husband? or how knowest thou, O man, whether thou shalt save thy wife?" (1 Cor. 7:16). Most of the time these unequally yoked marriages are the results of one in the marriage being saved after they were married and the other has not. Paul says you should let the person stay in the relationship if he or she wants to because there is a good chance he or she may also end up being saved. On the other hand, if the person doesn't want to stay, it's probably because he or she doesn't want anything to do with God and isn't going to change his or her mind.

"But as God hath distributed to every man, as the Lord hath called every one, so let him walk. And so ordain I in all churches" (1 Cor. 7:17).

Not Everyone Will Be Saved

This is a very significant statement made in a short sentence. "As God hath distributed to every man." Not everyone has a calling from God to be saved. Jesus said, "All that the Father giveth me shall come to me; and him that cometh to me I will in no wise cast out." (Jn 6:37) Not all are called by God, and not all will come. This may not sound fair to some of us, but God is the potter, and we are the clay. Some would call this "predestination," and some would call that "Calvinism" (the belief that not everyone is called to be saved). The Calvinist believes if you are predestined to be saved, you will be and if you are not, then you won't.

Here is what I think. Though God knows all those who will or won't be saved even before they are born, that doesn't mean He controls their decision. God is omniscient; that means He knows all things, even before they happen. God knows what decisions we are going to make in every aspect of our lives before we make them. Does that mean He controls every decision we make? When I see a car traveling at a high rate of speed and out of control and I know it is going to crash, does that mean I made the crash happen because I knew ahead of time it was going to? Even if it were true that God controls every decision concerning salvation and we have no say about it, which I don't believe is the case, then it wouldn't change anything as far as we are concerned. That is because God would know who could be saved, but we wouldn't; therefore, our mission as Christians remains the same. We should try to reach everyone with the Gospel.

> All that the Father giveth me shall come to me; and
> him that cometh to me I will in no wise cast out.
> For I came down from heaven, not to do mine own
> will, but the will of him that sent me. And this is the
> Father's will which hath sent me, that of all which
> he hath given me I should lose nothing, but should

> raise it up again at the last day. And this is the will
> of him that sent me, that every one which seeth the
> Son, and believeth on him, may have everlasting
> life: and I will raise him up at the last day. (John
> 6:37–40)

"As the Lord hath called every one, so let him walk." If you were married when you got saved, you should stay married unless the unbelieving partner chooses to leave you. If you were single when you got saved, then you should stay single, unless you can't control your desires. If you are divorced, then you should stay single unless you can't control your desires and your ex-husband or ex-wife has committed adultery or remarried. Then you are also free to remarry but are not required to.

> "Is any man called being circumcised? let him
> not become uncircumcised. Is any called in
> uncircumcision? let him not be circumcised."
> Circumcision is nothing, and uncircumcision is
> nothing, but the keeping of the commandments
> of God. Let every man abide in the same calling
> wherein he was called. Art thou called being a
> servant? care not for it: but if thou mayest be made
> free, use it rather. For he that is called in the Lord,
> being a servant, is the Lord's freeman: likewise also
> he that is called, being free, is Christ's servant. Ye
> are bought with a price; be not ye the servants of
> men. Brethren, let every man, wherein he is called,
> therein abide with God. (1 Cor. 7:18–24)

Paul concludes these instructions by reiterating the fact that this isn't a new concept. It applies to many areas, not just marriage. He says it twice more. Concerning your marital status, unless it is not possible, you should remain as you were when you got saved. In some cases, this would not be possible because you may have been living in a sinful situation at the time you were saved, and that would have to change. (A homosexual marriage would be an example.) In God's eyes, this is not the definition of a marriage; therefore, you are living in sin.

You Should Continue in Whatever Marital Status You Were in When You Got Saved

> "Now concerning virgins I have no commandment of the Lord: yet I give my judgment, as one that hath obtained mercy of the Lord to be faithful. I suppose therefore that this is good for the present distress, I say, that it is good for a man so to be. Art thou bound unto a wife? seek not to be loosed. Art thou loosed from a wife? seek not a wife. But and if thou marry, thou hast not sinned; and if a virgin marry, she hath not sinned. Nevertheless such shall have trouble in the flesh: but I spare you. (1 Cor. 7:25–28)

See verses 25–28. In this passage, Paul is talking about the unmarried, (pure men and women), but *virgin* usually means young unmarried women who still live with their fathers. Paul says if you are a virgin, it is good for you to stay pure and single. If you're single, don't look for a wife or husband. If you're married, don't seek a divorce. He also says that if you are loosed from a wife, then don't seek after another wife, but if you do remarry, you have not sinned. We already know that by "loosed" he means freed by a divorce that falls into Jesus' or Paul's legal description of divorce which is by death or adultery on the part of your ex.

When We Go to Heaven, Our Marital
Status Will Be Irrelevant

"But this I say, brethren, the time is short: it remaineth, that both they that have wives be as though they had none; And they that weep, as though they wept not; and they that rejoice, as though they rejoiced not; and they that buy, as though they possessed not; And they that use this world, as not abusing it: for the fashion of this world passeth away" (1 Cor. 7:29–31).

The time will soon come when none of this will matter because at the resurrection, when we have received our incorruptible bodies, we will be as the angels (asexual) without gender. We will not be married or given in marriage. This is why our marriages with our fleshly mates are for the duration of our fleshly lives. But the duration of our spiritual marriages—that is, our marriages to Jesus Christ—is for eternity.

> Saying, Master, Moses said, If a man die, having no children, his brother shall marry his wife, and raise up seed unto his brother. Now there were with us seven brethren: and the first, when he had married a wife, deceased, and, having no issue, left his wife unto his brother: Likewise the second also, and the third, unto the seventh. And last of all, the woman died also. Therefore in the resurrection whose wife shall she be of the seven? For they all had her. Jesus answered and said unto them, ye do err, not knowing the scriptures, nor the power of God. For in the resurrection they neither marry, nor are given in marriage, but are as the angels of God in heaven. (Matt. 22:24–30)

Single Persons Can Spend All Their Time Serving God

> But I would have you without carefulness. He that
> is unmarried careth for the things that belong to the
> Lord, how he may please the Lord: But he that is
> married careth for the things that are of the world,
> how he may please his wife. There is difference also
> between a wife and a virgin. The unmarried woman
> careth for the things of the Lord, that she may be
> holy both in body and in spirit: but she that is
> married careth for the things of the world, how she
> may please her husband. And this I speak for your
> own profit; not that I may cast a snare upon you,
> but for that which is comely, and that ye may attend
> upon the Lord without distraction. (1 Cor. 7:32–35)

In verses 32–35, Paul essentially says we should consider this before we get married or even look for a spouse. The unmarried man and unmarried woman have a great opportunity to be sanctified and dedicated to serving God only in the body and spirit, while the married man or woman has to spend a lot of time attending to things of this world to please his or her spouse. If a man takes a wife, he is responsible for her spiritual guidance, sanctification, provision, protection, physical needs, and desires. If a woman gets married, she is responsible for her husband's well-being, reputation, health, the keeping of the home, his physical needs and desires, and raising the children. All these responsibilities are to be taken seriously, and they are all important. Paul says we should do these things for each other if we are married. He isn't suggesting that it's wrong for us to attend to the needs of our wives or husbands; he is just saying that if we are married, we will be obligated to meet these needs. If we stay single, we don't have to worry about those.

The Father Who Refuses to Give His Daughter in Marriage

"But if any man think that he behaveth himself uncomely toward his virgin, if she pass the flower of her age, and need so require, let him do what he will, he sinneth not: let them marry. Nevertheless he that standeth stedfast in his heart, having no necessity, but hath power over his own will, and hath so decreed in his heart that he will keep his virgin, doeth well. So then he that giveth her in marriage doeth well; but he that giveth her not in marriage doeth better" (1 Cor. 7:36–38).

These verses (36–38) are talking about a father giving his daughter away in marriage. If a suitable marriage partner has been found, then the father can give his daughter away if he so chooses. Hopefully this would be to someone whom she desires to be with, and hopefully he has asked the father for her hand in marriage. Of course, he would be someone who wants the daughter for his wife as well. If this has been established, then the father can let her go if he so chooses. However, if he doesn't want to let her go for whatever reason, it is his right to refuse to give her away. I say good luck to a father who tries to hold on to a daughter these days. In God's eyes the father has this right, but in our society and under our laws, this wouldn't be acceptable, and God knows we have to obey the laws of our land.

"The wife is bound by the law as long as her husband liveth; but if her husband be dead, she is at liberty to be married to whom she will; only in the Lord. But she is happier if she so abide, after my judgment: and I think also that I have the Spirit of God" (1 Cor. 7:39–40). Finally, if the daughter does marry, she will be bound to her husband as long as he lives, unless he commits adultery. If he dies or commits adultery, she is free to remarry anyone else as long as he is saved. Then Paul adds something here at the end: if she becomes free from her husband, she would probably be happier if she stayed single. Later on Paul says that the younger widows should remarry but that the older widows should stay single. We will discuss that topic in the future.

We Are All Guilty of Some Sin—Our Hope Is in Forgiveness

Now that I have reviewed these scriptures with you concerning the laws dealing with marriage and divorce, I want to make sure we aren't missing the main issue. There were many more laws dealing with this topic in the Old Testament, but most of us aren't able to find justification for the sins we have already committed based on what we already know when it comes to this topic. Very few people save themselves sexually for marriage anymore; this is another topic we will deal with later, but it illustrates the fact that none of us can be justified by the law. If you have surmised from this scripture that you are already guilty (so there is nothing you can do about it), then you have gotten the point. You see, the law was written to point out the fact that we are guilty and need to be saved. No man is justified by the law.

"Knowing that a man is not justified by the works of the law, but by the faith of Jesus Christ, even we have believed in Jesus Christ, that we might be justified by the faith of Christ, and not by the works of the law: for by the works of the law shall no flesh be justified" (Gal. 2:16). Regardless of your current marital status, consider the following:

Jesus told the Samaritan woman at the well that she had been with five husbands and that the one she was currently with wasn't her husband. But then He told her that if she asked Him for the water He offered, she could have everlasting life. This meant she would be forgiven and have a clean slate concerning her sins in the sight of God.

> Then cometh he to a city of Samaria, which is called Sychar, near to the parcel of ground that Jacob gave to his son Joseph. Now Jacob's well was there. Jesus therefore, being wearied with his journey, sat thus on the well: and it was about the sixth hour. There cometh a woman of Samaria to draw water: Jesus

saith unto her, Give me to drink. (For his disciples were gone away unto the city to buy meat.)Then saith the woman of Samaria unto him, How is it that thou, being a Jew, askest drink of me, which am a woman of Samaria? For the Jews have no dealings with the Samaritans. Jesus answered and said unto her, If thou knewest the gift of God, and who it is that saith to thee, Give me to drink; thou wouldest have asked of him, and he would have given thee living water. The woman saith unto him, Sir, thou hast nothing to draw with, and the well is deep: from whence then hast thou that living water? Art thou greater than our father Jacob, which gave us the well, and drank thereof himself, and his children, and his cattle? Jesus answered and said unto her, Whosoever drinketh of this water shall thirst again: But whosoever drinketh of the water that I shall give him shall never thirst; but the water that I shall give him shall be in him a well of water springing up into everlasting life. The woman saith unto him, Sir, give me this water, that I thirst not, neither come hither to draw. Jesus saith unto her, Go, call thy husband, and come hither. The woman answered and said, I have no husband. Jesus said unto her, Thou hast well said, I have no husband: For thou hast had five husbands; and he whom thou now hast is not thy husband: in that saidst thou truly. The woman saith unto him, Sir, I perceive that thou art a prophet. Our fathers worshipped in this mountain; and ye say, that in Jerusalem is the place where men ought to worship. Jesus saith unto her, Woman, believe me, the hour cometh, when ye shall neither in this mountain, nor yet at Jerusalem, worship the Father. Ye worship ye know not what:

we know what we worship: for salvation is of the Jews. But the hour cometh, and now is, when the true worshippers shall worship the Father in spirit and in truth: for the Father seeketh such to worship him. God is a Spirit: and they that worship him must worship him in spirit and in truth. The woman saith unto him, I know that Messias cometh, which is called Christ: when he is come, he will tell us all things. Jesus saith unto her, I that speak unto thee am he. (John 4:5–26)

Jesus Said Neither Do I Condemn Thee, Now Go and Sin No More.

I believe this is why Paul told us that even though this is what the law says concerning marriage, it really doesn't matter all that much in eternity. We need to know what the law says because through the law is the knowledge of sin. If you are saved, then you should also try to keep yourself clean from sin so it doesn't affect your fellowship with God, but it doesn't have anything to do with your salvation. Now let me give you one more example: the woman who was caught in the act of adultery in the book of John. At the end of the story, Jesus told her, "Neither do I condemn thee, now go and sin no more" (John 8:3–11). So I believe when Paul tells us back in 1 Cor. 7:29–31 that this will not matter much longer because marriages only last while we are here on earth and by saying that whatever your marital status was or is when you get saved you should try to maintain that status unless you meet one of the conditions already discussed. Then combine that with what Jesus said in John 8:3-11 the point is that when you get saved all sin is forgiven and you should maintain that sinlessness to the best of your ability, but if or when you slip up, your fellowship with God may suffer but your relationship (your salvation) will stay intact. No matter what you have done, when you get saved or when you ask God for forgiveness, the slate is wiped clean. You are forgiven; now go and sin no more. In whatever situation you are in now, consider it where God wants you to be because He just accepted you. But go and don't do anything you know is sinful anymore. The stipulation is that you cannot live sin free if you continue to live in a sinful situation. If you are living with someone and aren't married to him or her, when you get saved, you should move out and keep yourself pure until you are married. That is just one example.

Interracial Marriage

I mentioned earlier that for Christians, the definition of a mixed marriage is when a saved person is married to an unsaved person. According to the apostle Paul, this is an acceptable reason for the couple to split up. Light and darkness cannot abide in the same household. This is the reason a Christian cannot be demon possessed; the devil cannot reside in the same place that the Holy Spirit occupies. So if this is what Christians call a "mixed marriage," then why do so many preachers teach that God is against interracial marriages as well? I have heard preachers from many different religions and races teach this. In the Old Testament God forbade a lot of these marriages between different races when it came to His chosen people, the Israelites. I think there are two basic reasons for that. The first is that God had to keep the bloodline pure regarding the house of David because of the prophesying of the Messiah's coming. Second, the other people the Israelites were getting married to were from other parts of the world and were therefore in many cases a different race. Most of these foreigners didn't know or worship the one true God (Jehovah), so God forbade these marriages because of the influence of false religions, not because these people were of a different race.

To some degree, this is still true today. Many times different parts of the world still have their own false gods, which they worship and pray to; therefore these are false religions. To God this is just idolatry because there is only one true God; anyone or anything else you worship is forbidden. If this is true about a potential mate for a Christian, then this person, unless converted, should be disqualified. Another reason is the basic argument of incompatibility. This is still the main reason used in our society as the primary cause for divorce, although I believe this is true only because it is the easiest divorce to get approved by the courts. It is also most often used because neither party wants to take the blame for the real reason.

I believe all men and women are incompatible to some degree, but that is what makes us compatible. People are looking at this the wrong way. Men and women are incompatible because they were created for two different purposes by God's design. Their differences should not conflict with each other but rather complement each other. It only makes sense that my wife and I don't like all things the same. Instead of this becoming a problem for us, we use it to our advantage. She is an excellent housekeeper, so I let her run with it. On the other hand, I am a fairly good provider, so she lets me deal with that. Are you and your spouse complementing one another, or are your differences a point of conflict? So anyhow, this incompatibility can be an obstacle concerning a potential marriage partner under certain circumstances. When it comes to racial differences, which are actually cultural differences, they can be significant, sometimes even enough so it makes it very difficult for these interracial marriages to survive. I believe there is some merit to this argument, and in some extreme cases, it could be true that this marriage should have never happened.

Some preachers will also tell you that interracial marriages are man's attempt to undo what God has done. This is because of the story about the Tower of Babel, so let's take a look at it.

> And the whole earth was of one language, and of
> one speech. And it came to pass, as they journeyed
> from the east, that they found a plain in the land of

Shinar; and they dwelt there. And they said one to another, Go to, let us make brick, and burn them thoroughly. And they had brick for stone, and slime had they for mortar. And they said, Go to, let us build us a city and a tower, whose top may reach unto heaven; and let us make us a name, lest we be scattered abroad upon the face of the whole earth. And the LORD came down to see the city and the tower, which the children of men builded. And the LORD said, Behold, the people is one, and they have all one language; and this they begin to do: and now nothing will be restrained from them, which they have imagined to do. Go to, let us go down, and there confound their language, that they may not understand one another's speech. So the LORD scattered them abroad from thence upon the face of all the earth: and they left off to build the city. Therefore is the name of it called Babel; because the LORD did there confound the language of all the earth: and from thence did the LORD scatter them abroad upon the face of all the earth. (Gen. 11:1–9)

Do Interracial Marriages Undermine God?

We can see from these verses that when all the people of the earth were of one race and one language, they apparently set out to do evil in God's sight, so God confounded them by separating them to all different parts of the earth. He also made them speak different languages so they wouldn't be able to coordinate an effort to rejoin one another. They were trying to build a tower to reach the heavens— to what end, I'm not certain—but apparently God knew they were up to no good. It says they had imagined to do things God didn't approve of. We know they couldn't have built a tower tall enough to reach God, but that doesn't change the fact that they were trying to. Some scholars have suggested that back during this period many people were worshipping the heavenly bodies such as the sun, the moon, and the stars. Perhaps they were trying to reach the heavenly bodies. Regardless of what their intentions were, God put an end to it. Because of this, some preachers say that interracial marriage is wrong because it is an effort to undermine God's deliberate actions to separate the human races. To me, that simply sounds like someone making up an excuse to support his or her own prejudices.

I don't believe there is much of a chance that all people of the earth will somehow become one race again. If this is true, then there are much more serious things going on today than interracial relationships. What about the United Nations and the one-world government that seems to be in the making? I think if God found a way to keep men from joining together for evil purposes back in this time, then He could do that again if He deemed it necessary. To summarize, in extreme cases of incompatibility based on cultural differences, it may be wise not to marry outside your own culture. There should never be any marriages between the saved and the unsaved, and if you are concerned that a marriage could result in a pact to do evil in God's sight, then it shouldn't take place. Before you marry someone, you should make certain he or she isn't entangled with false religions or false gods. Other than these reasons, I see no others in the scriptures to suggest that interracial marriage is sinful.

Cultural Differences

I wanted to give you an example of cultural differences in a way you will understand. I have a couple of rental properties in Orange Texas, where my wife and I live. One of my properties is occupied by an elderly black lady and her adult daughter. One month when the rent was due, my apartment manager told me this lady wasn't going to be able to pay her rent for that month because of some unexpected expenses that had arisen with her daughter. My manager also told me this lady had been living at the apartment with no electricity for several days because the power had been shut off. I called my wonderful wife and asked her if she would go over and find out how much the electric bill was and take care of it for the lady. I also told her I was going to let the lady skip the rent payment for that month because she had been a good tenant for several years, and everyone needs help on occasion. So my wife went to the apartment and took care of the electric bill right on the spot.

It just so happened that Thanksgiving day was only a few days away, so my wife, being the sweet, generous person that she is, asked the lady whether she had what she needed for her Thanksgiving. The lady replied that they didn't have anything. So my wife told the lady she would buy Thanksgiving dinner for them and asked the lady to send her a list of what she wanted. My wife was so excited about doing this (because she loves helping people as much as I do) that she didn't wait for the list. She went straight to the store and bought all the traditional items we buy for ourselves on Thanksgiving. After she got home, she checked her messages, and the lady had sent her the list. That was a while back, so I don't recall all the exact details, but the list went something like this; turkey neck bones, sweet-tator pie, mustard greens, and chitlins. My wife called me and told me about the list because she had never heard of some of these things, and we had a big laugh. Anyhow, she went back to the store and got the lady the additional items, and then she went to her house and gave her all of the things from both lists. The thing I love about my wife the most is her big heart. My point is that sometimes cultural differences can be difficult to overcome. I don't think I will ever be ready to celebrate Thanksgiving with turkey neck bones, sweet-tator pie, and chitlins, not to suggest that there is anything wrong with that menu but it wouldn't work for me.

What Does "Saved" Mean to You?

I think it would be a good time to summarize what we have covered concerning the search for a lifetime mate and partner. Most important of all, he or she should be a saved person. Then I think it is necessary to mention that not everyone has the same definition of "saved." According to God's Word, to be saved means to recognize your sinful condition, turn from your sinful ways (repent), believe in Jesus, the Son of God, and call on Him to save you from your sinful lifestyle. Another person's definition of salvation may be totally different than this. Some religions even teach that Jesus was a God and not the one and only true God and that anyone can become a God. The Bible warns us not to listen to anyone who offers a different definition of salvation than what the Word of God teaches. If we shouldn't listen to them, then we should certainly not marry them. Jesus is the only way to heaven, and we should not marry anyone who is not a saved, born-again Christian (John 14:6).

Even though we have seen that interracial marriage isn't wrong in itself, it is important that many people from different parts of the world, even those of the same race, could have been influenced by false religions and doctrines. Regardless of what race others are or what religion they grew up with, they must be converted to Christianity before they can be considered marriage candidates for born-again children of God. Sometimes even if others with a culture like this get converted, they will still carry some of their heathen practices with them. There are even some so-called Christian religions that don't have the same definition of salvation the Bible teaches. Be aware of this fact and don't be allured into idolatry, cultism, or a false religion by someone you are physically attracted to.

He or she should be someone who illustrates the fruit of the Spirit in his or her life. Not everyone who claims to be saved is (Matt. 7:23). When you are dating those who are interested in you, they will always put their best face forward. They will pretend to be someone they aren't just to get on your good side. They are trying to impress you, and their true selves are often hidden. If someone is really a Christian, you will be able to see this fact based on his or her good works. Remember, Christians don't do good works to get saved, but they will do good works *because* they are saved. If this person is always showing you all the good things he or she does but doesn't give the credit to God, then he or she is probably just trying to impress you. You can learn a lot about others by finding out what they enjoy doing. If their favorite thing to do is to hang out at bars, then they probably aren't the type of person you want to date. My daddy used to say, "If you find a wife in a bar, then you will be married to barfly. If you find a wife in a brothel, then you will be married to a harlot."

Incompatibility

You have probably heard the saying that every woman gets married, hoping her husband will change; and every man gets married, hoping his wife doesn't. Neither of these is likely to become a reality. If you marry someone who lives a life for the devil, I wouldn't expect that to change. I can only relate to you from my personal experiences, but I am a person who doesn't like a dirty house or clutter. If you are like me and are dating someone, then try making a surprise visit to the person's house and see how well it is kept. This is true whether we're talking about a man or a woman. Single men who want an orderly home will keep their homes orderly. It may not be as clean as a lady would keep it, but it won't be cluttered or filthy. If you go to your potential mate's home and find it disorderly, filthy, or cluttered (or if there are animals all over the place and it smells like animal feces), this won't change after you marry the person. I'm not saying there is anything wrong with having animals in the home, but I am saying that the home shouldn't smell like animals. "Can the Ethiopian change his skin, or the leopard his spots? then may ye also do good, that are accustomed to do evil"(Jer. 13:23).

Now here is some practical advice. If you want to know how a potential husband or wife is going to treat you after you get married, then take some time to check out his or her mother, father, and siblings. I will show you later that many bad behaviors are taught from our parents or other people who have influenced us at a younger age, such as older siblings. If the mother tries to rule over everything or is abusive, then her daughter may very well be the same way. If a father is abusive in the way he treats his wife and children, then his son will probably be the same way. This isn't always true but probably more often than not. If the father isn't a good provider, then his son may well turn out the same way. If the mother isn't a good housekeeper, then the daughter is likely to be the same.

"Beauty Is Only Skin Deep"

It goes without saying that you will pursue only those you are attracted to, but beauty is only skin deep. It really doesn't matter how attractive others are on the outside if they are bad people who are ugly on the inside. The Bible tells us these types of people will pursue, seek, and hunt for the righteous person to take advantage of and destroy him or her. "To keep thee from the evil woman, from the flattery of the tongue of a strange woman. Lust not after her beauty in thine heart; neither let her take thee with her eyelids. For by means of a whorish woman a man is brought to a piece of bread: and the adulteress will hunt for the precious life" (Prov. 6:24–26).

Christians Should Know Never to Date a Married Person

Under no circumstances should a Christian ever consider dating a married person. These verses are written to men about the types of women to avoid, but the same holds true for women looking for the right kind of man. "Can a man take fire in his bosom, and his clothes not be burned? Can one go upon hot coals, and his feet not be burned? So he that goeth in to his neighbour's wife; whosoever toucheth her shall not be innocent" (Prov. 6:27–29).

Fooling around with a married person is like playing with fire. If you keep playing around with others long enough, you will eventually get burned. They will always try to lure you by telling you how bad their husbands or wives are to them. They want to justify their actions and try to make you feel sorry for them. There are even those who will tell you they are just getting even for what their spouse did to them. In their eyes, they are justified in what they are doing because of something their spouses did. Two wrongs don't make a right. When a married person tries to seduce you, you should do what Joseph did with Potiphar's wife when she tried to seduce him. Run!

> And it came to pass after these things, that his master's wife cast her eyes upon Joseph; and she said, Lie with me. But he refused, and said unto his master's wife, Behold, my master wotteth not what is with me in the house, and he hath committed all that he hath to my hand; There is none greater in this house than I; neither hath he kept back any thing from me but thee, because thou art his wife: how then can I do this great wickedness, and sin against God? And it came to pass, as she spake to Joseph day by day, that he hearkened not unto her, to lie by her, or to be with her. And it came to pass about this time, that Joseph went into the house to do his business; and there was none of the men of the house there within. And she caught him by his garment, saying, Lie with me: and he left his garment in her hand, and fled, and got him out. And it came to pass, when she saw that he had left his garment in her hand, and was fled forth, That she called unto the men of her house, and spake unto

them, saying, See, he hath brought in an Hebrew
unto us to mock us; he came in unto me to lie with
me, and I cried with a loud voice: And it came to
pass, when he heard that I lifted up my voice and
cried, that he left his garment with me, and fled,
and got him out. And she laid up his garment by
her, until his lord came home. And she spake unto
him according to these words, saying, The Hebrew
servant, which thou hast brought unto us, came in
unto me to mock me: And it came to pass, as I lifted
up my voice and cried, that he left his garment with
me, and fled out. And it came to pass, when his
master heard the words of his wife, which she spake
unto him, saying, After this manner did thy servant
to me; that his wrath was kindled. And Joseph's
master took him, and put him into the prison, a
place where the king's prisoners were bound: and
he was there in the prison. (Gen. 39:7–20)

Joseph was a godly man, and he ran just as any other Christian
should, but as you saw, if you mess around with a married person,
even if you don't do anything wrong, you are putting yourself in a
vulnerable position. Joseph rightly proclaimed to Potiphar's wife that
this was a sin against his master and God. This is why you should
never spend any time alone with a married person. It is a good
practice to spend time with the opposite sex only when both of you
are single or if the spouses are also present. I'm sure this is a much
bigger problem for people who aren't saved, but even Christians
aren't above temptation. Don't risk it; you never know what other
people will do when given the opportunity. I am also sure you
think that if that happened to you, you could walk away. Don't be
so sure; don't test the theory. "Thou shalt not tempt the Lord thy
God." (Mtt 4:7)

Since the harlot will seek after the precious seed, most preachers will take precautions to prevent this type of situation from ever happening. If you pay attention, most pastors will have an office surrounded by windows so people can see in. This measure isn't accidental. Pastors often have to counsel women who are having relationship problems, and therefore these men can sometimes be vulnerable to more temptation than normal. I wish I could tell you that a man of God is above falling into this trap, but too many preachers have already been destroyed by this very thing. They may be men of God, but they are still men and are not above temptation. If pastors are giving someone like this counsel, then they should do so in a place where everyone can see what is going on in the room. Of course this is personal and private information and should be kept confidential, but the counseling itself should be done in plain sight. It is also a good idea for this type of counseling to include the woman's husband, if at all possible, and/or the pastor's wife. Not only does this protect the vulnerable woman from temptation, but it also protects the pastor's reputation. "Abstain from all appearance of evil" (1 Thess. 5:22).

The other day a friend of mine told me he had started dating his ex-wife again. He said it was going pretty well until she found out he was only going after her for *his money*.

CHAPTER 3

The Structure of a Christian Marriage

God's Chain of Command for the Home

Man Is Head over the Woman

God has given us a chain of command in the home and our lives. I'm not going to pretend I know all the reasons why this is true, but I do know a few I believe. First, we see in 1 Corinthians that "the head of every man is Christ; and the head of the woman is the man; and the head of Christ is God" (1 Cor. 11:3).

I believe this is the key verse to understanding this entire chapter. We know it's the head that is properly equipped to make decisions for the entire body. It is therefore necessary for the body to be subject to the decisions the head makes. With this in mind, let's look at the following verses in a new light. I have read these verses over and over in the past and never really understood what the author was trying to teach me.

"Every man praying or prophesying, having his head covered, dishonoureth his head" (1 Cor. 11:4). In this verse we learn that if a man prays or preaches with his head covered, he dishonors his head, which is Christ. Since the woman's hair is given to her for a covering (11:15), it could be deduced that when a man who has long hair like a woman prays or preaches, he brings dishonor to Christ. The Old Testament tells us that a woman shouldn't wear clothing that pertains to a man (Deut. 22:5). I think it is important to God that a man dress and look like a man and a woman dress and look like a woman.

Not to get off topic, but I should say that this doesn't mean a woman can't wear pants, in my opinion. Some pants are made for women, and men wouldn't look right wearing them. I like to see a lady wearing a dress, but if she is doing certain kinds of work, a dress wouldn't be appropriate. I think some ladies' pantsuits and other outfits that do not make their physical attributes draw attention are appropriate for all activities including church. Men shouldn't wear clothes made for women, and women shouldn't wear clothes made for men. I believe this is referring to cross-dressing, and this type of behavior is considered an abomination to God. Perhaps God doesn't want men to have long hair like a woman or a woman to have short hair like a man for the same reason. Now we will look at verses 5 and 6, which basically say the same thing about the woman. But she dishonors her husband when she prays or prophesies with her hair cut short like a man's. "But every woman that prayeth or prophesieth with her head uncovered dishonoureth her head: for that is even all one as if she were shaven. For if the woman be not covered, let her also be shorn: but if it be a shame for a woman to be shorn or shaven, let her be covered" (1 Cor. 11:5–6).

She Dishonors Her Husband

Since the head of the woman is the man, in particular her husband, when she practices her worship duties toward God and she has short hair, she is dishonoring her head, which is her husband. It also says that if she has short hair, this is the same as if she were shaven, and a shaven head is symbolic of shamefulness and embarrassment. Did you ever wonder why all the women wore what looked like doilies on their heads when they were in church back in the old days? Back then they took these verses seriously and felt that the wife was bringing dishonor to her husband if she didn't have something covering her head. I believe that if a woman has short hair like a man, then she should probably cover her head with something while in the church service; but if she has long hair, like the Word of God says she should, then her head is covered.

So when it comes to hair, what is considered long or short? If a man has hair that makes people think he is a woman when they approach him without seeing his face, then he has hair like a woman. If a woman has hair that is short enough that people think she is a man when they approach her without seeing her face, then she has short hair. For some people, you have to spell everything out in detail. In most cases men and women who do this intentionally are simply displaying their rebellion against their husbands, their wives, or their God.

God Made the Woman for the Man

Verse 7 of the same chapter explains that man is the image and glory of God. That is, man was made for God's glory and created in God's image. I told you earlier that gender was created for humans to join two people together and make them one for procreation. God is a spirit and must be worshipped in spirit (John 4:24). However, Jesus is the body of God; therefore, God is made manifest (visible) in a man's body. Man was made after the image and for the glory of God (so others could see the beauty emanating from God's character), but the woman was made for the glory of man. In other words, God made man for Himself, but He made the woman for the man.

This truth doesn't diminish the value or worth of either sex; it simply illustrates the fact that we were created under different circumstances and for different roles in God's plan, but God created us all with equal importance. The way I read this, God made the woman to be man's helper so she could help others see the beauty emanating from her husband's character. I think this will occur naturally if both the husband and wife live for God. She will sing his praises just as he will sing hers. "For a man indeed ought not to cover his head, for he is the image and glory of God: but the woman is the glory of the man" (1 Cor. 11:7).

Paul, the apostle, also points out here that the woman was created from the man and not the man from the woman. "For the man is not of the woman; but the woman of the man. Neither was the man created for the woman; but the woman for the man" (1 Cor. 11:8–9).

Women Will Desire to Have Man's God-Given Authority

In the last part of Genesis 3:16, we see this statement: "And thy desire shall be to thy husband and he shall rule over thee." "He shall rule over thee" is the source Paul uses in the verse in 1 Corinthians we just looked at. Note: Prior to "He shall rule over thee" is the statement "And thy desire shall be to thy husband." I have heard that this refers to a woman's natural desire to please her husband. After a little further study, I'm convinced it means something totally different. What I believe it means is that women will always have the desire to be in the position of authority God gave to men. That is, women will always desire to have positions of authority over men, but this is not the role God created for them.

This same statement is used in Genesis 4:7, when God said to Cain, "And unto thee shall be his desire and thou shalt rule over him." God said that Abel would have to serve Cain because Cain was the firstborn and that Abel would always desire to have Cain's position. Needless to say, Abel didn't always have a natural desire to please his brother, Cain, and women don't always have a natural desire to please their husbands. They want to rule by nature, but this is not God's way.

"For this cause ought the woman to have power on her head because of the angels" (1 Cor. 11:10). In verse 10, Paul uses the angels as an example for women to follow. He says women shouldn't argue with God about the order of things as He designed them, just like the angels don't argue with God in heaven. "Power on her head" refers to her desire to have authority over her husband. Just so men don't get too boastful here, Paul adds verses 11 and 12 to clarify the fact that even though God gave the man the position of authority, he needs to understand that this doesn't mean he is better than the woman.

Men and Women Are Equal Because Neither Can Exist without the Other

> Nevertheless neither is the man without the woman, neither the woman without the man, in the Lord. (1 Cor. 11:11)

> For as the woman is of the man, even so is the man also by the woman; but all things of God. (1 Cor. 11:12)

He says in verse 11 that the man cannot exist without the woman; nor can the woman exist without the man, and therefore in the Lord they are still equal. Then he stresses again that the woman was created for the man; however, the man is now born of the woman. They are equal, and both need each other to exist in the eyes of God. Paul concludes this topic in verses 13 through 15 by restating the same things he already said. "Judge in yourselves: is it comely that a woman pray unto God uncovered? Doth not even nature itself teach you, that, if a man have long hair, it is a shame unto him? But if a woman have long hair, it is a glory to her: for her hair is given her for a covering" (1 Cor. 11:13–15).

We already know that a woman shouldn't pray while she is uncovered. Her exposure brings shame and dishonor to her husband. Even nature itself tells us it's shameful for a man to have long hair like a woman. However, if a woman has long hair, it brings glory to her because it testifies to everyone that she has accepted the role God created her for and that she is in subjection to her husband and God. This glorifies her and her husband and God. Now I want to show you some other supporting verses.

Women Should Not Have Positions of Authority over Men in the Church

"Let the woman learn in silence with all subjection, but I suffer not a woman to teach nor usurp authority over the man, but to be in silence. For Adam was first formed, then Eve. And Adam was not deceived, but the woman being deceived was in the transgression" (1 Tim. 2:11–14). To "usurp," by the way, means to take away the power or authority belonging to someone else illegally or by force. God gave men power over women from the start, but Paul warns again here in the letter to Timothy that women will try to take that power away from men. He also gives two more reasons why God made man the head over the woman.

Because of the Order of Creation

First, there is because of the order of creation. "For Adam was first formed, then Eve." We already saw in Genesis 2:18 that the woman was created because the man needed a helper. I'd be the first person on earth to agree with that. Paul could also only be saying the same thing he already said in 1 Corinthians 11, that man was made for the glory of God, and later the woman was made for the glory of man.

Because the Woman Was Deceived by Satan

The other reason he gives here is the fact that the woman was deceived by Satan, not the man; therefore, she was in the transgression. *Transgression* is just another word for "sin," which is simply disobedience to God's laws. Surely we know that both the man and the woman sinned when they partook of the forbidden fruit, but Paul is saying that the woman was deceived by Satan and was convinced to commit the offense; then she gave the fruit to her husband. It doesn't say here whether Adam knew the fruit was from the forbidden tree, but if he did, it was still Eve who gave the fruit to him and convinced him to eat it. If he didn't, she deceived him into eating it. Either way, it appears that the woman is accredited with the bulk of the blame here; however, all three participants were punished for their part in the event, which would suggest that they all knew what they were doing.

> And the man said, the woman whom thou gavest to be with me, she gave me of the tree, and I did eat. And the Lord God said unto the woman, What is this that thou hast done? And the woman said, The serpent beguiled me, and I did eat. And the Lord God said unto the serpent, Because thou hast done this, thou art cursed above all cattle, and above every beast of the field upon thy belly shalt thou go, and dust shalt thou eat all the days of thy life: And I will put enmity between thee and the woman, and between thy seed and her seed; it shall bruise thy head, and thou shalt bruise his heel. Unto the woman he said, I will greatly multiply thy sorrow and thy conception; in sorrow thou shalt bring forth children; and thy desire shall be to thy husband, and he shall rule over thee. And unto Adam he said, Because thou hast hearkened unto the voice

of thy wife, and hast eaten of the tree, of which I commanded thee, saying, Thou shalt not eat of it: cursed is the ground for thy sake; in sorrow shalt thou eat of it all the days of thy life; Thorns also and thistles shall it bring forth to thee; and thou shalt eat the herb of the field; In the sweat of thy face shalt thou eat bread, till thou return unto the ground; for out of it wast thou taken: for dust thou art, and unto dust shalt thou return. (Gen. 3:12–19)

It appears here that the woman's subjection to her husband is part of the punishment for her allowing Satan to deceive her and then talking her husband into doing the same thing. Even though this is part of the reason, I know it sounds harsh to women to put it this way without any further explanation, so I'm going to try to explain a little better what is going on here and why. One thing I want to point out is that the devil was punished for deceiving the woman. The woman was punished for disobeying her husband, and the husband was punished for trying to please his wife over God.

Marriage Pictures Our Relationship with God

I think the best Bible verses to explain this part aren't actually talking about the marriage between a husband and wife but rather the marriage between Christ and the church. Nevertheless, this is one of the reasons why marriage between husband and wife is so important; it symbolizes or pictures the Christian's relationship with God. "Wives, submit yourselves unto your own husbands, as unto the Lord. For the husband is the head of the wife, even as Christ is the head of the church: and he is the saviour of the body" (Eph. 5:22–23).

The head over Jesus Christ is God the Father. Jesus said many times that He was here on earth to do the will of His Father, not

His own will. Even when He went to the cross, He asked the Father to save Him if it were possible; but then He said, ".....Nevertheless let not my will, but thine be done." (Lk. 22:42) We see here that everyone except God the Father has to answer to someone; even though Jesus was and is God and is equal to the Father, He still submitted to the Father's will.

We know that Jesus was with God in the beginning, but His form at the time was the Word of God. He didn't exist in worldly flesh at the time. Therefore, Jesus was the first man on earth to have the Spirit of God and also the first to be resurrected. Even though Jesus existed in the beginning, the body of Christ was created to represent God on the face of the earth through Mary. Man was created first in the image of God and for God. The woman was created second, but she was created for the man, not for God. Notice the verse says that the husband is the savior of the wife's body. He is not the savior of the soul or spirit of the wife but of the body. This means he is held accountable to God for her sanctification as long as she is in her natural body and is subject to his authority.

> Jesus saith unto them, My meat is to do the will of him that sent me, and to finish his work. (John 4:34)

> And he went a little farther, and fell on his face, and prayed, saying, O my Father, if it be possible, let this cup pass from me: nevertheless not as I will, but as thou wilt. (Matt. 26:39)

The head over the church (the body of Christ) is Christ. As Jesus was manifested in the flesh to do the will of God the Father, so the church was created to do the will of God the Son, Jesus. Then the woman was created to do the will of man. The Son cannot do the will of the father unless He is subject to the Father. The church cannot do the will of the Son unless it is subject to the will of the

Son, and the wife cannot do the will of her husband unless she is subject to the will of her husband. The Son was and is equal to the Father, the church was and is equal to the Son, and the wife was and is equal to the husband.

Wives Are Subject to Husbands in Everything

"Therefore as the church is subject unto Christ, so let the wives be to their own husbands in everything" (Eph. 5:24).

Husbands, Love Your Wives Enough to Die for Them

"Husbands, love your wives, even as Christ also loved the church, and gave himself for it" (Eph. 5:25). Husbands are told they should love their wives as they love themselves. A man should be willing to sacrifice his life for his wife just as Christ sacrificed Himself for the church. By the way, when a wife is subject to her husband, this means she is entitled to his guidance, provision, and protection. But wait, that's not all.

Wives Are Sanctified by Their Husbands

"That he might sanctify and cleanse it with the washing of water by the word, That he might present it to himself a glorious church, not having spot, or wrinkle, or any such thing; but that it should be holy and without blemish" (Eph. 5:26–27).

If a wife is subject to her husband, then her husband is also responsible for her sanctification. This doesn't mean salvation. Jesus saves, not man; but if she is to live by her husband's rules, then he is held accountable for her acceptance to God in the flesh. The verse above is talking about Jesus being responsible for the sanctification of His bride, the church. This is talking about the fact that after

Jesus died, He ascended into heaven and now acts as our high priest, making intercession for us because of our daily sins (Heb. 7:22–28). Just as Christ intercedes for the church, so the husband intercedes for his wife. Just as Christ prepares His bride to go to heaven, so also the husband prepares his wife to meet God.

We must comprehend the difference between sanctification and justification here. The husband doesn't save the wife just as the high priest doesn't save the people, but the job is to keep them sanctified or clean and therefore presentable to God. *Justified* means we are forgiven for being sinners, past tense; this is the finished work Christ did on the cross. Sanctification (being set apart for God's use; *holy* means the same thing) is a continual, ongoing cleansing that keeps us separated from the world to do God's work because God can't use an unclean vessel. Jesus is the intercessor for the church, and the husband is the intercessor for the wife. You may ask, "Just how is the husband supposed to do that?" The verse tells us that too: "With the washing of water by the word." She is cleansed by teaching her the Word of God. That is why Paul said that if the woman is to learn about spiritual things, she should ask her husband at home.

> By so much was Jesus made a surety of a better testament. And they truly were many priests, because they were not suffered to continue by reason of death: But this man, because he continueth ever, hath an unchangeable priesthood. Wherefore he is able also to save them to the uttermost that come unto God by him, seeing he ever liveth to make intercession for them. For such an high priest became us, who is holy, harmless, undefiled, separate from sinners, and made higher than the heavens; Who needeth not daily, as those high priests, to offer up sacrifice, first for his own sins, and then for the people's: for this he did once, when he offered up himself. For the law maketh men high priests which

have infirmity; but the word of the oath, which was since the law, maketh the Son, who is consecrated for evermore. (Heb. 7:22–28)

And if they will learn anything, let them ask their husbands at home: for it is a shame for women to speak in the church. (1 Cor. 14:35)

If the wife is to be obedient to or in subjection to her husband, then God holds the husband accountable for her sanctification. This is how it has to be because a wife's husband cannot be held accountable for her actions if she refuses to do what he asks. This is why God usually leads the family (spiritually speaking) through the husband, as I will illustrate later.

Christians' Bodies Are the Temple of God (Where God Lives)

"So ought men to love their wives as their own bodies. He that loveth his wife loveth himself. For no man ever yet hated his own flesh; but nourisheth and cherisheth it, even as the Lord the church. For we are members of his body, of his flesh, and of his bones" (Eph. 5:28–30).

Since the Holy Spirit lives inside Christians, we are the body of Christ. Therefore we are now the flesh and bone of God. We are God's temple not made with hands. Just as we are the flesh and bone of Christ through marriage, the wife and the husband are the flesh and bone of each other through marriage as well. This explains why the husband not only should be the head over the wife but also should be responsible for her guidance, sanctification, provision and protection, and her intercession and satisfaction.

"For this cause shall a man leave his father and mother, and shall be joined unto his wife, and they two shall be one flesh. This is a great mystery: but I speak concerning Christ and the church. Nevertheless let every one of you in particular so love his wife even as himself; and the wife see that she reverence her husband" (Eph. 5:31–33).

The Husband Is the Head of the Christian Home

There are a few things I'd like to mention about this verse. First, there is the leave-and-cleave principle. God intends the man to grow up and switch families, to leave his father and mother and cleave to his wife. Second, they are joined to one another and become one flesh. The Greek and Hebrew words used here and in Genesis mean two people stop being two people and become one person. There was the male and female version of humans, and after they joined, they became a third person. This third type of person is a complete person, which would indicate to me that the husband and wife are intended to make each other complete. The Word of God doesn't say this in so many words, but I believe that is what is insinuated. To sum it up, the husband should love his wife even as he loves himself, because they are one flesh, and the wife should respect her husband for the position of spiritual leadership God has placed him in. As the bishop is head of the church, the husband is the spiritual head of the Christian home.

In these last verses, we are told that this is why a woman should be in submission to her husband, why a husband should love his wife more than anyone other than God, and why a wife should reverence her husband. Ladies, if you consider the fact that your husband has to answer to God for your sanctification, your spiritual guidance for the entirety of your life, your provision, and your protection, "For no man ever yet hated his own flesh; but nourisheth and cherisheth it, even as the Lord the church:" (Eph 5:29), then is it really all that hard for you to follow his lead and respect him for all he does for you? The word *reverence* simply means to show respect. If your husband doesn't do any of these things for you, then he doesn't deserve the respect God is talking about here; but maybe if you pray for him to become a man of God and show him the respect anyhow, it will happen. The change has to start somewhere, and if he is saved, he should already be doing this for you; if not, then you should pray for his salvation.

One of my brothers told me a few days ago that he and his wife had been working out their differences for so long that he now knew how to get along with her without so much as a disagreement. He said that whenever they didn't see eye to eye on something, he just said he was sorry and admitted he was wrong, and she always agreed. He did add, however, that he always got the last word when they did have an argument. It was usually "Yes, ma'am," but still, he did get the last word.

God Gives Spiritual Guidance to the Husband

God Instructed Adam, Not Eve

God gave spiritual guidance to Adam first in the Garden of Eden. When these instructions were given to Adam concerning the tree of good and evil, Eve hadn't even been created yet. There is no record of God giving these instructions again to Eve. We know Eve received these instructions, however, because she was punished for not following them. We would have to assume then that Adam gave the instructions to Eve. These were instructions concerning spiritual matters God gave to the husband and the husband gave to the wife. Adam was eventually punished for listening to his wife instead of to God, and Eve was punished for listening to Satan instead of to her husband.

"And the LORD God took the man, and put him into the garden of Eden to dress it and to keep it. And the LORD God commanded the man, saying, Of every tree of the garden thou mayest freely eat: But of the tree of the knowledge of good and evil, thou shalt not eat of it: For in the day that thou eatest thereof thou shalt surely die. And the LORD God said, It is not good that the man should be alone; I will make him an help meet for him" (Gen. 2:15–18).

I know you are going to say this can't be true because Adam and Eve didn't die when they ate the fruit like God said they would. Actually they did die. They died a spiritual death. As I explained earlier, the word *death* means "to separate." In the beginning, Adam and Eve had spiritual life because they lived in God's continual presence. But when they ate the fruit, they were spiritually separated from God. Now let us continue the discussion concerning spiritual guidance in the marriage.

God Instructed Abram, Not Sarai

In this next example, God gave instructions to Abraham.

> Now the LORD had said unto Abram, Get thee out of thy country, and from thy kindred, and from thy father's house, unto a land that I will shew thee: And I will make of thee a great nation, and I will bless thee, and make thy name great; and thou shalt be a blessing: And I will bless them that bless thee, and curse him that curseth thee: and in thee shall all families of the earth be blessed. So Abram departed, as the LORD had spoken unto him; and Lot went with him: and Abram was seventy and five years old when he departed out of Haran. And Abram took Sarai his wife, and Lot his brother's son, and all their substance that they had gathered, and the souls that they had gotten in Haran; and they went forth to go into the land of Canaan; and into the land of Canaan they came. (Gen. 12:1–5)

The Bible says God chose Abraham because He knew Abraham would command his whole household to follow Him. I think I should mention a qualification here; if your husband is saved, then God will lead the family through him. If a man is going to claim the right to be the head over the wife based on God's Word concerning spiritual matters, then it should be made clear that God has given him this authority only if he is a man of God (or saved). We already saw in 1 Corinthians that if the husband isn't saved, the saved wife will assume the responsibility for the spiritual leadership in the home. Still, she is told to lead by example, not by assuming the authority God gave to the husband. Okay, I understand this gets complicated, trying to lead without having authority, but we are talking about spiritual matters here, not the head over the family in all matters. I will tell you that the husband doesn't have the authority to have the wife do something that is against God's laws. We don't have to be geniuses to know his authority isn't greater than God's.

"For I know him, that he will command his children and his household after him, and they shall keep the way of the Lord, to do justice and judgment; that the Lord may bring upon Abraham that which He hath spoken of him" (Gen. 18:19).

The Bible teaches that women should be in subjection to their husband's leadership just as Sarah obeyed Abraham.

> Likewise, ye wives, be in subjection to your own husbands; that, if any obey not the word, they also may without the word be won by the conversation of the wives; While they behold your chaste conversation coupled with fear. Whose adorning let it not be that outward adorning of plaiting the hair, and of wearing of gold, or of putting on of apparel; But let it be the hidden man of the heart, in that which is not corruptible, even the ornament of a meek and quiet spirit, which is in the sight of God of great price. For after this manner in the old

time the holy women also, who trusted in God, adorned themselves, being in subjection unto their own husbands: Even as Sara obeyed Abraham, calling him lord: whose daughters ye are, as long as ye do well, and are not afraid with any amazement. (1 Peter 3:1–6)

God Instructed Joshua, Not His Wife

Perhaps one of the most often-quoted verses in the Bible is Joshua's proclamation that, regardless of what anyone else did, he and his household were going to serve God. Joshua didn't ask his wife whether that would be okay with her. "And if it seem evil unto you to serve the LORD, choose you this day whom ye will serve; whether the gods which your fathers served that were on the other side of the flood, or the gods of the Amorites, in whose land ye dwell: but as for me and my house, we will serve the LORD" (Josh. 24:15).

Joshua, the man of God, most often doesn't receive the credit he deserves being in the shadows behind Moses. Joshua was a great man who served in the background as Moses' military captain as long as Moses lived. After Moses died, Joshua took over, and there are as many miraculous accomplishments recorded in the Word of God done through Joshua's leadership as there are through Moses'. I have listed some of the most prominent ones.

1. He brought down the walls of the great city of Jericho. (Josh. 6:20–21).
2. He parted the Jordan River to allow the Israelites to cross over on dry land. (Josh.4:10–18).
3. He made the sun stand still for twenty-four hours. (Josh.10:12–21).
4. He defeated five armies and five kings in one day. (Josh.10:12–21).

David Boudreaux

5. He led the children of Israel into the Promised Land. (Josh. 26:43–45).

God Instructed Joseph, Not Mary

Now I know what you are going to say: all this was in the Old Testament, and things are different now. Okay, so let me give you a New Testament example. Let us talk about the one woman who was so righteous in the sight of God that God chose her to be the mother of His only Son, Jesus. God chose Mary above all women, and rather than personally give her instructions concerning spiritual guidance, He led her through her future husband, Joseph. God waited until Mary was betrothed or engaged to be married before He allowed her to become pregnant with the Lord Jesus Christ. I believe this is true because God wanted Mary to have a husband to lead her spiritually as well as to provide for her and protect her. When two people became engaged to be married during this time period, this betrothal was just as binding as a marriage but lacked only the consummation. Therefore, God waited until Mary had submitted to Joseph's spiritual guidance.

> Now the birth of Jesus Christ was on this wise: When as his mother Mary was espoused to Joseph, before they came together, she was found with child of the Holy Ghost. Then Joseph her husband, being a just man, and not willing to make her a publick example, was minded to put her away privily. But while he thought on these things, behold, the angel of the LORD appeared unto him in a dream, saying, Joseph, thou son of David, fear not to take unto thee Mary thy wife: for that which is conceived in her is of the Holy Ghost. And she shall bring forth a son, and thou shalt call his name JESUS:

68

for he shall save his people from their sins. Now all this was done, that it might be fulfilled which was spoken of the Lord by the prophet, saying, Behold, a virgin shall be with child, and shall bring forth a son, and they shall call his name Emmanuel, which being interpreted is, God with us. Then Joseph being raised from sleep did as the angel of the Lord had bidden him, and took unto him his wife: And knew her not till she had brought forth her firstborn son: and he called his name JESUS. (Matt. 1:18–25)

So God gave Joseph charge over Mary, and it came to pass that as the time came for Mary to have the baby, Joseph had to go to be taxed in Jerusalem; and he took Mary with him. Now we know that it was prophesied that Jesus would be born in Bethlehem, but had Joseph not led Mary, how would she have gotten there? It is interesting to see how God works. God even used the government and taxes, of all things, to get Joseph and Mary where they needed to be to fulfill the scriptures. Incidentally, this is another passage of scripture that proves God intends for His children to obey the laws they are subjected to and even to pay taxes to a government they don't necessarily agree with all the time.

"And Joseph also went up from Galilee, out of the city of Nazareth, into Judaea, unto the city of David, which is called Bethlehem; (because he was of the house and lineage of David)To be taxed with Mary his espoused wife, being great with child. And so it was, that, while they were there, the days were accomplished that she should be delivered. And she brought forth her firstborn son, and wrapped him in swaddling clothes, and laid him in a manger; because there was no room for them in the inn" (Luke 2:4).

Later, after Jesus was born, God told Joseph to take the mother and child, and flee into Egypt because King Herod was going to try to find the child and have him killed. Again, God told Joseph, not Mary, to flee.

> And when they were departed, behold, the angel of
> the Lord appeareth to Joseph in a dream, saying,
> Arise, and take the young child and his mother, and
> flee into Egypt, and be thou there until I bring thee
> word: for Herod will seek the young child to destroy
> him. When he arose, he took the young child and
> his mother by night, and departed into Egypt: And
> was there until the death of Herod: that it might
> be fulfilled which was spoken of the Lord by the
> prophet, saying, Out of Egypt have I called my son.
> (Matt. 2:13–15)

After the death of Herod, again God told Joseph to take the mother and child back to Israel. He didn't tell Mary; He told Joseph. "But when Herod was dead, behold, an angel of the Lord appeareth in a dream to Joseph in Egypt, Saying, Arise, and take the young child and his mother, and go into the land of Israel: for they are dead which sought the young child's life. And he arose, and took the young child and his mother, and came into the land of Israel" (Matt. 2:19–21).

I have often thought about how this story would have worked out if Mary had been like most women are today. I can hear her saying to Joseph, "Why in the world can't we stay in one place? I'm tired of having to pack up everything and move over and over just because you say you had another dream. God never said anything to me about it. That's enough. I'm not doing it anymore."

Before Women Made a Vow to God, They Were to Check with Their Husbands

I think it's obvious at this point that God has made the man head over his wife, and through him God leads, provides, and protects. This can also be seen in the fact that the Bible teaches that a woman should be provided for by her father until she is married and then by her husband. The woman was even instructed that she shouldn't even make a vow to God that would interfere with her relationship between her and her father or her and her husband, depending on whether or not, she was married. If her husband objected to the vow, then God would release her from it. If a woman is widowed or divorced, however, then she will be held accountable to God for keeping her vow. If a woman makes a vow to God and her father or husband hears it and doesn't object, then she will be required to keep the vow. If the father or husband decides that he objects to her vow at a later date and tries to keep her from fulfilling her vow, then the husband or father will be held accountable for it. The bottom line is that God expects the wife or daughter to seek spiritual guidance through her father or husband.

> If a woman also vow a vow unto the LORD, and bind herself by a bond, being in her father's house in her youth; And her father hear her vow, and her bond wherewith she hath bound her soul, and her father shall hold his peace at her; then all her vows shall stand, and every bond wherewith she hath bound her soul shall stand. But if her father disallow her in the day that he heareth; not any of her vows, or of her bonds wherewith she hath bound her soul, shall stand: and the LORD shall forgive her, because her father disallowed her. And if she had at all an husband, when she vowed, or uttered ought out of her lips, wherewith she bound her soul; And her husband heard it, and held his peace at her in the day that he heard it: then her vows shall stand, and her bonds wherewith she bound her soul shall stand. But if her husband disallowed her on the day that he heard it; then he shall make her vow which she vowed, and that which she uttered with her

lips, wherewith she bound her soul, of none effect: and the LORD shall forgive her. But every vow of a widow, and of her that is divorced, wherewith they have bound their souls, shall stand against her. And if she vowed in her husband's house, or bound her soul by a bond with an oath; And her husband heard it, and held his peace at her, and disallowed her not: then all her vows shall stand, and every bond wherewith she bound her soul shall stand. But if her husband hath utterly made them void on the day he heard them; then whatsoever proceeded out of her lips concerning her vows, or concerning the bond of her soul, shall not stand: her husband hath made them void; and the LORD shall forgive her. Every vow, and every binding oath to afflict the soul, her husband may establish it, or her husband may make it void. But if her husband altogether hold his peace at her from day to day; then he establisheth all her vows, or all her bonds, which are upon her: he confirmeth them, because he held his peace at her in the day that he heard them. But if he shall any ways make them void after that he hath heard them; then he shall bear her iniquity. These are the statutes, which the LORD commanded Moses, between a man and his wife, between the father and his daughter, being yet in her youth in her father's house. (Num. 30:3–16)

This doesn't in any way suggest that women are incapable of making decisions for themselves or that their vows are less important than men. It's just how God wants things done. I should mention here that these scriptures point out that when a woman follows God's instructions, she will not be held accountable for anything she does or shouldn't do if her father or husband tells her to do it. However, if she is widowed or divorced and commits a sin, she will be held accountable to God for what she did. The man may be given the privileges that go with leadership, but he is also given the responsibilities. This is one area in which the husband serves as intercessor between his wife and God.

I own an aviation business, and I know this isn't exactly the same thing, but imagine that one of the people working for me did something wrong and the Federal Aviation Administration discovered it. Since that individual did the work under my authority, I would be the one held accountable for his or her actions. The woman may be subject to the man's authority, but she is also entitled to his guidance, provision, and protection. This may include protection from God's wrath for something she did wrong. This doesn't mean God doesn't listen to the wife's prayers or answer them—or that He doesn't provide her with spiritual guidance. But I do believe that when it comes to major spiritual decisions that will affect the affairs of the household, including the husband's personal ministry or issues concerning the man's responsibilities, such as provision or protection for the family, God will most likely communicate to the man what He wants regarding these matters. At the same time, I believe God will give the wife guidance concerning issues such as taking care of her husband, managing the home, or raising the children. These are her primary responsibilities.

I have seen God reveal certain things to my wife that He didn't tell me, and I have seen Him answer her prayers concerning things I didn't even know about until she told me. I know God listens to her, and He considers the issues she deals with in her life just as important as the ones I deal with. Last night she told me that God had communicated with her about being involved in starting a new ministry. I explained to her that if God wanted us to start a new ministry involving preaching, then I believed God would eventually tell me what He wanted me to do; and when He did, I would obey. In the meantime, I believe God may be preparing her for something He hasn't even revealed to me yet. This can be illustrated by the fact that God told Mary that she was going to become pregnant with the Son of God before He told Joseph what his responsibilities would be concerning the child's birth in Jerusalem. So God may give the wife some guidance, even concerning spiritual things, that He doesn't reveal to the husband right away. But He will not tell her anything contradictory to God's Word or to what He has told or will tell her husband.

A father gave his young Christian daughter in marriage to a young man who seemed to be a good man at the time. The young woman tried to do everything she thought would please her husband, but he never seemed to be satisfied with her efforts. The longer they were together, the harder she tried, and the meaner he became. After a while of being treated disrespectfully like she wasn't good enough for him, she began to hate her life and was depressed all the time. Even though she continued to try to please him in every way she could think of, his mistreatment of her continued to grow worse.

One day she was doing his laundry, and she became so upset that she began to cry and pray to God about what she should do. She sat down at the table and wrote a list of all the things she did for him every day and how much she had come to resent every part of it. She continued because it was what she thought God wanted her to do, but she hated every minute of it. When she was done with the list, she sat there for a while and then heard her husband coming. She had planned on giving the list to him but decided it would probably just make the situation worse, so she folded it up and put it in the bottom of her dresser drawer under some clothes and forgot all about it.

Eventually her husband became so disgruntled in the marriage that he left her, and soon he married someone else. Eventually, she also remarried a man from her church. I do believe it is permissible for a woman to remarry under certain conditions after her husband has divorced her, as we have already seen. Anyhow, after they had been married for several years, she was doing spring cleaning one day and decided to clean out all the dressers and get rid of clothes she didn't wear anymore. While doing so, she found the note she had written to her previous husband all those years ago, and after she had read the list, she started laughing. One of her friends who was helping her clean asked her what was so funny. She replied, "I wrote this list of all the things I hated to do as a wife many years ago. I found this list, and now I realize I am doing all those things I did then and even many more things I didn't do then, and now I love every minute of it. I love taking care of my husband, and these things I hated doing back then I now enjoy because I love making my husband happy."

So you see, men, if your wife isn't happy being your wife and doing wifely things, maybe, just maybe, it's not her fault.

CHAPTER 4

The Woman's Role at Church

The Head of Every Woman Is Man

I don't want to beat a dead horse to death by continuing to bring up the order of creation, but to ensure that I'm thorough in this discussion and to make sure I'm not taking anything out of context, it will be necessary to mention some things over again. Three main portions of scripture cover the topic of the woman's role in the church: 1 Corinthians 11:3–16; 1 Corinthians 14:1–35; and 1 Timothy 2:9–15. I will cover each of these passages in detail, but in doing so, there are a few things that will be mentioned several times. Since I have already spent a significant amount of time explaining these things, I will leave them in context but will not spend much time discussing them.

> But I would have you know, that the head of every man is Christ; and the head of the woman is the man; and the head of Christ is God. *Every man praying or prophesying, having his head covered, dishonoureth his head. But every woman that prayeth or prophesieth with her head uncovered dishonoureth her head*: for that is even all one as if she were shaven. For if the woman be not covered, let her

> also be shorn: but if it be a shame for a woman to
> be shorn or shaven, let her be covered. *For a man*
> *indeed ought not to cover his head, forasmuch as he*
> *is the image and glory of God: but the woman is the*
> *glory of the man.* For the man is not of the woman:
> but the woman of the man. Neither was the man
> created for the woman; but the woman for the man.
> (1 Cor. 11:3–9 emphasis added)

Because of the Order of Creation and the Reason for Creation

This is just another way of saying the same things I already explained in the previous chapter, simply that Christ is head of the church, God the Father is the head over Christ, and the husband is head over his wife for two basic reasons. Those are the order of creation and the reason they were created. What we didn't pay attention to before is that women should have their heads covered when *praying or prophesying.* Here it would indicate that it isn't forbidden for women to preach or pray, but as we shall see later, they shouldn't be placed in positions of authority over men in the church. The reason we are given in the verse is that this usurps the authority of her husband and therefore dishonors him. Perhaps this would indicate that they should be allowed to preach or teach other women or children at home or in the church. The reason they should not do so with their heads uncovered is because this gesture signifies rebellion against their husbands. This could also suggest that it would be okay for the wife to pray or even speak in the church if she does so under her husband's authorization, and that is because her purpose is to bring glory to her husband (help other people to see his attributes).

"For this cause ought the woman to have power on her head because of the angels" (1 Cor. 11:10). The woman doesn't have authority over men at the church, and her long hair is symbolic of her submission. "Because of the angels" just means she should show her submission without argument just as the angels do not argue with God concerning their submission to Him.

"Nevertheless neither is the man without the woman, neither the woman without the man, in the Lord. For as the woman is of the man, even so is the man also by the woman; but all things of God. Judge in yourselves: is it comely that a woman pray unto God uncovered?" (1 Cor. 11:11–13).

Men and Women Are Equal but Not the Same

To reiterate, this does not in any way suggest that the woman is not equal to the man. Paul states here that even though the woman came from the man, the man comes from the woman. Submission is supported by the order of creation, but equality is supported by procreation. They are both true and not contradictory.

"Doth not even nature itself teach you, that, if a man have long hair, it is a shame unto him? But if a woman have long hair, it is a glory to her: for her hair is given her for a covering. But if any man seem to be contentious, we have no such custom, neither the churches of God" (1 Cor. 11:14).

Long Hair on Men and Short Hair on Women

In these last four verses, Paul says that if a man has long hair, it is shameful because he is symbolically denying the position of authority God gave him. But if a woman has short hair, she is symbolically rebelling against God's plan for her. I think it is interesting that all the movies throughout the years have portrayed Jesus as having long hair. We know this isn't true because the Bible says doing so would be shameful. This isn't really important, just an observation.

Most theological scholars say that the last part of this verse should be interpreted to mean that we can argue about long hair on men if we want, but this is the only custom that is acceptable in all churches. I'm not convinced of that interpretation. To me it seems to be saying that, based on the scriptures, this is how God wants us to wear our hair because of what it signifies. However, if a man or woman chooses to do his or her hair differently, this is more of a preference than a conviction. In other words, the church shouldn't make a scene or ban someone from attending services because of this issue. This is just my opinion, of course.

The Role of Women in the Church

Now let us take a look at 1 Corinthians14, where Paul gives more specific instructions concerning how women should behave at church. These instructions were given specifically concerning the use of gifts in the church, but we can learn a lot more than that from this passage of scripture.

> Follow after charity, and desire spiritual gifts, but rather that ye may prophesy. For he that speaketh in an unknown tongue speaketh not unto men, but unto God: for no man understandeth him; howbeit in the spirit he speaketh mysteries. But he that prophesieth speaketh unto men to edification, and exhortation, and comfort. He that speaketh in an unknown tongue edifieth himself; but he that prophesieth edifieth the church. I would that ye all spake with tongues but rather that ye prophesied: for greater is he that prophesieth than he that speaketh with tongues, except he interpret, that the church may receive edifying. Now, brethren, if I come unto you speaking with tongues, what shall I profit you, except I shall speak to you either by revelation, or by knowledge, or by prophesying, or by doctrine? And even things without life giving sound, whether

pipe or harp, except they give a distinction in the sounds, how shall it be known what is piped or harped? For if the trumpet give an uncertain sound, who shall prepare himself to the battle? So likewise ye, except ye utter by the tongue words easy to be understood, how shall it be known what is spoken? for ye shall speak into the air. There are, it may be, so many kinds of voices in the world, and none of them without signification. Therefore if I know not the meaning of the voice, I shall be unto him that speaketh a barbarian, and he that speaketh shall be a barbarian unto me. Even so ye, forasmuch as ye are zealous of spiritual gifts, seek that ye may excel to the edifying of the church. Wherefore let him that speaketh in an unknown tongue pray that he may interpret. For if I pray in an unknown tongue, my spirit prayeth, but my understanding is unfruitful. What is it then? I will pray with the spirit, and I will pray with the understanding also: I will sing with the spirit, and I will sing with the understanding also. Else when thou shalt bless with the spirit, how shall he that occupieth the room of the unlearned say Amen at thy giving of thanks, seeing he understandeth not what thou sayest? For thou verily givest thanks well, but the other is not edified. I thank my God, I speak with tongues more than ye all: Yet in the church I had rather speak five words with my understanding, that by my voice I might teach others also, than ten thousand words in an unknown tongue. Brethren, be not children in understanding: howbeit in malice be ye children, but in understanding be men. In the law it is written, With men of other tongues and other lips will I speak unto this people; and yet for all that will they not hear me, saith the Lord. Wherefore tongues are for a sign, not to them that believe, but to them that believe not: but prophesying serveth not for them that believe not, but for them which believe. (1 Cor. 14:1–22)

Concerning the Practice of Speaking in Tongues

1. It was never intended to be used during the church service.

    In these verses we see that Paul is specifically commenting on the gift of tongues. He is not saying there is anything wrong with speaking in tongues but rather that you should understand that this particular gift was not intended to be used in the church. It was given as a sign to the unbeliever that the Holy Spirit was given to the gentiles the same as it had been given to the Jews. This was necessary at the beginning of the church age because the Jewish people didn't believe God was offering salvation to anyone except the descendants of Abraham. He goes on to say that speaking in tongues edifies (lifts up) only oneself and that it would be better to prophesy (preach) in the church so everyone is lifted up. He emphasizes that in the church it is better to speak five words people understand than ten thousand words they don't.

    "And when there had been much disputing, Peter rose up, and said unto them, Men and brethren, ye know how that a good while ago God made choice among us, that the Gentiles by my mouth should hear the word of the gospel, and believe. And God, which knoweth the hearts, bare them witness, giving them the Holy Ghost, even as he did unto us; And put no difference between us and them, purifying their hearts by faith" (Acts 15:7–9).

2. Tongues in their true form are not gibberish.

One last point: it was prophesied that the gift of tongues would be given, but this gift wasn't gibberish that no one could understand. Rather, it was a gift that prophets could use to communicate the gospel (the good news) to people in their own languages, even though the prophets had never learned them.

Now when this was noised abroad, the multitude came together, and were confounded, because that every man heard them speak in his own language. And they were all amazed and marvelled, saying one to another, Behold, are not all these which speak Galilaeans? And how hear we every man in our own tongue, wherein we were born? (Acts 2:6–8)

If therefore the whole church be come together into one place, and all speak with tongues, and there come in those that are unlearned, or unbelievers, will they not say that ye are mad? But if all prophesy, and there come in one that believeth not, or one unlearned, he is convinced of all, he is judged of all: And thus are the secrets of his heart made manifest; and so falling down on his face he will worship God, and report that God is in you of a truth. (1 Cor. 14:23–25)

3. Speaking in tongues during the service will make unbelievers think you're mad.

Here Paul says that if you speak in tongues at church, unbelievers or people uneducated in the Word of God will think you are mad. But if you preach the gospel of Christ to them, they will be convicted of their sins and be converted. From this verse, I want to show you the power of prophesying (preaching) to the unbeliever:

a. "He is convinced of all" (persuaded to believe the gospel).
b. "He is judged of all" (convicted of his own sin).
c. "The secrets of his heart made manifest" (will understand his need for a savior).
d. "Falling down on his face he will worship God" (he will repent and turn to God).
e. "And report that God is in you of a truth" (he will know that God lives inside Christians and that the church is real).

4. Regardless of what gift is used, everything should be done in order; therefore, there should be no tongues without an interpreter.

How is it then, brethren? when ye come together, every one of you *hath a psalm, hath a doctrine, hath a tongue, hath a revelation, hath an interpretation.* Let all things be done unto edifying. If any man speak in an unknown tongue, let it be by two, or at the most by three, and that by course; and let one interpret. But if there be no interpreter, let him keep silence in the church; and let him speak to himself, and to God. Let the prophets speak two or three, and let the other judge. If anything be revealed to another that sitteth by, let the first hold his peace. For ye may all prophesy one by one, that all may learn, and all may be comforted. And the spirits of the prophets are subject to the prophets. *For God is not the author of confusion*, but of peace, as in all churches of the saints. (1 Cor. 14:26–33 emphasis added)

In these verses, we are told that no matter what gift you have and exercise in the church, use it in a way that will lift the whole church, not just yourself. If you are going to use tongues, then two or three at the most may speak, one at a time; and then there must be an interpreter. If there is no interpreter, then don't speak in tongues in the church at all. He continues by saying that if there are preachers, they should speak with only two or three in a row, one at a time of course, while the other preachers hold their peace and judge what is being said. If one of them wants to speak, he should wait until others are finished. This way everyone will learn and be comforted. Then he makes a very profound and important statement: "And the spirits of the prophets are subject to the prophets." This means no one should be controlled by the spirit that is in them if the spirit is from God. The order will be easily maintained if it is of God. If the service appears to be out of control, then it is not from God. It seems to be apparent that they were having trouble keeping order in the church; these last few verses seem to indicate there was disorder because the church was being orchestrated by women professing to be speaking in tongues. Paul says if they can't maintain order in practicing this gift, then it is not from God. This is because God isn't the author of confusion, which is the opposite of order.

5. Some believe several of the gifts needed at the beginning of the church age ended with the completion of the Word of God, which ended the apostolic age. Several gifts are listed (1 Cor. 14:26), as we have already seen above. This is the main difference between the Pentecostal religion and other protestant religions. Those gifts listed include the following:

a. "A psalm" (musical talent or ability): still active
b. "A doctrine" (ability to comprehend and expound on doctrine or instruct): still active
c. "A tongue" (ability to speak in a foreign language without having been taught the language): no longer active
d. "A revelation" (the revealing or writing of new scripture, prophesying, or foretelling): no longer active
e. "An interpretation" (ability to interpret a foreign language without learning it): no longer active

The inactive gifts listed above are speaking in tongues, prophesying, and interpreting tongues. Most religions believe these gifts were done away with when the last scripture was written. This belief is based on the following verses.

God, who at sundry times and in divers manners spake in time past unto the fathers by the prophets, Hath in these last days spoken unto us by his Son, whom he hath appointed heir of all things, by whom also he made the worlds; Who being the brightness of his glory, and the express image of his person, and upholding all things by the word of his power, when he had by himself purged our sins, sat down on the right hand of the Majesty on high. (Heb. 1:1–3)

Charity never faileth: *but whether there be prophecies, they shall fail; whether there be tongues, they shall cease; whether there be knowledge, it shall vanish away.* For we know in part, and we prophesy in part. *But when that which is perfect is come, then that which is in part shall be done away.* When I was a child, I spake as a child, I understood as a child,

I thought as a child: but when I became a man, I put away childish things. For now we see through a glass, darkly; but then face to face: now I know in part; but then shall I know even as also I am known. And now abideth faith, hope, charity, these three; but the greatest of these is charity. (1 Cor. 13:8–13 emphasis added)

The Pentecostals believe the reference "when that which is perfect is come" refers to the Second Coming of Christ. Most other religions believe "that which is perfect" is referring to the perfect Word of God, which is the completed Bible. This was accomplished with the writing of the book of Revelation, which occurred around AD 95–96 by the apostle John. It says, "when *that* which is perfect is come," not "when *He* who is perfect has come."

Women Are to Be Silent in Church

"Let your women keep silence in the churches: for it is not permitted unto them to speak; but they are commanded to be under obedience as also saith the law. And if they will learn anything, let them ask their husbands at home: for it is a shame for women to speak in the church" (1 Cor. 14:34).

1. This church was out of control and being run by women.

   Paul intended to get this church back in order through these instructions. He felt that to do that he needed to remind the church that women were supposed to stay silent in the churches. If they wanted to learn something spiritual, they should ask their husbands at home. The husband should be the pastor of the home.
2. They shouldn't have authority over men.

   He also said it was shameful for women to speak in

the church. I don't think he meant they weren't allowed to speak at all but rather that they shouldn't be running the church service. They shouldn't speak in tongues, be in positions of authority over men, or preach to men. We already know that the husband is held accountable for the spiritual guidance of his wife. I believe when the Bible was finished, the gifts of prophecy (foretelling), speaking in tongues, interpreting tongues, and the gift of knowledge (refers to the proclamation of doctrine) were done away with, but when this epistle of Paul was written, they were still active. We can also deduce that since women can't pray or preach with their heads uncovered, that they can do so with their heads covered. The stipulation would be that they were never allowed to usurp authority over the men, especially not their husbands.

The Way Women Should Dress in Church

The last portion of scripture we will look at concerning the woman's role in the church is 1 Timothy 2:9–15. In this passage the apostle Paul is writing a letter (epistle) to one of his converts, so it is believed, concerning instructions on running a church. Timothy was a young, inexperienced pastor at the church in Ephesus.

"In like manner also, that women adorn themselves in modest apparel, with shamefacedness and sobriety; not with broided hair, or gold, or pearls, or costly array" (1Tim. 2:9).

1. She doesn't draw attention to her body.

    This is talking about the way a woman should dress in church. She should actually dress the same way anywhere in public. Modest apparel is just what it sounds like. Women should not dress in a way that brings attention to their physical attributes. Alluring attire is meant for their husbands in private. Women can dress nicely without trying to show off their bodies. This is what I suggested earlier when I said women can wear pants, in my opinion, as long as they don't bring attention to their bodies. You know what I'm talking about. Some women's clothes leave little to the imagination.

2. She still gets embarrassed.

"Shamefacedness" describes someone who is able to show shame. She is a woman who is offended to see someone improperly dressed. She isn't used to vulgar language and so forth.

3. She has a sound mind (nothing influencing her clear thinking).

Sobriety means a sound mind, not one altered by alcohol, drugs, or anything else.

4. She isn't worldly.

"Broided hair" means hairdos that represent worldliness such as mohawks, purple or green hair, men's haircuts, and so forth.

5. She dresses like a lady.

She also shouldn't wear anything considered vulgar, cheap, or showy such as expensive jewelry or excessive makeup. (She shouldn't dress like a harlot; you ladies know what that means.) In my opinion, Some of the ladies representing Christianity in the past were good examples of how women should *not* dress or wear makeup.

A fellow told me last week that he saw his wife put on her seductive undergarments that morning. He said that could mean only one thing; it was laundry day. Yes, this is a serious topic, but there is no reason why we can't have fun talking about it. You know God has a sense of humor.

6. She has godliness.

"But (which becometh women professing godliness) with good works" (1Tim. 2:10).

7. She has a good testimony.

     She should have a good testimony in her personality, dress, appearance, and character.

In Subjection to and Not in Authority over Men

"Let the woman learn in silence with all subjection. But I suffer not a woman to teach, nor to usurp authority over the man, but to be in silence. For Adam was first formed, then Eve. And Adam was not deceived, but the woman being deceived was in the transgression" (1Tim. 2:11–14).

She should learn in silence in the church, showing subjection to her husband. She is strictly forbidden to teach or exercise any kind of authority over a man. But she should remain silent, because Adam was made before Eve, and she was the one deceived by Satan, resulting in the fall of mankind. If the woman spoke with the permission or authority of the pastor or her husband, then she wasn't usurping his authority.

Women Have a Significant Role to Bear and Raise Their Children

"Notwithstanding she shall be saved in childbearing, if they continue in faith and charity and holiness with sobriety" (1Tim. 2:15).

He summarizes by saying women have a worthy purpose, and that is bearing children (which was mentioned earlier as a way of proving their equality) if they stay faithful, loving, holy (sanctified), and chaste. This verse also refers to their salvation, which is accomplished through their faith, love, and sanctification. Faith is required for salvation and love, and sanctification is proof of salvation. This concludes the verses that pertain to women's behavior in the church, but still other scriptures pertain to the woman's role at home.

Older Women Should Teach and Train Younger Women

These next verses in the book of Titus were instructions given to older women as to the things they should teach younger women. As we have already seen in the book of Proverbs under the description of the perfect wife, many of these things aren't taught anymore.

"The aged women likewise, that they be in behaviour as becometh holiness, not false accusers, not given to much wine, teachers of good things" (Titus 2:3).

Lead by Example

1. Be holy.
    "Behaviour as becometh holiness" means they should act like Christians, separated from the unrighteousness practiced by the unsaved world we live in.
2. Don't be false accusers.
    "Not false accusers" means they shouldn't spread rumors or talk about people behind their backs.
3. Don't be given to much wine.
    (Personally I believe "not given to much wine" verifies the fact that God says it's okay to have a bit of alcohol on occasion.) The idea is to stay sound minded. I think it is sinful to let anything control you, which happens when you overdo it. I also believe some people can't control the amount they consume or the way they act when they do so. That is the reason for the terminology to stay sober, meaning in your right mind. If some people have a problem in these areas, they shouldn't open themselves up to allow the devil to tempt them. Just for the record, neither my wife nor I drink, but I don't judge those who do provided that they maintain a sound mind.

Teachers of Good Things

Finally, this verse concludes with "teachers of good things." I believe this passage would also authorize women to teach younger women and children in the church. Some of the things they should teach are mentioned in the following verses.

"That they may teach the young women to be sober, to love their husbands, to love their children" (Titus 2:4).

1. Teach them to be sober.

    "Teach the young women to be sober" means to keep a sound mind. This precludes the use of drugs or alcohol to the point that it causes others to do things they wouldn't do if they hadn't taken them. I believe moderate use of alcohol or certain drugs is still allowed so long as they don't alter the ability to behave normally. Keep in mind the fact that some people may need some medication to act normally.

2. Teach them to love their husbands and children.

    Sometimes love doesn't come naturally. Sometimes love has to be taught and earned. I still know women who tell me they were married when they were very young because they wanted to get out of the house, or their parents wanted them out; but they didn't love the men they had married. Over time they learned to love them because of the love their husbands showed them through the years. Sometimes it takes years to get there. The Bible says we learn to love God because He first loved us (1 John 4:19). I think this is true. How can you love someone you don't really know that well? Most women love their children right away, and I think this is how God intended it to be, but that isn't always true either. This is one form of what God refers to as lacking natural affection. (2 Tim. 3:3).

    Some situations can make this difficult for some women as well, such as postpartum depression or the terrible twos.

Too often these days, women have children before they are ready, and they feel as though the child just gets in the way of how they want to live their lives at the time. It's important to get married when you are ready to be married and to have children when you are ready to have children. When people say this child was a mistake or that he or she was the result of a drunken party one night, this statement makes it obvious that this woman isn't yet ready to be a mother. Unfortunately, it's the child who pays the price. This is why it's important for women to teach their daughters to be sober, chaste, and loving to their husbands and children.

A census taker came to one home, and when he knocked on the door, a young woman answered. The man explained that he was there for the census and proceeded to ask her whether she was married. She replied that she wasn't married but lived there with her five children, so he asked her what the children's names and ages were. She replied that the names of her five boys were Dennis. The man asked her what the rest of the names were, and she said they were all named Dennis. So the man asked her, "Well, then how do you call them in for dinner in the evening?"

She replied, "I just call out, 'Dennis, it's time for dinner,' and they all come in."

The man asked her, "Well, what do you do if you only want one of them?"

She replied, "Well, in that case, I would use his last name."

This is a funny story, but at the same time, it's not very funny. It illustrates the moral condition of our society. Too often this is the reality today, and again it is the children who suffer. This is the result of a society that teaches that morality is a joke, that people should act on their immoral impulses without concern for the final results. These days many people live as though there are no consequences for their actions. It is a society where the government takes care of those who have acted irresponsibly and therefore forces those who act responsibly to pay their way. This is a society in which every person does what is right in his or her own eyes with no regard for God (Judg. 20:25).This is what is now being referred to as democratic socialism, where all of them feel like they are entitled to a free ride in life no matter how they act.

According to God, these people should be cared for by their families first; and if there is no family, then the church should step in. Socialistic societies cannot support themselves for any extended period. You can take from those who have earned their own way for only so long before they either run out of resources or move to another country. I didn't mean to get off on a side trail, but it's important to understand what the breakdown of the family unit results in. Ladies, the things you should be teaching your daughters are vital in the struggle to maintain the family unit and preserve a godly society and nation.

More Good Things They Should Teach the Younger Women

> "To be discreet, chaste, keepers at home, good, obedient to their own husbands, that the word of God be not blasphemed" (Titus 2:5).

1. Be discreet.

     Be careful to avoid being offensive to anyone, especially if it is done to gain an advantage.
2. Be chaste.

     Be sexually pure. There should be no sex if they are single and sex only with their husbands if they are married.
3. Be keepers at home.

     Be keepers at home (the woman's main job is to take care of her husband, children, and home). I will show you later that a woman's home is where she is the ruler. This doesn't mean she should be confined to the house.

4. "Be good" is self-explanatory (righteous).
5. Be obedient to their own husbands.

How can the wife be the ruler of her house if she has to be obedient to her husband? I believe as a married couple, most decisions should be made together, even though the husband should have the final say. However, there are things I do that I don't ask my wife about, such as running my business. On the other hand, I know the home is her domain and that she pretty much does anything and everything she wants to there. She is much better at taking care of the house, the children, the grand children and the yard than I am. Every good boss knows that the key to running a successful business is not knowing how to do everything himself or herself but rather how to hire people who are good at what they do and let them do it. If they are better at it than you are, stay out of their way and let them do it. My wife is way better at running the home than I could ever be.

6. Refrain from blaspheming the Word of God.

This simply refers to the fact that God intended the husband to be head over his wife, and to break this rule is to blaspheme the Word of God. To "blaspheme" simply means to speak out against or ill of something. The wisdom is displayed by the way the husband exercises that right and responsibility.

General Instructions for Women

This next passage of scripture is talking about widows and the responsibility of the church family regarding their care, but we can learn several other things about the roles of women in general from these verses.

"Rebuke not an elder, but intreat him as a father; and the younger men as brethren; The elder women as mothers; the younger

as sisters, with all purity. Honour widows that are widows indeed"
(1Tim. 5:1–3).

1. Respect elders.

   You should not rebuke or correct elders but treat them
   like you would your own father. This is talking about older
   men in the church. In some places, the word "elders" means
   church leaders, but here it is only referring to older men, not
   bishops or deacons.
2. Treat younger men in the church as brothers.

   This isn't talking about Christian brothers, even though
   that would also be true, but it is saying we should treat a
   Christian brother like we would a brother in your fleshly
   family.

Respecting Your Elders

When I was growing up, this was called "respecting your elders."
Of course, it wasn't talking about church elders because I grew up
as a Catholic and we didn't call the ministers in the church "elders."
Anyhow, we were taught to treat older people with respect. Wow,
what a strange concept! Yes, sir, when I was young, every child
answered adults with "Yes, ma'am" or "Yes, sir." It was normal to
say "please" and "thank you."Nowadays, don't expect children to do
this. They will act like you are asking them to commit some sort of
sin if you expect any kind of respect from them.

My son Paul was accepted into a military program where only
a very few special people were chosen. It was a program of the
US AirForce, where the intention was to recruit certain people to
become military officers. If they were chosen, the military would
pay for the rest of their college degrees if they served for a couple of
years as officers in the service of their country afterward. I told him
that I was very proud of him for his achievements. He replied that

it was because of me that he had been accepted. I asked him, "How so?" He told me that he had been asked to write an essay about why he should be chosen over other candidates, and he chose to write a story about something that had happened when he was a child. The story he told went something like this:

> My dad was driving down the road one day, and he had me and a couple of my brothers with him in the vehicle. We drove by this house and saw an old man who's riding lawnmower was stuck in the ditch in front of his house. (Yes, they had riding lawnmowers when my kids were young.) He drove to the next street, turned the car around, went back to the man's house, and pulled off to the side of the road in front of his house. We got out of the vehicle and helped the old man pull his lawn mower out of the ditch. Then we cleaned it up and had him start it back up to make sure everything still worked. After asking him if he was okay and if he needed anything else, we got back in the car and proceeded on our way. This is how I was taught you should treat your elders.

My son Paul told me that he had been selected for this special military program based on this story. I never got the chance to read the story he submitted, but I'm sure he told it more elegantly than I did here.

Treatment of Women in the Church

Older Women

The older women should be treated as you would your mother. Women are spoken of with equality to men as they should be. I feel like I have to keep pointing this out because women today seem to feel as though they are being treated as second-class citizens because God doesn't want them to rule over men. That is simply not true; they are equal to men in every way, but they are created to serve a different purpose in God's plan. Remember, I told you God had to create for man a worthy adversary—oops, I meant companion. (I'm just kidding around.)

Don't think that my son who went into the air force is perfect, by the way. He told me another story a while back that proves otherwise. He said he and his wife were having breakfast, and something unexpected happened. You know how sometimes your mind is wandering when someone asks you an unrelated question? You intend to say one thing, but something else comes out. Well, he meant to ask his wife, "Honey could you please pass me the Post Toasties, but what came out was, "You ruined my life." Paul is such a good boy! He and his wife actually get along very well.

Younger Women

We should treat the younger women as we would a sister. That is with all respect and purity.

Widows Indeed

Honor widows who are "widows indeed." Women whose husbands have died and are cared for by the church deserve to be honored because they have proven themselves worthy by meeting the qualifications of "widows indeed."

Qualifications of Widows Indeed

"But if any widow have children or nephews, let them learn first to shew piety at home, and to requite their parents: for that is good and acceptable before God. Now she that is a widow indeed, and desolate, trusteth in God, and continueth in supplications and prayers night and day" (1Tim. 5:4–5).

1. She is desolate (left without means of support).
2. She trusts in God to take care of her; she has no family.
3. She continues in prayer and supplication (begging God) day and night.

If the widow has surviving children (specifically sons) or nephews, then the family should accept the responsibility to take care of her, not the church. If she doesn't have any family who can take care of her and she is left desolate, trusts in God, and continues in prayer and supplication (the act of begging or pleading, asking for her needs to be met) day and night, then the church should care for her.

Widows Who Live for the Things of the World (and Not God) Are Not the Church's Responsibility

"But she that liveth in pleasure is dead while she liveth" (1 Tim. 5:6).

To live in pleasure is talking about a woman who denies God and denies her responsibilities; she lives for the pleasures of a sinful lifestyle. To be dead while she lives refers to the fact that she remained unsaved (separated from God) during her lifetime. This is not suggesting that a life for God shouldn't be pleasurable, but the author of Hebrews said it is better to suffer affliction for God than to serve the pleasures of sin for a season. If Moses would have claimed to be Pharaoh's daughter's son, he would have been entitled to a life of pleasure, leisure, and luxury.

"By faith Moses, when he was come to years, refused to be called the son of Pharaoh's daughter; Choosing rather to suffer affliction with the people of God, than to enjoy the pleasures of sin for a season" (Heb. 11:24–25).

More Qualifications of the Widow Indeed

> And these things give in charge, that they may be blameless. But if any provide not for his own, and specially for those of his own house, he hath denied the faith, and is worse than an infidel. Let not a widow be taken into the number under threescore years old, having been the wife of one man. Well reported of for good works; if she have brought up children, if she have lodged strangers, if she have washed the saints' feet, if she have relieved the afflicted, if she have diligently followed every good work. (1 Tim. 5:7–10).

For the church to take responsibility for the widows, they needed to be blameless in the eyes of the people. The church should care only for those without family. If the families don't care for their own, including wives and parents and widows, then they are worse than unbelievers. The widow had to be at least sixty years old, having had only one husband at a time during her lifetime. She should be known for her good works, including raising her children godly, providing shelter for strangers, serving in the church, providing relief for the less fortunate, and taking advantage of every opportunity to do good works for God. This doesn't mean the church denies helping anyone in need, but they take into full care only those who were "widows indeed."

1. Be blameless in the eyes of the people.
2. Have no family.
3. Be at least sixty years old.
4. Was married to only one man at a time.
5. Was known for her good works.
6. Raised her children godly.
7. Provided shelter for strangers.
8. Served in the church (washed the saints' feet; though this was usually done by servants, Jesus did this for His apostles).
9. Helped the poor.
10. Took advantage of every opportunity to do good.

The Younger Widows Should Not Be the Church's Responsibility

"But the younger widows refuse: for when they have begun to wax wanton against Christ, they will marry; Having damnation, because they have cast off their first faith. And withal they learn to be idle, wandering about from house to house; and not only idle, but tattlers also and busybodies, speaking things which they ought not. I will therefore that the younger women marry, bear children, guide the house, give none occasion to the adversary to speak reproachfully. For some are already turned aside after Satan" (1 Tim. 5:11–15).

The church shouldn't take in younger widows because when their sexual desires become stronger than their desire to serve Christ, they will leave their first love (turn from serving God) and seek out ways to satisfy their worldly desires. After a young person has tasted sexual pleasure, living without it is more difficult. This is another reason why young women and men should stay pure until they are married. Then it goes on to say they will learn to be the lazy, tattlers (gossipers), and busybodies (sticking their noses in everyone else's business), spreading rumors. Therefore younger widows should remarry, bear children, and guide the house (this comes from the Greek word that can be translated to mean "manage" or "rule over"). This is why I told you earlier that a woman's house is her domain to rule over. A man's house is his wife's castle. If the younger women will do this, it will prevent the devil from tempting them to satisfy their sexual desires outside of marriage. This is the passage I was referring to earlier when I said Paul later said it is better for younger widows to remarry. Therefore, the church shouldn't take in young widows for the following reasons:

1. Their sexual needs will eventually become stronger than their desire to live for God.
2. They will become idle (lazy).
3. They will be tattlers (gossipers).
4. They will be busybodies (getting in everyone else's business).
5. They are better off getting remarried.
6. They will have children (one of the most honorable things to do).
7. They will guide the house (the wife's home is her domain to rule over).

Taking Care of Widows Should Be the Responsibility of Family First

"If any man or woman that believeth have widows, let them relieve them, and let not the church be charged; that it may relieve them that are widows indeed" (1 Tim. 5:16).

If any men or women who are Christians have a widow in their family, they should assume responsibility for her care so the church can care for those that don't have family. Finally, the last portion of scripture that deals with the role God intended for women is found in 1 Peter 3. For some people, going through these scriptures has probably been painstaking and maybe even offensive, but it is necessary to get the full picture of what God's intentions are.

Saved Wives Should be in Subjection to Their Lost Husbands Because This Could Lead to Their Conversion

"Likewise, ye wives, be in subjection to your own husbands; that, if any obey not the word, they also may without the word be won by the conversation of the wives; While they behold your chaste conversation coupled with fear" (1Peter 3:1–2).

In these verses, the apostle Peter reiterates the importance of the wife being in subjection to her husband, but he gives us a different reason. If any wife has a husband who is not a believer, she may be able to convert him by her godly, pure behavior along with her fear of God, which he will learn to respect. Here it is plainly pointed out that she should still be in subjection to her own husband, even if he is not saved. It is also saying she should not be in subjection to all men or even to all husbands, just hers. If she is not married, then she should be in subjection to her own father, not any father and not any man. Still, even if her husband is not saved, she should still be in subjection to him but not expect him to provide spiritual guidance. In this case (the same as if her husband were saved), her subjection to him doesn't require her to do anything contrary to God's Word.

> Whose adorning let it not be that outward adorning of plaiting the hair, and of wearing of gold, or of putting on of apparel; But let it be the hidden man of the heart, in that which is not corruptible, even the ornament of a meek and quiet spirit, which is in the sight of God of great price. For after this manner

> in the old time the holy women also, who trusted in
> God, adorned themselves, being in subjection unto
> their own husbands: Even as Sara obeyed Abraham,
> calling him lord: whose daughters ye are, as long as
> ye do well, and are not afraid with any amazement.
> (1 Peter 3:3–6)

She will not win him over by dressing and acting worldly or by wearing a lot of seductive makeup or costly jewelry or clothing. She will win him over to God by being a godly person. This includes having a meek and quiet spirit, which God says is worth a great deal. No one likes a loud-mouthed, obnoxious, bickering, nagging wife. No one wants that in a man either, but we are talking about wives here. Throughout history, the Bible talks about the behavior of godly women such as Sarah, Abraham's wife. She is a great example of a godly woman who obeyed her husband and even called him lord, and then Peter goes on to say you all have the heritage of Sarah if you also do what is right without fear. Some translations render this passage to say that women should do right without fearing their husbands. I believe this is a true statement, but I'm not certain that is what the verse is saying. I believe it is saying if they obey and serve their husbands as unto the Lord, then they should be able to do so without being afraid because he wouldn't put them in danger, as he must also answer to God for their safety.

"Likewise, ye husbands, dwell with them according to knowledge, giving honour unto the wife, as unto the weaker vessel, and as being heirs together of the grace of life; that your prayers be not hindered" (1 Peter 3:7).

Husbands Dwell with Their Wives according to Knowledge

This last verse is for husbands, but I don't think there is any mistake made by placing it here in this portion of scripture intended for wives. It is saying that you husbands should consider all the things I just told your wives, and based on that, dwell with them according to what you now know." Then he says to give "honour unto the wife, as unto the weaker vessel." The word *honour* comes from a Greek word meaning "to hold in high esteem, that which is of great value, precious or of great worth." (Isn't that kind of like putting her on a pedestal?) "As unto the weaker vessel," I believe, is emphasizing the fact that her husband is responsible for her protection. "As being heirs together of the grace of life" means God has given the two of them the privilege and responsibility of creating life in their children.

Husbands should acknowledge certain things about their wives. First, they are in subjection to their husbands because God told them to be, and wives fear God and want to please Him. Second, a wife is being submissive because she is doing this for her husband's benefit so he will become a Christian if he is not already saved, or he will try to obey God following her example. Third, she is following the example of other godly women who have lived in the past and have set the standard. Fourth, she is trying to serve God by doing what is right without having to fear the consequences from her husband, God, or the world. If she does right, God will defend her. I think he is also saying, "If you are smart, you will let your wife rule the household and raise the children in the way that she sees fit because God has given her that authority and responsibility." The husband is still the overseer, but if he is smart, he will let her do what she is good at. Jesus obeys God, and man obeys Jesus. The wife obeys the husband, and the children obey the wife. The verse ends with a warning to husbands: In essence it is saying if you don't figure out how to treat your wife the way you should, then God will not hear your prayers.

The Husband's Responsibility to Provide and Protect

Man's Responsibility to Provide

We already saw in 1 Timothy 5, that the church's responsibility is to take care of the widows and that the men's responsibility is to take care of their families, but the fact is, this task was given to man long before then. Man's responsibility to provide for his family came with the curse at the fall; prior to this God provided everything.

> And unto Adam he said, Because thou hast hearkened unto the voice of thy wife, and hast eaten of the tree, of which I commanded thee, saying, Thou shalt not eat of it: cursed is the ground for thy sake; in sorrow shalt thou eat of it all the days of thy life; Thorns also and thistles shall it bring forth to thee; and thou shalt eat the herb of the field; In the sweat of thy face shalt thou eat bread, till thou return unto the ground; for out of it wast thou taken: for dust thou art, and unto dust shalt thou return. (Gen. 3:17–19)

Prior to the fall, the earth yielded forth its fruit naturally. Adam didn't have to plant, irrigate, fertilize, or do any of the things we have to do now to produce food. It was already there in abundance. But when Adam sinned, the ground was cursed to punish man. It is a man's responsibility to provide for his wife until death and for his daughters until they are grown and married. Notice, it says that the man, not the woman, was to earn a living by the sweat of his brow. God never intended a woman to forsake the responsibility of caring for her husband and children to have a career. The woman was intended to guide the house, to be a keeper at home, to be a mother and a wife. Don't get mad at me, ladies. God said this, not me; I'm just the messenger. The role that most women fill today is far from what God created them for. Have I become your enemy because I tell you the truth? I suppose many will read this book because they are trying to figure out what went wrong in their marriages.

I'm not going to sugar coat what God said. If you are not being the wife or husband God intended you to be, this is why your marriage isn't working. I'm not saying a wife cannot have a career, but I am saying that if the career keeps her from fulfilling her God-given responsibilities, then the career needs to go. Today our society has a tendency to look down on those young women who want to be housewives and take care of their families. I say, "Great shall be their reward in heaven." Not only have they discovered the truth about God's role for them, but they have found the secret to a happy and successful marriage and life. These are the ladies who have chosen a path that is pleasing to God, and they shall be rewarded.

On the other hand, no one can ensure that a young woman, or man for that matter, will ever find the right person to marry. For that reason, I believe everyone should be prepared to support him or herself provided that this is how life turns out for him or her. According to God's Word, the father should be responsible for the well-being of his daughter until she marries, but daddy will not always be around. There is nothing wrong with a woman having a career, but it should just not be her top priority if she is married, especially if she has children. Personally, I believe there is a man for every woman who seeks to please God in this capacity, but that isn't guaranteed. Therefore, she should be prepared to support herself, but that isn't what she should desire. Of course, we saw already that if she can stay pure and dedicate her life to serving God, then her father remains responsible for her provision, protection, and guidance; and this is the most honorable goal. Most women who choose to live a life dedicated to God usually end up working for a church in some capacity; therefore, they are supporting themselves through the service of the church.

Man's Responsibility to Protect

God has also given the husband the position of protector for his wife and family. I don't believe God intended it to be a punishment for women to be the weaker vessel and for them to have the right to the man's provision and protection. This is a position of honor and respect. Instead of looking at this as a woman being inferior to a man, it seems to me that God is telling the man that he should put his woman on a pedestal, sort to speak. He is told he should be willing to give his life for her provision and protection. I don't recall seeing any place in the Bible where God tells the woman that she should be willing to do this for her man. I ask you, how can that be considered a position of inferiority?

About twenty-five years ago, when I first began to work on this book, a young woman, Shannon Faulkner, took the military academy, The Citadel, to court to gain the right to attend this all-male academy. When she finally won her case in court, she attended the school for approximately one week before she dropped out. I don't understand why any woman would want to degrade her God-given position of privilege and honor to join a group of raunchy, rough military men. I personally spent almost nine years in the military, and I can tell you from experience that this is no place for a lady. But then I guess she never claimed to be a lady, did she? I remember one woman telling me that she wasn't a lady because if she was, she wouldn't have nearly as much fun as she did. Who said ladies don't have fun?

It is better to suffer for Christ than to enjoy the pleasures of sin for a season. Those who live for God will find happiness, but those who live for themselves will find damnation. Nevertheless, God never intended women to be warriors. This should be obvious by the way they are created physically. I know what I'm saying isn't popular, and some would consider it prejudiced, but I'm telling you what God says about the matter. My opinion, like yours is irrelevant.

Women Shouldn't Be on the Front Lines of War

In Judges 4, the Bible tells us about a woman named Deborah, whom God had made a judge over the children of Israel. Deborah was also a prophetess in the land at the time. Now remember that women aren't allowed to usurp authority over men in the church or in the home, but I never said they couldn't lead in other areas. I don't believe women who serve in government or companies where they are put in positions of authority are breaking God's rules.

Anyhow, my point here is that I don't believe women should be in battle. If they want to be in the military, then that is their business as well, but they shouldn't be on the front lines. So Deborah led an army to battle for the Israelites with Barak, but she didn't go down to where the fighting was. There are numerous battles recorded in the Bible and several where women were present, but it never mentions women being in the battles because they are entitled to men's protection. I'm not suggesting that women can't hold their own; I know several that I'd rather not confront. My point is that this isn't God's intended purpose for them. The Bible is filled with numerous examples of men being sent to war while the women and children stayed home. I will give you just a couple to check out for yourselves (Deut. 3:18–20; Josh. 1:14–15). Women have not been allowed in the military very long yet, but in the United States, the women who have served in the military are seeking help with emotional problems, such as post-traumatic stress disorder (PTSD) and other emotional disorders like extreme depression and anxiety, twice as often as men. Some say this could be because women are more likely than men to admit they have a problem and seek help. In either case, this is an indicator that God didn't design most women to fill this position.

Man Is the Woman's Intercessor between Her and God

There is one last thing that needs to be said about man's obligation to protect. I already briefly mentioned that men are to be intercessors between their wives and God. A man's job is to sanctify his wife so she will be presentable to God, clean and without wrinkle or spot. He is trying to keep her clean to stay God's chastisement from her body. This is the ultimate form of protection. In the book of Ruth, Ruth asked her kinsman redeemer to cover her with his skirt. This action signified two things: first, his pledge to marry her; and second, his acceptance of the responsibility to protect her.

> And she went down unto the floor, and did according to all that her mother in law bade her. And when Boaz had eaten and drunk, and his heart was merry, he went to lie down at the end of the heap of corn: and she came softly, and uncovered his feet, and laid her down. And it came to pass at midnight, that the man was afraid, and turned himself: and, behold, a woman lay at his feet. And he said, Who art thou? And she answered, I am Ruth thine handmaid: Spread therefore thy skirt over thine handmaid; For thou art a near kinsman. And he said, Blessed be thou of the LORD, my daughter: for thou hast shewed more kindness in the latter end than at the beginning, inasmuch as thou followedst not young men, whether poor or rich. And now, my daughter, fear not; I will do to thee all that thou requirest: For all the city of my people doth know that thou art a virtuous woman. (Ruth 3:6–11)

To cover her nakedness with his skirt signified a God-ordained, proper, innocent marriage just as to uncover someone's nakedness in the Old Testament referred to sinful sexual relations. God spoke of this same responsibility to protect when He took Israel and claimed her for His own, Israel as his bride. "Now when I passed by thee, and looked upon thee, behold, thy time was the time of love; and I spread my skirt over thee, and covered thy nakedness: yea, I sware unto thee, and entered into a covenant with thee, saith the Lord GOD, and thou becamest mine" (Ezek. 16:8).

Man as the Protector Is Not a New Idea

God took on Himself the responsibility of protecting Israel, and she became His bride, the same as the church is the bride of Christ. Christ protects the church. This concept of the males being the protectors is not a new one for me. When I was growing up in the great state of Texas, things were always done a certain way. In our family, we had five boys and three girls, all born in eight years. There was one set of twins, Joyce and John, who are one year older than I. Then there is my oldest sister, Carol Anne; she is two years older than Joyce and John. Then there is my oldest brother, James; he is one year older than Carol Anne. Under me is my brother William, or Billy, who is one year younger than me. Then comes my youngest sister, Vivian Rose, who was named after my mom, Vivian Minnie. We call Vivian Rose "Rosey." Then the youngest is my brother Richard Collins, who goes by Ricky.

The boys always did boy things like clean the yard and build things. We hung out with Daddy all the time. We learned how to work on things and fish and hunt and do guy things, while the girls hung out with mom, went shopping, and bought clothes and groceries and so forth, like girls used to do. I guess you could say Daddy taught the boys how to be men and do men things, and Momma taught the girls how to be ladies and do lady-like things. One of those things we were taught as boys was to be protective of our family members, especially our sisters. If anything bad were to happen to one of our sisters, we were expected to do whatever needed to be done to protect them. If we didn't, then we would have to answer to Daddy's "Why not?" Trust me when I tell you that Daddy had a way of making us regret not doing the right thing when it came to looking out for the women in our family. Some of those lessons I will never forget. We were taught that if anything happened to the ladies in our family, it was our fault.

After we were grown, one of my brothers-in-law told me that everyone had been scared to take advantage of any of the Boudreaux girls at school. Apparently, they were quite nervous about the reputation of the Boudreaux boys. Daddy made it very clear that protecting our sisters was our job. He took the protection of my mom and his responsibilities as the protector and provider of the family just as seriously. I think in our society today chivalry has become a lost standard, but it needs to be reintroduced because this is how God says it should be. From a Christian perspective, a woman who asks for equal rights to a man has in fact requested a demotion from her God-given privileged status.

CHAPTER 5

Relationships Christians Should Avoid

Mixed Marriages

We have already seen in 1 Corinthians 7 that Christians shouldn't be married to unbelievers. The following verses make this even clearer—not only the fact that we shouldn't marry unbelievers but also that we should separate from them altogether.

> Be ye not unequally yoked together with unbelievers: for what fellowship hath righteousness with unrighteousness? And what communion hath light with darkness? And what concord hath Christ with Belial? Or what part hath he that believeth with an infidel? And what agreement hath the temple of God with idols? For ye are the temple of the living God; As God hath said, I will dwell in them, and walk in them; and I will be their God, and they shall be my people. Wherefore come out from among them, and be ye separate, saith the Lord, and touch not the unclean thing; And I will receive you. And will be a Father unto you, and ye shall be

my sons and daughters, saith the Lord Almighty.
(2Cor. 6:14–18)

Because of Their Lifestyle

These following verses describe the lifestyle of the unsaved. Based on what we already know, as far as how God wants Christians to live is concerned, it should be obvious that Christians shouldn't be close friends with these people.

Because that, when they knew God, they glorified him not as God, neither were thankful; But became vain in their imaginations, and their foolish heart was darkened. Professing themselves to be wise, they became fools, and changed the glory of the uncorruptible God into an image made like to corruptible man, and to birds, and fourfooted beasts, and creeping things. Wherefore God also gave them up to uncleanness through the lusts of their own hearts, to dishonour their own bodies between themselves: Who changed the truth of God into a lie, and worshipped and served the creature more than the Creator, who is blessed forever. Amen. For this cause God gave them up unto vile affections: For even their women did change the natural use into that which is against nature: And likewise also the men, leaving the natural use of the woman, burned in their lust one toward another; men with men working that which is unseemly, and receiving in themselves that recompense of their error which was meet. And even as they did not like to retain God in their knowledge, God gave them over to a reprobate mind, to do those

things which are not convenient; Being filled
with all unrighteousness, fornication, wickedness,
covetousness, maliciousness; full of envy, murder,
debate, deceit, malignity; whisperers, Backbiters,
haters of God, despiteful, proud, boasters, inventors
of evil things, disobedient to parents, Without
understanding, covenant breakers, without natural
affection, implacable, unmerciful: Who knowing
the judgment of God, that they which commit such
things are worthy of death, not only do the same,
but have pleasure in them that do them. (Rom.
1:21–32)

1. They worship false gods. (If you put anything above God,
   you're guilty.)
2. God gave them up to uncleanness because of the lust in
   their hearts.
3. They dishonored their own bodies, which usually refers to
   adultery.
4. They changed the truth of God into a lie and worshipped
   the creature (maybe talking about the false gods they had
   created or the fact that man trusts scientists more than God).
5. God gave them over to vile (morally corrupt) affections.

   a. The women did immoral acts with each other
      (corrupting their natural use of their bodies). These are
      acts of lesbianism.
   b. The men did immoral acts with each other (leaving the
      natural use of the woman and turning to each other).
      These are acts of homosexuality.
   c. This is unseemly behavior (inappropriate or immoral
      acts or behavior).
   d. There is recompense; they will have to pay restitution
      for their actions.

6. Because they denied God, He turned them over to a reprobate (unacceptable or rejected) mind.

7. They did those things that aren't convenient (improper, repulsive, or immoral). What are those things?

    a. Acts full of unrighteousness

    b. Fornication, sex outside of marriage

    c. Wickedness, what is evil or immoral

    d. Covetousness (lusting after something that belongs to someone else)

    e. Maliciousness, the intent or desire to do evil

    f. Fullness of envy, excessive jealousy

    g. Murder

    h. Debate (being argumentative)

    i. Deceit (concealing something or being sneaky)

    j. Malignity, an intense ill will, spite or hatred

    k. Being whisperers, those who spread rumors

    l. Being backbiters, malicious talk or intent toward someone not present

    m. Being haters of God, those who not only deny God but also intentionally commit acts in defiance against Him (devil worshippers in apostasy)

    n. Being despiteful, derogatory, or mean spirited

    o. Being proud, having an unnaturally high opinion of one's self or one's accomplishments

    p. Being boasters, showing excessive pride, or bragging

    q. Being inventors of evil things, inventions built to harm others physically, mentally, emotionally, or morally (tools used to perform abortions, do torture, and so forth)

    r. Being disobedient to parents (this is where rebellion against authority begins)

    s. Being without understanding, denying God's authority

t.   Being covenant breakers, liars, those you can't trust their words, or promise breakers

u.   Being without natural affection, women who lust after women, men who lust after men, and women or men who have no affection for their own children

v.   Being implacable, unappeasable, always angry

w.   Being unmerciful, those who have no compassion for others

8.   Those who do such things are worthy of death.

9.   Those who take pleasure in seeing others do such things are no better.

This Separation Extends beyond Marriage

According to the scriptures, these are the sorts of things unbelievers do. It should be obvious why a Christian shouldn't be bound to such a person in any kind of partnership, much less a marriage.

I believe this means we shouldn't have any kind of close fellowship or partnership with unbelievers at all. We shouldn't marry them, go into business with them, hang out with them, attend any kind of service with them, or have any kind of partnership with them. We shouldn't fellowship or party with them. I know that what I am about to say should go without saying for a Christian, but I'm not naïve and I know what people are doing these days. You shouldn't have a "friends with benefits" arrangement with them. A saved person shouldn't live with an unsaved person, especially if he or she is the opposite sex. If you claim to be saved and yet feel more comfortable around lost people than with Christians, something is wrong. "I wrote unto you in an epistle not to company with fornicators" (1 Cor. 5:9).

As far as attending services with them, if they attend any kind of church that teaches anything other than that Jesus is the only begotten Son of God and that there is no other way to be saved but through Jesus, then you shouldn't have anything to do with them spiritually speaking either.

> Whosoever transgresseth, and abideth not in the doctrine of Christ, hath not God. He that abideth in the doctrine of Christ, he hath both the Father and the Son. If there come any unto you, and bring not this doctrine, receive him not into your house, neither bid him God speed: For he that biddeth him God speed is partaker of his evil deeds. (2John 1:9–11)

> Be it known unto you all, and to all the people of Israel, that by the name of Jesus Christ of Nazareth, whom ye crucified, whom God raised from the dead, even by him doth this man stand here before you whole. This is the stone which was set at nought of you builders, which is become the head of the corner. Neither is there salvation in any other: for there is none other name under heaven given among men, whereby we must be saved. (Acts 4:10–12)

Do Not Wish Them Success

Not wishing them Godspeed means not wishing them a prosperous or successful journey. I am trying not to say anything that is offensive to any true believers, but you should be aware that there are many false prophets and false religions who teach false doctrines. If they teach anything other than the basic truth of who Jesus is, then they are false prophets and should be avoided. That doesn't mean you should go around asking every person you see what he or she believes about God before you can talk to the person or even be friendly.

It does mean, however, that you should know these things before you become close friends with them or do anything else with them. Another thing that was briefly mentioned is that you shouldn't have sexual relations with either believers or unbelievers before you are married, and you shouldn't have intimacy with anyone besides your spouse after you are married.

Do Not Be So Heavenly Righteous That You're No Earthly Good

Several years ago, I was driving across the country when I saw a saying on a church sign that left a lasting impression on me. Yes, I do think that being separated from the world is very important in our Christian lives; however, we should be in the world but not of the world. As we have already seen, Jesus spent a lot of time with sinners because His goal was to reconcile them to God. Our goal is the same, and we can't do so if we don't spend any time among them. I have seen so many Christian people who, meaning well, isolated themselves from all sinners including their own family members. They thought they were doing the right thing, but this isolation makes other people feel as though you think you are better than they are; and it eliminates any possibility of you witnessing to them. I think you should still attend family events and get-togethers, but don't participate in questionable activities. This allows you to let your light shine on your family. They should know something is different about you but not feel as though you think you are too good to be around them.

Several years ago I wrote an illustration concerning adultery. I'd like to share that with you here.

Heart Strings

When two hearts are bonded together, it is like they are secured with an adhesive. When you try to pull two items apart that are bonded that way, the adhesive will allow the two hearts to separate to a degree, forming adhesive, elastic-like strings between the two. These elastic strings can be stretched only so far before the bond fails.

For the sake of illustration, I want to compare the heart strings to rubber bands or bungee cords. These bungee cords can be stretched and pulled apart a long way before they start to strain, and when the pressure is relieved, they pull the two hearts back together like there was never any opposing pressure applied. The stretching of the two hearts apart is done every day by normal everyday pressures such as finances, the stress of a job, or unruly children. These types of pressures seldom ever apply enough stress to break even one of the bungee cords much less all of them. As long as none of them are broken, the overall strength of the bond remains the same, and they always come back together with the same closeness as before. If the hearts do get pulled apart enough to cause a string or cord to break by some dramatic event such as bankruptcy or a medical disaster, then the overall bond will become a bit weaker, but the remainder of the cords are still adequate to hold the hearts together. It is also possible sometimes to repair these broken strings by applying more adhesive or tying them back together, but remember, repaired cords are still never as strong as the original, leaving the relationship more vulnerable to other outside influences.

When there is cheating or infidelity of any sort (in my opinion), it is like intentionally taking a pair of scissors and severing the cords. If people would only realize the destruction this causes, maybe they would think a little more before committing such an offense against their partner. When the cords are cut, the overall bond is instantly weakened. That doesn't mean it is weak enough to tear the hearts all the way apart, but it will now not be able to handle the same amount of stretching as it did before. Every time an act of infidelity is committed, another cord is cut, and the less ability the overall bond has of taking even everyday stresses. When enough cords are cut, the hearts will rip apart, and it is generally too late for repairs. That is why I think that when marriages are destroyed most of the time, there is some sort of infidelity involved. Even that innocent little dream about another man or woman in my view is a sign that the cords are being stretched beyond their normal, everyday pressure. It is irrelevant, by the way, whether the act of infidelity actually occurred or is only perceived to have occurred. This is why jealousy is so damaging, and it is important that your partner know at all times that your dedication to him or her is above mere infatuation. Now let me interject another aspect of this illustration. It is usually the person who has committed the offense of infidelity who decides to end the marriage. As I said before, when infidelity takes place, the cords are being cut one at a time until enough are destroyed that the hearts can now be ripped apart. These two hearts, in addition to being cut apart, are also being stretched during the entire process. The person committing the illicit act, even though he or she may not know it, is attaching his or her cords to someone else at the same time. This new attachment pulls in the opposite direction, thereby doubling the stretching of the original bond and accelerating its inevitable failure. When the heart attaches to the new lover, it now becomes an unfair tug of war with two hearts tugging against the one. Many times some of these strings or cords are ripped apart by the stretching and are not cut. These cords are attached with such amazing strength that when they are ripped off the heart, they tear off pieces of the heart with them. If there was a large number of the cords still attached, then a large piece of the heart can be ripped out, leaving behind a broken heart.

The person responsible for the separation has little regard for the pieces he or she tore off. For a while, he or she may drag along a few dangling strings of guilt or some feeling of remorse, but with the person's cords now attached to someone new, these dangling strings soon wither and fall off as well, and life goes on. For the person who had large pieces of the heart ripped out, he or she has a severely wounded or broken heart. The healing of a wounded heart may take many years, the same as any other severe flesh wound. Even when the healing is complete, some pieces (such as the desire to find a new heart to attach to) may still be missing similar to a limb being lost in a car accident. For those hearts that were lucky enough not to have any large pieces ripped out, they are still left with ugly scars (fear to try) when in actuality this may not have been their fault at all.

The Strange Woman (Refers to Relations with Someone Other Than Your Spouse)

So now let's look at some scriptures that talk about the same things.

> To deliver thee from the strange woman, even from the stranger which flattereth with her words; forsaketh the guide of her youth, and forgetteth the covenant of her God. For her house inclineth unto death, and her paths unto the dead. None that go unto her return again, neither take they hold of the paths of life. (Prov. 2:16–19)

> My son, attend unto my wisdom, and bow thine ear to my understanding: That thou mayest regard discretion, and that thy lips may keep knowledge. For the lips of a strange woman drop as an honeycomb, and her mouth is smoother than oil: But her end is bitter as wormwood, sharp as a two-edged sword. Her feet go down to death; her steps take hold on hell. Lest thou shouldest ponder the path of life, her ways are moveable, that thou canst not know them. Hear me now therefore, O ye children, and depart not from the words of my mouth. Remove thy way far from her, and come not nigh the door of her house: Lest thou give thine honour unto others, and thy years unto the cruel: Lest strangers be filled with thy wealth; and thy labours be in the house of a stranger; And thou mourn at the last,

when thy flesh and thy body are consumed, And say, How have I hated instruction, and my heart despised reproof; And have not obeyed the voice of my teachers, nor inclined mine ear to them that instructed me! I was almost in all evil in the midst of the congregation and assembly. Drink waters out of thine own cistern, and running waters out of thine own well. Let thy fountains be dispersed abroad, and rivers of waters in the streets. Let them be only thine own, and not strangers' with thee. Let thy fountain be blessed: and rejoice with the wife of thy youth. Let her be as the loving hind and pleasant roe; let her breasts satisfy thee at all times; and be thou ravished always with her love. And why wilt thou, my son, be ravished with a strange woman, and embrace the bosom of a stranger? (Prov. 5:1–20)

For the commandment is a lamp; and the law is light; and reproofs of instruction are the way of life: To keep thee from the evil woman, from the flattery of the tongue of a strange woman. Lust not after her beauty in thine heart; neither let her take thee with her eyelids. For by means of a whorish woman a man is brought to a piece of bread: and the adultress will hunt for the precious life. Can a man take fire in his bosom, and his clothes not be burned? Can one go upon hot coals, and his feet not be burned? So he that goeth in to his neighbour's wife; whosoever toucheth her shall not be innocent. (Prov. 6:23–29)

My son, keep my words, and lay up my commandments with thee. Keep my commandments, and live; and my law as the apple of thine eye. Bind them upon thy fingers, write them upon the table of thine heart. Say unto wisdom, Thou art my sister; and call understanding thy kinswoman: That they may keep thee from the strange woman, from the stranger which flattereth with her words. For at the window of my house I looked through my casement, And beheld among the simple ones, I discerned among the youths, a young man void of understanding, Passing through the street near her corner; and he went the way to her house, In the twilight, in the evening, in the black and dark night: And, behold, there met him a woman with the attire of an harlot, and subtil of heart. (She is loud and stubborn; her feet abide not in her house: Now is she without, now in the streets, and lieth in wait at every corner.) So she caught him, and kissed him, and with an impudent face said unto him, I have peace offerings with me; this day have I payed my vows. Therefore came I forth to meet thee, diligently to seek thy face, and I have found thee. I have decked my bed with coverings of tapestry, with carved works, with fine linen of Egypt. I have perfumed my bed with myrrh, aloes, and cinnamon. Come, let us take our fill of love until the morning: let us solace ourselves with loves. For the goodman is not at home, he is gone a long journey: He hath taken a bag of money with him, and will come home at the day appointed. With her much fair speech she caused him to yield, with the flattering of her lips she forced him. He goeth after her straightway, as an ox goeth to the slaughter, or as a fool to the correction of the stocks; Till a dart strike through his liver; as a bird hasteth to the snare, and knoweth not that it is for his life. Hearken unto me now therefore, O ye children, and attend to the words of my mouth. Let not thine heart decline to her ways, go not astray in her paths. For she hath cast down many wounded: yea, many strong men have been slain by her. Her house is the way to hell, going down to the chambers of death. (Prov. 7:1–27)

Other Forbidden Forms of Sexual Conduct

Old Testament Law concerning Improper Relationships

Keep in mind that these are laws written for the Jewish people, which are much more detailed and strict than the ones mentioned in the New Testament. It should also be mentioned that Christians don't live by the law because they are saved. This is a general guide to follow when dealing with issues not mentioned in the New Testament. Also one should remember that if you were guilty of these sins but you are now saved, then you have been forgiven. The thing to remember is that if there is something that was mentioned here and reinforced in the New Testament, then even after you get saved, you should not continue in this type of behavior as a Christian. It will not cause the loss of your salvation, but it will affect your fellowship with God.

What Is the Law For?

Why did God give us laws?

1. First, to preserve sanctification. God called Israel out to be separate from the evil found in the rest of the world.
2. Second, to preserve health. You have to realize that when these laws were given, there was no refrigeration. There

were no antibacterial soaps or sanitation wipes. There was no modern medicine with surgeons and disease specialists.

3. Third, to preserve the Israeli bloodline. This was because it would be necessary to prove that Jesus, the Savior of the world, came from pure blood and is a descendant of Abraham as God promised.

4. Fourth, so all people would become guilty before God and in need of a Savior. If the Israelites were going to stay healthy and pure, they were going to have to not do certain things. Many of these laws pertaining to preservation, sanitation, and hygiene don't apply today because there is no need for them. On the other hand, they may need to be reconsidered during a pandemic or some other sort of health crisis.

Sexual Sins

- Intimacy with a woman who was having her cycle (Lev. 15:24)
- Sexual sins with close relatives (incestual)
- Intimacy with a close relative such as a mother, stepmother, sister, granddaughter, half-sister on the father's side, paternal or maternal aunt, paternal uncle's wife, daughter-in-law, brother's wife, stepdaughter or grand stepdaughter, or a wife's sister as long as the wife lived. (There is some debate as to whether this means you shouldn't be intimate with your wife's sister if you are divorced from your wife and she is still living or if it means you shouldn't have intimate relations with your wife's sister while you are still married to the first. Back when these laws were written, it wasn't uncommon for men to have more than one wife, so this could be talking about being married to one sister and sleeping with another or marrying another at the same time.)

- Also intimacy with your neighbor's wife. Whatever is wrong for the man is wrong for the woman as well (Lev. 18:6–20).

Other Sexual Sins

1. Homosexuality is an abomination (something that causes disgust or hatred in God's eyes); bestiality is also forbidden. It is sinful for a man or woman to lie with an animal of any kind. (Lev. 18:21–23; 20:13).
2. Man should not be married to a woman and her mother, it is sinful to have intimate relations with both a mother and her daughter. (Lev. 20:14).
3. Again, intimacy with an animal is forbidden (Lev. 20:15–16).
4. Cross-dressing is sinful; this is women dressing like men or men dressing like women. (Deut.22:5).
5. Unfaithfulness on the part of the woman is prohibited. (Deut. 22:13–21).
6. A man caught sleeping with another man's wife is adultery; they were both put to death (Deut. 22:22).
7. If a woman who is engaged but is still a virgin lies with another man, this is considered adultery. Both man and woman were put to death. (Deut. 22:23–24).
8. If a woman is raped, the man was put to death, but the woman was innocent. (Deut. 22:25–27).
9. If a man seduced a virgin (a young woman still living with her father), he had to pay the father for her dowry and marry the girl. They weren't ever allowed to divorce. (Deut. 22:28–29).

The Significance of Chastity before Marriage

First, let me just say that sex doesn't constitute marriage in God's eyes regardless of what the government says about it. The Bible says that when men have relations with a harlot, they are joining their body to the harlot (1 Cor. 6:16), but then Paul goes on to explain that Christians shouldn't participate in this type of sexual sin because they are sinning against their own bodies. The following verses show that sex outside of marriage is sinful. If sex constituted marriage, then these would be marital relations and not be sinful. Sex outside of marriage is sin and not part of God's plan.

> All things are lawful unto me, but all things are not expedient: all things are lawful for me, but I will not be brought under the power of any. Meats for the belly, and the belly for meats: but God shall destroy both it and them. Now the body is not for fornication, but for the Lord; and the Lord for the body. And God hath both raised up the Lord, and will also raise up us by his own power. Know ye not that your bodies are the members of Christ? Shall I then take the members of Christ, and make them the members of an harlot? God forbid. What? Know ye not that he which is joined to an harlot is one body? For two, saith he, shall be one flesh. But he that is joined unto the Lord is one spirit. Flee fornication. Every sin that a man doeth is without the body; but he that committeth fornication sinneth against his own body. What? Know ye not that your body is the temple of the Holy Ghost which is in you, which ye have of God, and ye are not your own? For ye are bought with a price: therefore glorify God in your body, and in your spirit, which are God's. (1 Cor. 6:12–20)

We Should Not Defile Our Bodies Because We Are the Temples of God

I know Christians should abstain from all sin to maintain a good fellowship between themselves and God so they don't grieve the Holy Spirit, so they keep a good testimony in the world, and so they can be used in God's service. But it seems that sexual sins are even more grievous than other sins because they defile our bodies, which are God's temple. We already discussed the Samaritan woman at the well, but let's look at her in a different context.

"Jesus saith unto her, Go, call thy husband, and come hither. The woman answered and said, I have no husband. Jesus said unto her, Thou hast well said, I have no husband: For thou hast had five husbands; and he whom thou now hast is not thy husband: In that saidst thou truly" (John 4:16–18).

This woman had been intimate with five men before and was now living with her sixth. The word translated "husband" here from the Greek can mean "husband" or can just be translated to mean "man." So the best we can tell is that she had been with six men altogether, and as far as we know, none, or all of them were her husbands. In these verses, she admitted she had no husband, even though she was obviously having an intimate relationship with someone at the time. Then Jesus confirmed that what she had said was true; she didn't have a husband, and the man she was living with wasn't her husband either.

The point is that living with a man or woman, or having an intimate relationship with a man or woman, doesn't make someone married to that person. Therefore, by her own admission, she was living in sin and committing fornication. This act didn't preclude her from the possibility of being saved and becoming a Christian, but she wouldn't have been able to abide in this sinful situation. She would have had to break off the intimacy until after she married the man. Intimacy before marriage is forbidden and with good cause.

There Are Many Good Reasons to Wait Until after Marriage

Ladies, if a man really loves you and cares for you and he is a godly person, he will understand and agree with your reasons for wanting to wait. If he isn't a Christian, you shouldn't be with him to start with, but if he is a Christian, he shouldn't be trying to talk you into an intimate encounter before you are married. If you end up getting married, then you have the rest of your lives to share yourselves with one another, and if you do not, then you have saved yourself from much grief. If you are scared you will lose him if you don't give in to his worldly desires, then you probably shouldn't be with him to start with.

Men, if your lady starts off the relationship by offering herself to you, then she isn't so much a lady. I'm not saying that any woman who is not still a virgin is off limits because it depends on the circumstances. What I am saying is, if she is offering her body to you early in the relationship, it could be because she has no respect for her body, in which case you should avoid her. If she will offer herself to you, then she will offer herself to others. Or she may be doing so only because she is afraid of losing you. If you think this is the case, then you should explain the fact that you are a Christian man and that you have more respect for her than that.

If sex is what catches you, then it will most likely end up being the same thing that loses you. This goes for men and women; if the person you are dating or committing adultery with will defile him or herself for you, or cheat on his or her husband or wife with you, then the person will also defile him or herself with someone else or commit adultery with someone else. A relationship based solely on sex won't last. There are many good reasons why you should wait.

1. Fornication is defined as sexual relations between unmarried persons. There are numerous Bible verses that soundly condemn fornication as being immoral and sinful. "But

fornication, and all uncleanness, or covetousness, let it not be once named among you, as becometh saints" (Eph. 5:3).

2. The proper place for intimacy is between a man and a woman in God's good design of marriage. When God gives part of Himself (the Holy Spirit) to a person at the time of salvation, that person becomes one with God. It is the same with the husband and wife. When the husband and wife join intimately, the marriage is consummated, and the two become one. It is also for the purpose of two people bonding with one another, providing a means of procreation, and offering a means for married couples to enjoy each other's bodies. Physical relations in a marriage are intended to provide extreme joy and satisfaction for both the man and his wife. Any deviation from this sacred model, which is designed and approved by God, is a violation of God's law and a sin against your own body. This type of conduct will break your fellowship with God. You can't live in sin and have good fellowship with God at the same time. "Marriage is honourable in all, and the bed undefiled: but whoremongers and adulterers God will judge." (Heb. 13:4).

3. Sex without the binding commitment of marriage cheapens both the sanctity of the act itself and the sacred institution of marriage. It also cheapens oneself and the person the act was committed with. Love without commitment isn't really love at all; it is lust. It is also selfish and self-satisfying.

4. All violations of God's laws come with consequences. They include the following:

   a. Feelings of guilt
   b. Resentment toward the person who instigated the infraction
   c. Loss of respect and trust
   d. Unplanned pregnancy
   e. Abandonment

    f.   Forced marriages (shotgun weddings)

    g. Marriage to the unsaved (mixed marriages)

    h. Venereal diseases (STDs)

    i.   Lack of security in marriage

    j.   A greater risk of divorce

    k. Degradation of your personal testimony

    l.   The breaking of the laws of God and man

    m. The spreading of other diseases, such as cervical cancer and AIDS

Guilt Can Have Serious Consequences

I would like to expound for just a moment on this guilt thing. If you will wait till after you are married to consummate it, it will eliminate what always follows sin in the marriage that is to be. This one thing will make the marriage innocent and pure in the eyes of God and man. For some men, this may not seem like a big deal, even though, if you are a saved man, it should. It is a very big deal to most women, even if they don't realize it at the time. The loss of a woman's purity outside of marriage is almost always something that is mourned. It makes women feel dirty, cheap, and defiled. Some women never get over this loss, and if this relationship leads to a marriage between these two people, this guilt will be carried into the marriage as well. Some women will always blame their husbands for his violation of her; this is true even if she agreed to it because of pressure he applied before they were married. Many times the marriage will never stop having trust issues because the wife knows he violated her, and in her mind if he did that with her, then he may do it with someone else.

If a person is dating someone who has been married before, some may be thinking, *What is the big deal?* After all, they were married before, and they have already been with other people. Consider this. Maybe they got saved since all that happened. Maybe they asked God to forgive them and they have started over with a clear conscience. Maybe they have been forgiven and they want to do it the right way this time. Maybe for the first time in their life, they have been forgiven, and feel innocent and clean. Maybe they don't want to feel guilty and dirty again. Maybe they really care for this new person and don't want to go against God's words and end up losing them because of it. If someone is a saved person, they should feel guilty for even suggesting that their new potential partner surrender to physical desires prior to marriage.

Marriage Intended for Life

You should realize that regardless of whether your relationship started out the way God planned, you are now married, and this marriage is now God's will for your life. The sex in itself doesn't constitute the marriage, but a publicly announced commitment to one another for life, the consummation of the marriage bond, and the legal contract before witnesses does. It is always God's will for two people to be married if they intend to live together and have intimate relations with each other. On the other hand, divorce was never part of God's plan.

What about Common Law Marriage?

Next, we should consider the aspects of the law. In this case, I'm talking about the laws of man we are subject to as opposed to God's laws. If the law of the land says a couple is married after seven years of living together, then they are married. In some states today, there isn't even a time limit, but the law says if the two people have lived together as husband and wife and have done legal things together, such as filing their taxes jointly, then they are considered to be married by the state. This requires only a minimum of two years of cohabitation. The Word of God teaches us that we should be subject to the powers that have been placed over us because they wouldn't be allowed to have that authority over us without God giving it to them. (Rom. 13:1–2). If you fall into this category, I don't think that should hardly ever be the case if you are saved, but it does occur. The exception, of course, would be if you and your partner were both recently saved and you had already been living together for the given amount of time required to meet the legal definition of marriage.

If this is true, then I think you should still have a public ceremony to declare your love and commitment to one another before witnesses and God. This public announcement or testament will solidify the promises you have made to one another and bestow on each of you a certain amount of accountability. I don't think either partner in the marriage should ever be able to say, "I never promised you anything", because a promise is exactly what marriage should be based on. The marriage should be made official legally as well, which would require proper documentation. Some of you are now thinking that if this is true, then a legally recognized homosexual marriage is also a marriage according to God. That would not be true because, first, God says marriage is between a man and a woman (1 Cor. 7:2–3). Second, it isn't possible for two men or two women to join together, intimately becoming one and thereby creating life as God intended. They may be able to join physically, but this is considered an unnatural use of the body and a result of vile affections, not a marital bond (1 Peter 3:7). Finally, this kind of relationship is considered an abomination to God and therefore is considered living in a continual sinful situation. (Lev. 20:13).

What about Couples Who Were Together Long Enough to Be Considered Married but Are Now Split Up?

Should the couple split up prior to making the marriage official legally but were together long enough for the marriage to be considered binding according to the law, then I believe they are still married in the eyes of the law and of God. For the most part, these laws are put in place to protect the rights of women and children concerning provision and protection when a man refuses to accept responsibility for his actions. I believe every effort should be made in this case to reconcile the same as any other marriage; however, if the man refuses to take responsibility for his wife and children, then the law should be used to ensure their needs are still met. This is one of the benefits of being a wife, and if the split is because of the man, he is still held accountable for their well-being until someone else takes that responsibility.

Personally, I believe that if another man takes this woman as his wife, he should be willing to take the responsibility of supporting and taking care of her and her children as well. This doesn't mean the biological fathers of the children from these relationships are relieved of all their responsibilities concerning the children, but just as when a virgin marries, her father is no longer responsible for her. If a woman remarries her ex-husband, the father should no longer be responsible for her well-being.

Who Is Responsible for the Care of Single Women and Their Children?

There is no scripture I'm aware of that specifically details the care of the wife and children should the wife leave other than that we know men are responsible for the care of their wives and children so long as they are still married. The end of the marriage would have to be based on biblical grounds (adultery). At that point, a single woman would become the responsibility of her father once again. In our society today, however, it would be difficult for the woman to be obedient to her father again; therefore, if she won't do what he says, then he shouldn't be responsible for what happens to her.

Personally, I think the ex-husband should still be held accountable for the well-being of his children. To be plain, he should still provide support for his children whether they live with him, live with their mother alone or their mother and her father, or live with their mother and her new husband. At the same time, he shouldn't be cut off from parental privileges either. He should be allowed to have time with his children and have some say about how they are raised. These are my opinions based on what I know concerning the scriptures and what is best for the children. Boys who grow up without a proper male influence sometimes have a hard time learning how to be a man. Girls who grow up without the training of their mothers do not learn how to love, honor, and respect their husbands. While it is true that they can get these influences from other men and women, it is usually best if it comes from the biological mom and dad. I said "usually" because some biological moms and dads aren't suitable parents.

Christians Should Obey the Laws of the Land

We have already seen a lot of scripture pertaining to obedience to God's laws, but let me show you where the Word of God teaches we should also obey man's laws dealing with these issues.

> Let every soul be subject unto the higher powers. For there is no power but of God: The powers that be are ordained of God. Whosoever therefore resisteth the power, resisteth the ordinance of God: And they that resist shall receive to themselves damnation. For rulers are not a terror to good works, but to the evil. Wilt thou then not be afraid of the power? Do that which is good, and thou shalt have praise of the same: For he is the minister of God to thee for good. But if thou do that which is evil, be afraid; for he beareth not the sword in vain: For he is the minister of God, a revenger to execute wrath upon him that doeth evil. Wherefore ye must needs be

subject, not only for wrath, but also for conscience sake. For this cause pay ye tribute also: For they are God's ministers, attending continually upon this very thing. Render therefore to all their dues: tribute to whom tribute is due; custom to whom custom; fear to whom fear; honour to whom honour. (Rom. 13:1–7)

What Is God's Definition of a Marriage?

The apostle doesn't give room for any misinterpretation here. If the law says a couple is married by common law and God agrees that they should be because of intimacy between each other, then they are. God gives the law its authority, and it is put in place for good. In this case, it is good for a man to accept his responsibility for the provision and protection of his wife and family if applicable. A woman who has been abandoned by her husband is left without provision or protection, and so are the children. We should be honest here and admit that if there was no commitment to one another in the beginning, the woman and man wouldn't have moved in together. When people do this, they are accepting the responsibility that goes along with it. Two people don't have to live together to have sex. Since there obviously was some commitment, they should finish what they started and get married.

Marriage, therefore, consists of commitment, consummation, and testimony. When you get saved, you get baptized by water to announce to the world publicly that you have accepted Christ as your Savior. Jesus said, "If you confess me before men I will confess you before my Father in heaven" (Matt. 10:32).You should be willing to do the same thing for your wife and confess before men that you have accepted your wife to become one with you for life. This will hold both of you accountable for what you have promised to each other. Doing this publicly will also eliminate the appearance of living in sin. A Christian shouldn't want to be in a situation where it appears he or she is committing fornication on a continual basis (1 Thess. 5:22).To God, marriage is a lifetime commitment between a man and a woman, made before God and man in an open testimony. A marriage that isn't between a woman and a man isn't a marriage. A marriage that does not include a lifetime commitment to one another is not God's idea of marriage. A marriage that hasn't been proclaimed legally and publicly isn't what God intended. Anything that involves sexual intimacy between two people that doesn't include these elements is either adultery or fornication; or according to God, if it is between two people of the same sex, it is an abomination. *Abomination* means it is abhorrent or disgusting in God's sight.

> For this cause God gave them up unto vile affections: for even their women did change the natural use into that which is against nature: And likewise also the men, leaving the natural use of the woman, burned in their lust one toward another; men with men working that which is unseemly, and receiving in themselves that recompense of their error which was meet. And even as they did not like to retain God in their knowledge, God gave them over to a reprobate mind, to do those things which are not convenient. (Rom. 1:26–28)

> Thou shalt not lie with mankind, as with womankind: it is abomination. (Lev. 18:22)

David Boudreaux

Christians Must Judge between Good and Evil but Not Judge People

The Bible teaches that the spiritual man judges all things (1 Cor. 2:15). A spiritual person must be able to judge between good and evil in order to keep him or herself away from evil. The Bible also teaches that you shouldn't judge people unless you want to be judged (Matt. 7:1–5). The obvious conclusion is therefore that a spiritual person must be able to judge concerning good and evil activity, but he or she shouldn't judge people. Only God knows what people are going through in their lives and how He is dealing with them individually. We, therefore, do not have the required knowledge to formulate an accurate judgment.

I think I should make it clear that I do not have a phobia of gay people. I believe the Bible teaches that this type of sexual behavior is a sin, and if it is a sin, then it is not an acceptable alternative lifestyle. I know numerous people who are gay, and several of them are family members. I don't treat them like they are bad people. I think most of them have been deceived by this immoral world into believing that what they are doing is normal and therefore not wrong. I do not believe they were born gay. If a person were born gay, then that would mean God made him or her that way, but if that were true, then God wouldn't call it sinful behavior, which He most definitely does.

This is a good example of humankind believing the words of man over the words of their creator. God destroyed Sodom and Gomorrah because of sinful behavior just like this. If our nation continues to make believe that gay marriages and abortions are acceptable, then God will take the necessary actions to punish us. Being gay, cross-dressing, being a transvestite, stealing and lying, and doing all the other things listed as deeds of the evil influence of mankind and the devil are all equally sin. I will not say that these behaviors are normal or acceptable. The Supreme Court may have jurisdiction over the laws of our nation, but they do not have jurisdiction over the laws of God. To say that this is a protection of human rights is shameful. Humans don't have the right to live sinful lifestyles if they want to go to heaven; neither do they have the right to commit murder in abortion clinics. I just voted in the Republican primary election the other day, and there was a legislative proposal introduced to make it illegal for anyone in Texas to allow young children to have a sex change. I can't believe we have reached the point in our nation where we need to pass laws to keep people from destroying their own children's lives. We are also to the point where we have to pass laws to keep boys out of girls' restrooms in our schools and keep boys from playing on girls' sports teams and entering girls' dressing rooms.

I wonder if somebody makes an umbrella that will protect me from hail fire and brimstone. All sin should be dealt with in the same manner, it should be confessed as a sin; then the offender should demonstrate repentance and ask God for forgiveness. God can forgive us for any sin we ask Him to if we repent. We cannot be forgiven for sin if we refuse to admit it is a sin or refuse to stop living that way. I don't look down on people who are victims of sexual sin. I have had plenty of sin of my own, and no one is innocent. I am concerned for their eternal souls, because if they are convinced that these lifestyles are acceptable, then they won't recognize it for the sin that it is and seek forgiveness; and without forgiveness, they will be eternally lost. I don't wish that on anyone. To ensure that I am understood, I will end by saying this: I am not homophobic, but I am "theophobic." I'm not scared of gays, but I am scared of God's judgment on those that I care about. Being gay will not cause anyone to go to hell any more than being a liar will. It is not the sin that sends us to hell it is the rejection of Christ as the savior. As a saved person, any sin will cause you to lose fellowship with God but it will not cause you to lose your salvation.

"What I tell you in darkness, that speak ye in light: and what ye hear in the ear, that preach ye upon the housetops. And fear not them which kill the body, but are not able to kill the soul: but rather fear him which is able to destroy both soul and body in hell" (Matt. 10:27–28).

CHAPTER 6

Separation, Surrender, and Service

Putting God First Results in Separation from the World

The man as the spiritual leader is held accountable for maintaining standards of separation in the home. All those who profess the name of Christ as their Savior are called to be separated from the ways of this ungodly world in which we live. The Bible says the friends of the world are enemies of God. "Love not the world, neither the things that are in the world. If any man love the world, the love of the Father is not in him. For all that is in the world, the lust of the flesh, and the lust of the eyes, and the pride of life, is not of the Father, but is of the world. And the world passeth away, and the lust thereof: but he that doeth the will of God abideth for ever" (1 John 2:15–17).

How to Know the Will of God for Your Life

When we get saved, our bodies are bought and paid for and should be dedicated to God's service. For God to use us, we must be cleansed or sanctified (or made holy). *Holy* in the Greek is the word *hagios*. It means sacred, pure, blameless, consecrated, or saintly. This is separation, and the reason is that God can't use a dirty vessel for His work. That would be like putting purified water in a dirty glass.

"I beseech you therefore, brethren, by the mercies of God, that ye present your bodies a living sacrifice, holy, acceptable unto God, which is your reasonable service. And be not conformed to this world: but be ye transformed by the renewing of your mind, that ye may prove what is that good, and acceptable, and perfect, will of God" (Rom. 12:1–2). These verses alone say a lot, so let's take a hard look.

1. First, we must be willing to offer our bodies as living sacrifices to God for Him to use us in whatever way He chooses.
2. Second, we must separate ourselves from the world so we will be clean vessels for God's use.
3. Third, this shouldn't come as a shock that this is what God expects from us. After all He has done for us, this is a reasonable expectation.
4. We shouldn't try to conform or be the people the world expects us to be. We are expected to be better than that now. We should be transformed or changed into what God wants us to be.
5. How do we make this transformation take place? By renewing our minds. It's not enough to stop thinking the way the world wants us to think. We must train our minds to think about the things of God. This is done by studying the Word of God and allowing the Holy Spirit to guide us through life.
6. Finally, this is the only way we will ever know that we have found the perfect will of God for our lives, and then we can live it.

    You can never know what the perfect will of God is for your life until you give your body totally over to God for His use. This is a life separated from the world. "Having therefore these promises, dearly beloved, let us cleanse ourselves from all filthiness of the flesh and spirit, perfecting holiness in the fear of God" (2Cor. 7:1).

We Should Not Have Any Kind of
Binding Connection to the Lost

> Be ye not unequally yoked together with unbelievers: for what fellowship hath righteousness with unrighteousness? And what communion hath light with darkness? And what concord hath Christ with Belial? Or what part hath he that believeth with an infidel? And what agreement hath the temple of God with idols? For ye are the temple of the living God; as God hath said, I will dwell in them, and walk in them; and I will be their God, and they shall be my people. Wherefore come out from among them, and be ye separate, saith the Lord, and touch not the unclean thing; and I will receive you. And will be a Father unto you, and ye shall be my sons and daughters, saith the Lord Almighty. (2Cor. 6:14–18)

We Should Walk after the Spirit

To be separate from the world obviously doesn't mean to be taken out of the world. That will happen one day when the rapture takes place, and of course we, still being in corrupt bodies until then, will still commit sins from time to time. What God is telling us is that we should walk after the Spirit and not after the flesh. The flesh, as long as we carry it around with us, will be in a war against our spirits as we try to live lives that are pleasing to God. But we should always try to do the right thing; this is being separated from the lifestyle the world has to offer because the world seeks to please the desires of the flesh. *To live in God's will, just do right.*

If you are saved, then you should desire to live a life separated to God and serve Him. This change has taken place inside you because of the indwelling Holy Spirit of God now living inside you. You will determine that serving God and finding His perfect will for your life are more important than anything else you could ever do with your life. You must realize that only the things you do for God will count for eternity, for all that is in this world and pertains to this world will pass away (1 John 2:17). Only those who have been redeemed will be there to share eternity with you. You must concentrate on storing up treasures in heaven (Matt. 6:19–20). Stay focused on things above. This means Jesus must be more important than family, including mother, father, wife, and children. We mentioned this earlier, but it needs to be elaborated on.

The Importance of Right Priorities

Below is how your priorities should be arranged concerning other people in your life. I'm not trying to say people aren't important; they are the most important thing other than God. I'm just trying to emphasize how much more important God is than any person.

1. God
2. Spouse
3. Children
4. Others
5. Self

If you don't have right priorities, nothing else in your life and relationships with those around you will ever be right either.

Love God above All Others

"Jesus said unto him, Thou shalt love the Lord thy God with all thy heart, and with all thy soul, and with all thy mind. This is the first and great commandment. And the second is like unto it, Thou shalt love thy neighbour as thyself. On these two commandments hang all the law and the prophets" (Matt. 22:37–40).

Love Your Wife Like Christ Loved the Church

This is where it gets a little confusing because God says to put Him first and then your neighbor. It says God should be ahead of your wife, but it doesn't say here that your wife and children should be ahead of your neighbor. I think that is because in this context it is trying to emphasize the importance of putting God ahead of everyone else including your wife and kids. In this context, your wife and kids are part of the same group as your neighbors, but it doesn't distinguish among the neighbors which ones should come first, so we will have to find that in other scriptures. The Bible tells us in the book of Ephesians that you should be willing to sacrifice yourself to save your wife, but it doesn't say that about the rest of your neighbors. It does say we should be willing to die for our Christian brothers and sisters but not that we should nurture and cherish them like we do our wives and children. That makes it clear to me that she is the next priority after God and then the children. "Husbands, love your wives, even as Christ also loved the church, and gave himself for it" (Eph. 5:25).

It would be negligent of me not to include the fact that the scriptures say you should be willing to lay down your life for a brother in Christ as well. I believe, however, that in the way this is worded, it is referring to your willingness to die for Christianity, not specifically for an individual. I believe the wife should also be second because she is one with her husband, whereas the neighbors and brethren or not. "Hereby perceive we the love of God, because he laid down his life for us: and we ought to lay down our lives for the brethren" (1 John 3:16).

Those in Your House (Your Children) Are Third

Then in 1 Timothy God says that if we don't take care of those in our own household first, then we are worse than unbelievers and have denied Christianity. That sounds to me like our children should be next. "But if any provide not for his own, and specially for those of his own house, he hath denied the faith, and is worse than an infidel" (1 Tim. 5:8).

God clearly made the first commandment first because loving God more than anything else is the most important thing you can do. The next most important thing, is loving your neighbor. Jesus said that if you will do these two things, you will fulfill all the laws of God because love will cause you to keep God's commandments, and love will keep you from doing anything to hurt your neighbor (Rom. 13:10).To me this makes it obvious that being a good Christian involves two things: first, putting God where He belongs in your life; and second, treating other people with love, compassion, and respect. There is no mention of money, material objects, or wealth here. God doesn't care about any of those things. What is important to Him are people. Now for the importance of order:

> If any man come to me, and hate not his father, and mother, and wife, and children, and brethren, and sisters, yea, and his own life also, he cannot be my disciple. And whosoever doth not bear his cross, and come after me, cannot be my disciple. For which of you, intending to build a tower, sitteth not down first, and counteth the cost, whether he have sufficient to finish it? Lest haply, after he hath

laid the foundation, and is not able to finish it, all
that behold it begin to mock him, Saying, This
man began to build, and was not able to finish.
Or what king, going to make war against another
king, sitteth not down first, and consulteth whether
he be able with ten thousand to meet him that
cometh against him with twenty thousand? Or else,
while the other is yet a great way off, he sendeth an
ambassage, and desireth conditions of peace. So
likewise, whosoever he be of you that forsaketh not
all that he hath, he cannot be my disciple. (Luke
14:26–33)

Jesus wasn't saying that His followers should hate their parents,
wives, and children. The word translated "hate" here is a Greek word
meaning to love less. He is simply saying that if you place the value
of family over the value of God, then you aren't worthy of Him.
Jesus said that His mother and brothers were those who did the will
of His Father. This goes for your spouse as well. No one should be
more important than God. "There came then his brethren and his
mother, and, standing without, sent unto him, calling him. And
the multitude sat about him, and they said unto him, Behold, thy
mother and thy brethren without seek for thee. And he answered
them, saying, Who is my mother, or my brethren? And he looked
round about on them which sat about him, and said, Behold my
mother and my brethren! For whosoever shall do the will of God,
the same is my brother, and my sister, and mother" (Mark 3:31–35).

Examples of Wrong Priorities and the Results

Let's go back to Luke 24. Here Jesus goes on to say that anyone
who intends to be His disciple must count the cost and be willing
to sacrifice all else and put God and His work first. God should

always be first on your priority list. Getting your priorities wrong is probably the biggest destroyer of marriages throughout history. Money, jealousy, and almost any other marital problem you can think of can be traced back to wrong priorities. In the following paragraphs I have listed some examples of wrong priorities in a marriage and some possible results:

Men Putting Their Wives Ahead of God

This is what caused the fall of humankind from the beginning. I think Adam faced the same problem we do in that God is a spirit, and even though He was there with Adam, Adam couldn't see or touch Him. Eve, on the other hand, had been custom-made for Adam, and he loved her as much as he did himself just the way God intended. It's much easier to express your feelings to someone you can see.

This reminds me of the little girl who was put to bed and told it was time to go to sleep. Every time her mom left the room, the little girl started crying. Each time the mom went back in to comfort the little girl. Finally, the little girl told her mom she was scared in the room all by herself at night. The mom, being sympathetic and a born-again Christian, told her little daughter that she didn't need to be scared because she wasn't alone. She continued by saying, "You know that Jesus is here with you, and He will never leave you alone."

The little girl replied, "Yes, Mom, I know, but sometimes I need someone with skin."

I'm saying sometimes it's easier to trust and hold on to someone you can touch. I'm not saying Adam did anything any of the rest of us may not have done being in his position, but we must learn to trust God and put Him first above anyone else, even when we can't see Him or even feel Him for that matter. There are times when God's presence will be difficult to feel, but we must trust that He is there anyhow.

As I mentioned previously, before the fall of mankind, men didn't have to work to provide for their families; God did that for them. Women also didn't have to suffer during childbirth. These were punishments given to humankind because man listened to his wife rather than what God had told him to do. I believe for many men this is still happening, even if they don't realize what is going on. Men, it is a fact that you should love your wife more than any other person on earth but not more than God. The man is intended to be the head over the wife by God's plan; if you let your wife control every aspect of your life, especially concerning spiritual matters, then you have your priorities wrong, and so does your wife. Can your wife convince you to do something you know God doesn't want you to do? If so, then you are headed for trouble. The church looks to Christ for spiritual leadership, and the wife should look to her husband.

Men Put Others Ahead of Their Wives

A wife is a very jealous creature. This isn't necessarily a bad thing because we know that we also have a very jealous God. "But ye shall destroy their altars, break their images, and cut down their groves: For thou shalt worship no other god: for the LORD, whose name is Jealous, is a jealous God" (Ex. 34:13–14).

I think this verse calls for a bit of explanation. If you understand that the root word that God's name Jehovah comes from is also the same word that is translated jealous in English. The point is not only did God's name mean jealous but just like the rest of the names that God has been for Himself in Scripture, it describes one of God's attributes.

The thing is, men need to be aware of this and therefore be considerate of their wives' feelings and not do anything that would provoke jealousy. *Behind every angry woman is a man who has no idea what he did wrong.* I will tell you this: if your wife never gets jealous, it is probably because she has lost her first love for you. I don't mean she isn't in love with you anymore, but she has lost the deep emotional connection she had when you got married, and you need to work on getting it back. You shouldn't be looking at other women, even if you are not lusting. Sometimes men develop this bad habit as single men and have a hard time changing it. You had better get that under control. Some women will pretend it doesn't bother them for a while, but it does, and sooner or later you're going to hear about it. Sometimes even your good intentions can bring out jealousy. If your wife feels like you do more for other people than you do for her.

Men, if your wife feels like she is being neglected in some way while you are meeting the needs of others, then you have made another mistake. While God does expect us to help others, He doesn't expect you to treat others better than you do your wife. After all, she is one flesh with you, and you should cherish her. Putting others ahead of your wife will destroy her trust and faith in you as a provider and protector. It will make her reluctant to be in subjection to you as well. If a man wants his wife to fulfill the role God created for her in marriage, then he must fulfill his part first. I believe this is another tricky area because men are told to put themselves last on the list of priorities and that their wives are one with them. Because they are one with the husband the husband tends to not show them the priority that they deserve and that is second only to God.

Another thing you should do as a husband is always support your wife and the decisions she makes in public. Even if you don't completely agree with what she might be saying sometimes, you should make every effort to agree with her in front of other people. If she thinks you are taking someone else's side against her, you have just started a war in your marriage. I don't think you should go along with her concerning immorality, but in a marriage most issues don't have anything to do with morality. Again, if you want to live with her according to knowledge, then you need to learn how to pick your fights. No two people are going to agree on everything, but what you need to ask yourself is this: is it important enough to argue over? Most of the time the answer is no. A woman's home is her domain. She should always feel like she is more important to you than other people, especially other women. Don't tease her about other women trying to invoke jealousy; this will destroy your marriage. The deacon in our church, Darren Wagner, has a favorite saying: "Do you want to be right, or do you want to be happy?"

When my wife gets a *little upset*, all it takes is a "Calm down, sweetheart" in a soft, mellow, soothing voice to make her get a *lot upset*.

Men Put Others Ahead of Their Children

If you do this, your children will be offended. We are warned about provoking our children to wrath. "And, ye fathers, provoke not your children to wrath: but bring them up in the nurture and admonition of the Lord" (Eph. 6:4).

Notice that this command is given to fathers; I believe that is because you seldom ever need to tell a mother not to put other people ahead of her children. Children are a gift from God and should be treated as such (Ps. 127:3). I believe rather than being mistreated, most of the time children are more neglected these days. People's opinions still vary greatly on what is considered child abuse, and we will get into some of that later when we are talking about marital intimacy and having children, but here I'm just saying you should not put other people ahead of your children.

The only person more important than your children should be your spouse. I don't think your children should be spoiled to the point that they have everything they ever wanted and some, but they should not feel as though you think other people are more important than they are. They should never have to stand in line behind anyone else to get what they need from you. That includes your protection, provision, time, and affection. They are entitled to all the same things your wife gets from you. In the verse above, we see they are entitled to nurturing (caring for and encouraging growth or development) from you and admonition (giving authoritative guidance or counsel to).This will take time to do, and perhaps your time is the thing they need the most and are most likely to be resentful about if they don't get it.

Your time is the most valuable asset you have. Devoted time is the only thing you can give to only one person at a time. It is the only thing you have that you can give only once because once it is spent, you can't get it back. Time spent with someone will make the person feel like he or she is important to you. As much good as time does when it is well spent, the more damage it can do when not spent in the right way. One other thing I will mention here is that if you don't have a good relationship with your children, you won't have a good one with your wife either because other than you, they are the most important thing in her life as well. If you mistreat your children, your wife (their mother) will feel as though you are mistreating her as well. This is just part of being a mother. Oh yeah, just because the kids are grown and gone, that doesn't change either. She will still be protective of her grown kids as well as the grandkids. On the other hand, the best way to make a good impression on a mother is to be good to her children.

Men Will Sometimes Put Themselves Ahead of Their Wives

I do believe, as I said earlier, that God expects husbands to love, honor, cherish, provide for, and protect their wives. They should love them as much as they love themselves because they are one flesh. How can you nourish and cherish someone you don't love at least as much as you love yourself? Now, here is where I believe the Bible teaches you should cherish (love) her more than you do yourself. If I'm reading it right, it says that a man should love his wife enough to sacrifice himself to save her, just like Jesus sacrificed Himself to save the church. If you are going to sacrifice yourself to save her, then it's obvious that her life is worth more to you than your own. That means you will make sure all her needs are met before your own are. You will make sure she is protected better than you are. You will make sure she has food even when you don't. You will make sure she has a safe, warm, and comfortable place to live even if you don't. This is what I call a man putting his wife ahead of himself.

By the way, your children should also be put ahead of yourself and they should also be ahead of everyone else except your wife. He who doesn't provide for his family is worse than an unbeliever (1 Tim. 5:8). A selfish man, in my opinion, is the absolute worst kind. This is the man who demands that his wife work and take care of the house and the children while he sits around shouting orders. He usually doesn't want to have children regardless of what his wife wants because he wants her to give him all her attention and he doesn't want to be responsible for anyone or anything. He wants to control all the household finances and doesn't give her any money for herself without any accountability. All he thinks about is work, more money, more attention, and what new toy he will buy for himself next. This man generally has no regard for God or others, or doing right either; it is all about pleasing self. If this man claims to be a Christian, I would have my doubts about that being true. This man also gives no consideration to pleasing God in any aspect of his life. A selfish man is the worst kind.

The Wife Has a Cold

It is during the first year of marriage, and the wife has a cold. The husband says, "Hey my sweet, little sugar dumpling. Are you okay, sweetie pie? Is there anything I can get you, love cakes? I'm going to stay right here next to you until you feel better, okay, honeysuckle? Do you want me to make you some soup, sweetheart? Do you want me to get you some medicine or water or juice? Can I turn on the TV or go get you anything? Don't worry about anything, sweet pea. I will take care of everything until you feel better."

Five years after the wedding, the wife has a cold. "Hey, babe, I'm sorry you don't feel well. I'm going to the store. Do you want anything? Do you think you will be well enough to go back to work tomorrow? I can get one of the kids to come sit with you if you want. Do you need anything else before I go out with the guys tonight? I hope you will be okay."

It is ten years into the marriage, and the wife has a cold. "Hey you, Are you just going to lie around the house all day? I have to go to work all day and then come home and pick up after you. Can you quit snorting like a bull and leaving snotty rags lying around everywhere? I don't know how a little cold can put you out of commission. You act like you're dying all day long."

If your husband acts like this, then he is a self-centered brat with his priorities all messed up.

Women Will Put Their Children Ahead of Their Husbands

This can be the case whether the child is a blood relative of both the husband and wife or more often than not, if the child is only related by blood to the wife but not to the husband or related to the husband but not to the wife. Women have built inside them a natural instinct to protect their children, and sometimes this natural instinct, especially in new marriages, can be stronger than the love bond that has developed between the husband and wife.

We know the woman should put her husband ahead of her children because this is God's plan, but try to explain that to the heart. She hasn't had the benefit of seeing her husband and children interact with one another since the day of the child's birth. She knows her husband loves her or at least professes to, but he hasn't spent enough time with the child to prove he has the same kind of love for him or her. Love takes a little time to grow, and we all know that, so it is only natural to believe her new husband cannot love her child like she does. These feelings generally end up causing the mother to be over protective of her child, which puts a tremendous strain on the marriage.

Here is what I suggest if you are in this type of situation. Women should realize that their husbands may not know their children that well, but they have accepted the responsibility to provide for them and protect them; therefore, they should have some authority over them as well.

Personally, I don't think a husband and wife should ever take the side of the child over that of the parent, at least not in front of the child. If you don't agree with each other, put a pause on the situation and find a place away from the child where you can discuss it until you reach a mutually agreeable solution. Then go to the child together and render the solution. Third, I think men should realize their wives are better equipped by God to handle certain situations, and guiding the home and raising children or two of those areas. Again, the home is her domain, and the husband can let her handle these situations without feeling like he has lost his position as head over the family.

My wife makes the majority of the decisions concerning the home and the children and the grandchildren, and I gladly let her deal with them. I don't feel like this diminishes my authority at all. Both partners in a marriage should realize that marriage is a lifetime

David Boudreaux

commitment, and long after the children are gone, they will still be there to support one another.

One woman gets so mad at her husband that she tells him he needs to move out. The man gathers up his things and heads for the door. As he is leaving, his wife shouts out, "I hope you end up living a long, miserable, unhappy, lonely life."

The husband replies, "I thought you said you wanted me to leave."

Women Sometimes Put Husbands Ahead of God

More often than not, it is the husband's fault when this happens. Because God has made man head over his wife, many times the man will be so demanding that the wife has no time for God. He might even be jealous of the time she spends with God and intentionally does things to make her service to God difficult or impossible. This is why it's so important to marry a man who serves God and wants a wife who serves God as well. I think going to church is a great thing which Christian families should do together. If the husband won't go, there is a problem if he doesn't want his wife to go or causes problems for her every time she tries to. While it is true that the man is supposed to be the spiritual leader in the home, that doesn't mean he is always going to do what he should.

If it is a mixed marriage and the wife is a Christian but the husband is not, then she will have to take the position of spiritual leadership in the home. She obviously cannot order her husband to go to church and get saved, but she can possibly win him over by her Christian behavior. That is what the verse means when it say he may be won over by the conversation of his wife. 1 Pet. 3:1. Nevertheless, at the very least, she should be able to take the place of spiritual leadership in the home over her children since the husband won't do so.

If the husband will not allow his Christian wife to serve God, won't go to church, and won't try to raise the children in a Christian

158

manner, then perhaps this is the situation the apostle Paul referred to when he said the Christian is under no obligation to make the unbeliever stay. These types of marriages will seldom last, and if he chooses to leave, then let him go. If the wife is the unbeliever, then the husband should retain the position of spiritual leadership and try to win the wife and children over to Christianity. If that doesn't work, then he is not obligated to stay with the unbelieving wife either should she decide to leave (1 Cor. 7:15). If there has been no adultery committed in the marriage when the split takes place, then the believer should stay single until the unbelieving partner who left either commits adultery or finds someone else; then the person is free to marry whomever he or she wants as long as the new partner is saved. For goodness' sake, don't make the same mistake again. That reminds me of another illustration.

This man asked his wife the other day what she liked about him the most, his body or his face. After looking him up and down a couple of times, she smiled and answered, "Your sense of humor." Somehow I don't feel like she is putting him ahead of God.

Women Put Themselves Above Their Husbands and God

This is the woman who marries only for money, status, reputation, or possessions. She really has no regard for serving God or her husband but is in the relationship only for what she can gain from it. This is the woman who will stay with her husband until she has what she wants and gets bored with him or until she finds someone else she thinks is capable of giving her more. This is the harlot who seeks after the precious seed. She will take all you have and then dump you without a second thought. She will cheat on you, deceive you, abuse you, take advantage of you, and eventually leave you for her next victim. This woman is obviously not a Christian, and eventually she will commit adultery, and you will be free. The only question is how much she will take from you before she leaves.

Hopefully, a Christian man will never be caught in such a situation, but these women are deceitful and very good at hiding their true selves until it is too late. If she cheats on you before you get married, then she will also do so afterward. If she cheats with you on her husband, then she will cheat on you with her next victim. All you can do is hope you catch her before she destroys your life and takes all you have. This is the harlot described in Proverbs 7:1–27. I have already showed you these verses once, so I'm not going to include them here, but you may want to read them again. The reason all this is important in serving God is because you cannot have a good relationship with God if you don't have a good relationship with your spouse at home. I love to add a little illustrative humor.

An older gentleman had to go see his doctor because he was always overly tired. As always, his wife went with him because he needed a little help getting around from time to time, and she wanted to hear what the doctor told him anyhow. She always wondered whether he understood what the doctor was saying because he was hard of hearing as well. Anyhow, they went into the doctor's office, and the doctor did his usual physical checkup routine while the wife sat there quietly and watched every move.

After the checkup, the doctor told the wife, "Your husband needs complete peace and quiet for an extended period of time so he can rest. He is showing all the signs of exhaustion from the lack of rest." Then the doctor reached for his notepad and said, "I'm going to prescribe some sleeping pills I believe will help the situation."

The wife, while watching him write on the notepad, said to the doctor, "I think that is probably a good idea, but when should I give them to him?"

The doctor replied to the wife, "These are for you."

Look at what God says about living in a contentious household:

> As a jewel of gold in a swine's snout, so is a fair
> woman which is without discretion. (Prov. 11:22)

A virtuous woman is a crown to her husband: but she that maketh ashamed is as rottenness in his bones. (Prov. 12:4)

Every wise woman buildeth her house: but the foolish plucketh it down with her hands. (Prov. 14:1)

It is better to dwell in a corner of the housetop, than with a brawling woman in a wide house. (Prov. 21:90

It is better to dwell in the wilderness, than with a contentious and an angry woman.(Prov. 21:19)

It is better to dwell in the corner of the housetop, than with a brawling woman and in a wide house. (Prov. 25:24)

A continual dropping on a very rainy day and a contentious woman are alike. (Prov. 27:15)

The Bible says, "For three things the earth is disquieted, [Worried or Anxious] and for four which it cannot bear: For a servant when he reigneth; and a fool when he is filled with meat; For an odious [extremely unpleasant or repulsive] woman when she is married; and an handmaid that is heir to her mistress" (Prov. 30:21–23). Here is a little more humor:

A woman says to her neighbors, "I'm very concerned about my husband. It has been raining for three days now, and all he does is stand there by the window and stare. If this keeps up much longer, I'm going to have to let him come in."

The Surrender of Your Resources to God

You Must Be Willing to Sacrifice All

We have been talking about the surrender of yourself and your household along with the separation from the world God requires if you want to be used to do His work. This is what is necessary for you to fully obey God's will. In addition to surrendering yourself, you must also be willing to surrender your resources. This doesn't mean what God has planned for you will require you to forsake everything you have, including family, but it does mean you should be willing to do so if that is what He asks you to do.

> So likewise, whosoever he be of you that forsaketh not all that he hath, he cannot be my disciple. (Luke 14:33)

> And, behold, one came and said unto him, Good Master, what good thing shall I do, that I may have eternal life? And he said unto him, Why callest thou me good? There is none good but one, that is, God: but if thou wilt enter into life, keep the commandments. He saith unto him, Which? Jesus said, Thou shalt do no murder, Thou shalt not commit adultery, Thou shalt not steal, Thou shalt not bear false witness, Honour thy father and thy mother: and, Thou shalt love thy neighbour as thyself. The young man saith unto him, All these things have I kept from my youth up: what lack I yet? Jesus said unto him, If thou wilt be perfect, go and sell that thou hast, and give to the poor, and thou shalt have treasure in heaven: and come and follow me. But when the young man heard that saying, he went away sorrowful: for he had

great possessions. Then said Jesus unto his disciples, Verily I say unto you, That a rich man shall hardly enter into the kingdom of heaven. And again I say unto you, It is easier for a camel to go through the eye of a needle, than for a rich man to enter into the kingdom of God. When his disciples heard it, they were exceedingly amazed, saying, Who then can be saved? But Jesus beheld them, and said unto them, With men this is impossible; but with God all things are possible. Then answered Peter and said unto him, Behold, we have forsaken all, and followed thee; what shall we have therefore? And Jesus said unto them, Verily I say unto you, That ye which have followed me, in the regeneration when the Son of man shall sit in the throne of his glory, ye also shall sit upon twelve thrones, judging the twelve tribes of Israel. And every one that hath forsaken houses, or brethren, or sisters, or father, or mother, or wife, or children, or lands, for my name's sake, shall receive an hundredfold, and shall inherit everlasting life. (Matt. 19:16–29)

Learn to Be Content Wherever God Puts You

This total surrender won't always lead you to the most hospitable and desirable conditions. This is why Paul felt it was prudent to mention that he had learned to be content in every situation, realizing this was God's will for Him. "Not that I speak in respect of want: for I have learned, in whatsoever state I am, therewith to be content" (Phil.4:11).

My wife is from Oregon, and I am from Texas. We tease each other a lot about which state is better. I love Texas, and I don't intend to ever go anywhere else, but if God told me to sell everything we have and move to Oregon, I would do so in a minute. This illustrates two points. First, Paul wasn't talking about being in any certain place or territory; he was talking about being in a certain state of mind. That state of mind is this: if this is according to God's will for me, I will rejoice in it. Second, we must be willing to go anywhere or do anything God wants us to do, or we can't be in God's will.

> And when her masters saw that the hope of their gains was gone, they caught Paul and Silas, and drew them into the marketplace unto the rulers, And brought them to the magistrates, saying, These men, being Jews, do exceedingly trouble our city, And teach customs, which are not lawful for us to receive, neither to observe, being Romans. And the multitude rose up together against them: and the magistrates rent off their clothes, and commanded to beat them. And when they had laid many stripes upon them, they cast them into prison, charging the jailor to keep them safely: Who, having received such a charge, thrust them into the inner prison, and made their feet fast in the stocks. And at midnight Paul and Silas prayed, and sang praises unto God: and the prisoners heard them. And suddenly there was a great earthquake, so that the foundations of the prison were shaken: and immediately all the doors were opened, and every one's bands were loosed. And the keeper of the prison awaking out of his sleep, and seeing the prison doors open, he drew out his sword, and would have killed himself, supposing that the prisoners had been fled. But Paul cried with a loud voice, saying, Do thyself no harm: for we are all here. Then he called for a light, and sprang in, and came trembling, and fell down before Paul and Silas, And brought them out, and

said, Sirs, what must I do to be saved? And they said, Believe on the Lord Jesus Christ, and thou shalt be saved, and thy house. And they spake unto him the word of the Lord, and to all that were in his house. And he took them the same hour of the night, and washed their stripes; and was baptized, he and all his, straightway. (Acts 16:19–33)

As you can see from these verses, serving God isn't always pleasant, but Paul and his companions were rejoicing and singing praises unto God while they were in prison and in shackles after being beaten. The end result was that the jailer and his entire household were saved. Would you be rejoicing and praying and singing praises to God if you were cast into prison and put in shackles? First Corinthians 4:2 says, "It is required of stewards that a man be found faithful." You can't expect God to give you more work to do if you're not happy about doing what He has already given to you. Are you available to go anywhere, do anything, or answer any call God gives you? If there is a place where you have said you won't go, that is probably the place where God could have used you. A person who claims to be right with God should never say, "I won't do anything, or I won't go anywhere." If you want to fulfill God's perfect will in your life, then you will.

Everything Happens for a Reason

When I first moved to Orange, Texas, to start my business, I was all alone in this big world. At first, I lived in a small travel trailer and had very little to call my own. Being in the aircraft repair business, however, does have some advantages, and I was able to meet some very good people soon after arriving in the area. One of them was a man named Tom Foreman, who owns a local business called Foreman Construction. Anyhow, Tom owns a "V" Tail Bonanza aircraft, which is sometimes referred to as the "doctor killer" in aviation circles. That is another story for another time. Anyhow, I met Tom because I started working on his airplane, and it didn't take hardly any time at all before we became best friends. Through Tom, I met another man named Robert. Robert is a real estate fellow who owns several rental properties in Orange County. I asked Robert whether he had any rental properties available, and he said he didn't, but he had recently purchased a trailer house he was getting ready to rent out. I sort of pushed the issue because I wasn't going to be able to stay where I was for much longer. Robert, being a great guy, did his best to get the trailer ready for me as soon as he could, and I moved in a few days later.

After being in the trailer about three days or so, I was sleeping on the floor in the living room because I still had no furniture. I woke up around two in the morning and thought I smelled smoke in the house. It was pretty dark, and I couldn't see any smoke, but I thought I should get up and look around just to make sure. I went to the far end of the trailer where the circuit breaker box was located, and I could see a little smoke near the box. I went back to the living room to see whether I could find anything to open the box and see what the problem was. I found a screwdriver and went back to where the breaker box was, but I was too late. Now flames were shooting out of the wall on the left-hand side of the box and smoke was quickly filling the house.

I decided I needed to get out of the house, so I went back to the living room to get my phone, wallet, and keys. But by that time, the smoke was so thick that I couldn't find anything, so I grabbed my phone and ran out. I started heading for the front door, and the flames were already coming down the hallway. I couldn't believe the fire was spreading so fast, but I know what I saw. I ran out of the house without anything except the clothes I had been sleeping in. As I stood on the street corner, watching the house burn with everything I had still inside, I was in awe. The lady who lived across the street came out and stood with me, watching the house burn.

She asked me whether I was okay, and I replied that I was fine and that all was good.

She gave me funny look and said, "What could possibly be good right now?"

I grinned at her and said, "Well, for starters I'm pretty sure I just got a significant reduction in my rent."A good attitude means accepting the fact that everything that happens to you is part of God's plan. "And we know that all things work together for good to them that love God, to them who are the called according to his purpose" (Rom. 8:28).

God Will Give You What You Need

If God calls you into service, He will also give you the abilities you need to accomplish any task He gives you.

> And Moses said unto the children of Israel, See, the LORD hath called by name Bezaleel the son of Uri, the son of Hur, of the tribe of Judah; And he hath filled him with the spirit of God, in wisdom, in understanding, and in knowledge, and in all manner of workmanship; And to devise curious works, to work in gold, and in silver, and in brass, And in the cutting of stones, to set them, and in carving of wood, to make any manner of cunning work. And he hath put in his heart that he may teach, both he, and Aholiab, the son of Ahisamach, of the tribe of Dan. Them hath he filled with wisdom of heart, to work all manner of work, of the engraver, and of the cunning workman, and of the embroiderer, in blue, and in purple, in scarlet, and in fine linen, and of the weaver, even of them that do any work, and of those that devise cunning work. (Ex. 35:30–35)

God won't tell you to do something without giving you the ability to do it. Moses gave God all kinds of excuses at the burning bush, but God gave Moses what he needed to do the job. He can and will do the same thing for you. You have no talents, abilities, gifts, wisdom, understanding, or knowledge except what God has given you anyhow. If God gave it to you, then you should be willing to use it to serve Him. All Christians should prepare themselves for God to use them in any way He chooses. He may never call you into His full-time service, but you will never know what God could have done with you and your family if you don't surrender all. "I beseech you therefore, brethren, by the mercies of God, that ye present your bodies a living sacrifice, holy, acceptable unto God, which is your reasonable service. And be not conformed to this world: but be ye transformed by the renewing of your mind, that ye may prove what is that good, and acceptable, and perfect, will of God" (Rom. 12:1–2).

Doing God's Will Doesn't Come without Opposition

When I was in Bible College, we had to prepare three sermon outlines every week and preach at least three times a week somewhere. For the most part, this was a lot of fun, and it led to some interesting places and situations. At the same time, it was also exhausting at times with all the other school work that had to be done every week; plus I had a wife and four kids at the time. I was also working forty hours a week and supporting my family at the same time. Anyhow, it wasn't always easy to find a place to preach three sermons every week with all the other things going on. I have preached in nursing homes. I have preached in other churches. I have preached in the prisons. I have preached at the Salvation Army chapel. I have had to preach on the street corner. All these places had their unique challenges to deal with.

Perhaps the most challenging place at times was on the street corner. I have had people come up to me on the street while I was preaching and threaten to shut me up. I never stopped preaching, and they never went any further than threats, but it was an interesting experience. I even had a couple of people bully me and push me around a little, but I kept preaching; and when the cops drove by, they left. One time a car kept driving by with someone inside cursing at me. Once a girl in a car's back seat pulled up her blouse and hung herself out the window, screaming, "Save me! Save me." You don't really know how to react when people do things like that. I just thought, *Man, her parents must really be proud of her.* No, I've never had to suffer anything like Paul did, but if you intend to serve God, be prepared to face opposition. We live in an evil world; you never know what they will throw at you next. Every once in a while, however, I did get the opportunity to witness to people and even had the privilege to lead a few to accept Christ.

CHAPTER 7

Church Family

Where Two or More Are Gathered

While it may be true that the scriptures say if two or more are gathered together in the name of Jesus Christ that He will be with them, I'm not sure this is what He intended as a definition of church attendance. I would interpret the scripture this way: if two or more people are gathering together to start a church, then this is a good example of the correct application of this verse. However, if someone is using this verse as an excuse not to attend a regular church, that would be a misapplication. The point of the verse in its context is that the law requires two witnesses for a matter to be established as fact. Otherwise, it would just be one against one, and there would be no one to verify the truth. This authority is given to the church, so the proper interpretation would be, if two church brothers go to confront another brother who is out of line, they would have church authority behind them to do so.

> Moreover if thy brother shall trespass against thee, go and tell him his fault between thee and him alone: if he shall hear thee, thou hast gained thy brother. But if he will not hear thee, then take with thee one or two more, that in the mouth of two

or three witnesses every word may be established. And if he shall neglect to hear them, tell it unto the church: but if he neglect to hear the church, let him be unto thee as an heathen man and a publican. Verily I say unto you, whatsoever ye shall bind on earth shall be bound in heaven: and whatsoever ye shall loose on earth shall be loosed in heaven. Again I say unto you, that if two of you shall agree on earth as touching anything that they shall ask, it shall be done for them of my Father which is in heaven. For where two or three are gathered together in my name, there am I in the midst of them. (Matt. 18:15–20)

Many of you can probably already see from the passage that these verses aren't saying that anytime two or more people are gathered together in Christ's name that they are in church. Verse 17 even says that if this man to whom the two or three from the church went to talk to still has a problem, then they should take the man to the church to decide what to do about the matter. If this is true, then obviously the two or more who went to talk to the man only represented the church in this issue, but it is not the church itself. This passage is talking about how the church should deal with a person who is backslidden, as it is commonly called, someone who has slipped backward in his or her Christian growth. This term is used to describe those who are falling back into their old way of life or in some cases have just stopped moving forward in their spiritual growth. If you feel like a brother or sister has wronged you, you should first go to that person alone and try to settle the issue. If the person refuses to listen to you and repent of his or her trespass against you, then you should see him or her again with one or two other brothers from the church. If the person still refuses to make it right, then he or she should be turned over to the church for proper disciplinary action, if needed. If the person still will not listen, even to the church authorities, then he or she should be treated like a heathen person (lost person) by the rest of the church members. The church has been given the authority to do this. It is through the ministry of the church and its authority that the gospel is spread and people are saved.

Notice that it says the person is to be treated as a heathen person. This doesn't mean the church can take his or her salvation away. It means if the person is backslidden and living like a lost person, then the church members should treat him or her as though he or she were a lost person. If others in your church have had a falling out with the pastor in your church because of some sin in their lives and they leave the church because of it, you should break fellowship with them until they get right. This separation does several things: first, it may convince them that they have made an error. This, therefore, causes them to repent and do the right thing to restore fellowship. Second, it could prevent you from falling into the same trap they fell into if they are able to turn you against the church. Verse 18 here states the authority of the church the same as it did concerning Peter in the book of Mathew. This tells me authority was given to the church, which consists of all those who believe and confess Christ as the Son of God, but in this case, it is referring to the local church assembly. "And I will give unto thee the keys of the kingdom of heaven: and whatsoever thou shalt bind on earth shall be bound in heaven: and whatsoever thou shalt loose on earth shall be loosed in heaven" (Matt. 16:19).

The placement of this authority was repeated to all the apostles later in the book of John. This is why I believe this authority is given to all believers, but when it comes to church matters, it should involve the local church leadership. "Then said Jesus to them again, Peace be unto you: as my Father hath sent me, even so send I you. And when he had said this, he breathed on them, and saith unto them, Receive ye the Holy Ghost: Whose soever sins ye remit, they are remitted unto them; and whose soever sins ye retain, they are retained" (John 20:21–23).

What Is the Church?

The church has the authority to show people how to get saved and to discipline those who refuse to repent when they do wrong after they have been saved. The members of the church are subject to church leadership (the pastor or bishop is the intercessor between Christ and the church members) just as the wife is subject to the husband, who is the intercessor between her and God. We know God is with all Christians all the time through the presence of the Holy Spirit, who lives inside them, but they aren't always in church. The word *church* is the Greek word *eklasea*, which is translated to mean "a called-out assembly." The "called-out" part is addressing the fact that they are Christians, and they have been called out to be separate from the world. The "assembly" part refers to those who gather together to attend to spiritual matters, such as preaching the gospel, and includes the practicing of the church ordinances. If your assembly doesn't participate in church ordinances, such as baptism and the Lord's Supper, then it isn't fulfilling all the responsibilities of a church. The universal church (the body of all born-again believers of all religions who believe in Christ) won't be an assembly until the rapture occurs.

God Tells Believers Not to Forsake the Local Assembly

> Not forsaking the assembling of ourselves together, as the manner of some is; but exhorting one another: and so much the more, as ye see the day approaching. (Heb. 10:25)

> I was glad when they said unto me, Let us go into the house of the LORD. (Ps. 122:1)

> When I remember these things, I pour out my soul
> in me: for I had gone with the multitude, I went
> with them to the house of God, with the voice of
> joy and praise, with a multitude that kept holyday.
> (Ps. 42:4)

> And many people shall go and say, Come ye, and
> let us go up to the mountain of the LORD, to the
> house of the God of Jacob; and he will teach us of
> his ways, and we will walk in his paths: for out of
> Zion shall go forth the law, and the word of the
> LORD from Jerusalem. (Isa. 2:3)

It's important to understand that the church doesn't refer to a building. Even when the scripture is talking about a local church assembly, it is talking about the people in the church building, not the building itself. All the letters the apostle Paul wrote were epistles to the church in Rome, Corinth, Galatia, Ephesus, Philippi, Colossae, and Thessalonica. First and Second Timothy were written to one of Paul's converts, who was the pastor of the church at Ephesus. Titus was also one of Paul's converts and was left to pastor the church at Crete. Philemon was written to a slave owner to give instructions to the church at Colossae. In Revelations chapter 2, God sent messages to seven different churches that were actual local churches or local church assemblies of that day. He gave specific instructions to each individual church suited to their specific needs.

While the universal church is the body of all born-again believers, regardless of their religious affiliation, they will all one day be gathered together in heaven; it is obvious here that Jesus recognizes individual local churches as well. We all serve the same God and have the same redeemer and hope in the same salvation. We are commanded to go to church to worship God, to praise God, to practice the ordinances, to encourage the brethren, to receive instructions, to pray for one another, to practice the active gifts of the Holy Spirit, to pay tithes, to send out missionaries and church starters, and to spread the gospel. Christians who don't go to church are in danger of being overly influenced by the evil in this world and neglecting their responsibility of being separated from its influence. They are also denying themselves the opportunity to share with other Christians the privileges of church ordinances and the Christian fellowship God intended. Church membership isn't required to be saved or to stay saved, but it is highly recommended to ensure sanctification, surrender, and service.

The Devil Wants to Keep You out of Church

The devil will provide you with all the excuses you need to never go to church, but if you want to serve God or have His perfect will in your life, then you should find a church home. Men, if your wife happens to become disgruntled with the church you are attending and decides she wants to leave the church, if you agree with her, then you should find another church to attend as a family as soon as possible. If you don't agree with her, remember that God counts on you to be the spiritual leader of the household. You should keep going to church whether she goes or not, and you should ensure that the children keep going as well. You obviously cannot force her to go with you, but you can pray for her and hope she will come back or find some other church to go to. I believe families should go to church together, but any attendance is better than none. Hopefully, you will both be able to work out the situation.

Ladies, if your husband drops out of church but you want to keep going to the same church, then you should. You should also pray for him to return. Here is the difference; if the husband finds a different church he thinks is better suited for the family, remember that God has designated him as the spiritual leader of the home. You should follow his lead. I have to be careful when I give this advice because men aren't always right. If your husband wants you to go someplace where they don't preach Jesus Christ as the only name under heaven whereby man might be saved, then you should not follow him there (Acts 4:12). It may be hard for you to explain that to him, and it may be better to get the church leaders to speak to him about the issue. The point I'm trying to make is this: don't let the devil put a wedge between you and your husband to prevent you from going to church. For the most part, I believe that if you have a spiritual husband, you won't have a problem with this; and if you don't, then he probably won't go to church anywhere.

Majoring on the Minors

I don't believe you should ever leave a church because of high standards. Separation from the world is what God expects from us. I will say, however, that in my opinion, some things are more important than strict rules. If there is more emphasis put on how people dress or how they wear their hair than how dedicated they are to God and serve Him, then there is room for improvement. If the church spends too much time preaching rules and little time on saving souls, then in my opinion this is majoring on the minors and minoring on the majors. The Bible teaches Christian liberty and separation. If the church doesn't have high enough standards, then perhaps that is a good reason to look for another church.

The Most Important Aspect of Church Selection Is Doctrine

The most important issue to me is that your church preaches the true gospel of Christ and not an alternative method of salvation such as good works. Salvation is obtained as a gift from God through believing and confessing Jesus Christ as your Savior. There is no other way (Acts 4:10–12), and if you are at a church where they teach something different, then you need to leave. Churches are made up of people, and people aren't perfect; therefore neither are churches.

Every church should have a document commonly referred to as the "Statement of Faith". This document should contain the primary beliefs that are taught and preached at the church. Before joining a church you should ask to review their statement of faith to see if you agree with what the church believes. I have included the Statement of Faith from our church as an example of what you should be looking for. I can't tell you what to believe but you should agree with the majority of what your church teaches or go somewhere else.

The Statement of Faith for the Faith Bayou Fellowship Church

1. We believe there is only one true God and that He is the God of the Israelites (Jehovah). He is one God but consist of three distinct and separate parts, The Father, the Son (Jesus Christ) and the Holy Spirit.
    References: Isaiah 45:5-6, Acts 3:13, Matthew 28:19
2. We believe that Jesus Christ is the son of God and was God Himself in the flesh when He was here with us on the earth. Jesus is the manifestation of God. The part of God that could be seen and touched and heard.
    References: Colossians 2:9, John 1:1-14
3. We believe that the one and only unpardonable (unforgiveable) sin is the personal rejection of Jesus Christ as your savior. This rejection is the denial of the power of God through the Holy Spirit to provide spiritual life and therefore is blasphemous to the Spirit's authority.
    References: Matthew 12:32, Mark 3:29
4. We believe that the only means whereby one might be saved is through the belief in Jesus Christ as the Son of God and there is no other way.
    References: Acts 4:12, John 3:18

5. We believe that salvation is a free gift from God and no-one is capable of earning it through payment or through good works or through the keeping of the law.

   References: Ephesians 2:8-9, Galatians 3:11

6. We believe that our salvation is a gift from God and therefore once He has given it to someone they are saved for eternity and their salvation is kept by God..

   References: 1 Peter 1:5, John 1:12-13

7. We believe that when a person is born again of the Spirit of God that they are indwelt by the Holy Spirit. You must be born again of the Spirit to be saved.

   References: John 3:6-7, John 14:17, Romans 8:15

8. We believe that Jesus (The Son of God) came to the earth, suffered, died and was buried to pay the price for the sins of mankind. He was in the grave for three days and then He rose from the dead and ascended into heaven where He is seated at the right hand of God the Father.

   References: 1 Corinthians 15:3-8, Acts 1:9-11, John 3:13

9. We believe when a person is born again that they are baptized (indwelt) by the Holy Spirit, after that they should be baptized by water as their first step of obedience. This water baptism requires complete submersion to illustrate the death burial and resurrection of Christ.

   References: Matthew 28:19, Acts 8:25-38, Matthew 3:11

10. We believe that the universal church consist of the body of all born again believers regardless of their religion, race, gender or other affiliation. There are many different religions and a number of them believe that they must be saved through Jesus Christ. Those who believe this are saved and those who seek salvation through any other means are not saved even if they claim to be Christian.

   References: 2 John 10:11, Romans 10:13, Acts 2:21

11. We believe the main mission of the church should be to reconcile the lost world to God. To bring people to Christ, to spread the gospel.

    References: Mark 16:15, Acts 1:8, 2 Corinthians 5:18

The other purposes of the local church assembly

(1) Worship and praise of God
(2) Practice the New Testament ordinances (Water baptism and the Lord's supper)
(3) Encourage and edify one another
(4) Pray for one another
(5) To receive Spiritual guidance and instructions
(6) To practice the use of the active gifts of the Holy Spirit.

    We believe the gift of prophesying (fore-telling) and the gift of tongues are no longer active. John the Baptist was the last Old Testament prophet and the New Testament prophets ended with the Apostle John. There has been no scripture written since John's death. Tongues were used as a sign to the Jews to illustrate the fact that the Gentiles had received the gift of the Holy Spirit. Paul told us these gifts would cease and we believe they did when the Word of God was completed fulfilling the scripture saying "when that which was perfect had come". (1 Corinthians 13:10)

(7) To provide a means of financing God's work (to receive and distribute the tithes and offerings).

12. We believe in a pre-tribulation rapture meaning that the Christian (Those born again of the Spirit of God) will be taken off the earth prior to the beginning of the seven years of the tribulation period. It doesn't make any sense that God would leave His children here during the tribulation if the tribulation is for the purpose of punishing those who reject

Christ. We believe the only thing preventing the tribulation from beginning is the fact that the gospel must be heard throughout the whole world first. This prophecy could be fulfilled any day. After that the Christians will be raptured and the tribulation period will begin.

References: 2 Thessalonians 2:3-9, Mark 13:10

13. We believe in the miracle of healing as it is described in the Bible by the laying on of hands and anointing with oil and the effectual fervent prayer of the church members and the elders.

References: James 5:13-16,

14. We believe that just as God is real so is the devil and his demons. Therefore our spiritual battle is not against flesh and blood but rather against spiritual wickedness in high places.

References: Ephesians 6:12, 1 Peter 5:8

15. We believe that the God ordained institution of marriage is a relationship between a man and a woman and any physical relationships outside this description is sinful.

References: Romans 1:26-27, Ephesians 5:31-32

16. We believe in the sanctity of life and that life begins at conception. Therefore, if anyone takes a life from the time of conception on, unless the life has been convicted and sentence to death by the authorities, or in the case of self-defense, it should be considered murder. This includes the inalienable rights of the unborn child. Abortion is murder.

References: Jeremiah 1:5, Psalms 139:13

17. We believe that the Holy Bible (the Canonized Bible, excluding the Apocrypha) is the inspired Word of our Living God and is the only reliable source for our doctrine, for reproof, for correction and for instruction in righteousness.

References: 2 Timothy 3:16 (inspired by God means God breathed), Hebrews 4:12

18. We believe that the Israelites are still God's chosen people and God will fulfill all the promises made to them during the Millennial reign of Christ following the tribulation period.

    References: Romans 11:26-30, Hebrews 8:8-12

19. We believe that all born again Christians will one day live in heaven with Jesus. The church is the bride of Christ and only those who have been saved will be allowed to enter into the kingdom of God as the bride of Christ and live with God throughout all eternity.

    References: Revelations 21:27

20. We believe there will be a great white throne judgment when all the people who have ever lived and whose names are not written in the Lamb's Book of Life will be judged. The dead shall be judged and cast into the lake of fire which is the second death.

    References: Revelations 21:12

21. We believe Christians are commanded to be separated from this evil world and to live a life surrendered to God. If we are born of the Spirit we should walk after the Spirit. 1 peter 1:16

22. We believe in a close communion. There are three types of communion or ways of practicing the Lord's Supper.

    (1) Open communion- open to everyone weather they are saved or not

    (2) Close communion- Open to anyone who is saved, a born again child of God.

    (3) Closed communion- Open only to church members

    We believe that anyone who is saved should be allowed to participate in the Lord's Supper as practiced at our church. We would warn however that one should examine themselves prior to taking part in this ordinance as the

Bibles warns many are ill and some departed for partaking when they were unworthy.

Reference: 1 Corinthians 11:27-29

Tithing

The last thing I want to talk about concerning the church is the tithe. The tithe is generally considered 10 percent of your income, which is set aside to do God's work. If you are a church member, the tithe is usually given to the church to do God's work. Considering the fact that we all pay approximately 30 percent of all we make to the government every year for the things it provides for us, 10 percent doesn't sound like a lot to give God for all He does for us every day. "Tithing is God's way for God's people to do God's work." That is a direct quote from Dr. James Vineyard, former pastor of the Windsor Hills Baptist Church in Oklahoma City.

Husbands and fathers seem to be the ones who have the hardest time accepting this concept, but it is biblical as we shall see. Many would argue that the tithe was an Old Testament concept, and while it is true that it is first mentioned in the Old Testament, I have not found any place in the New Testament where we are told not to do it anymore. In fact, Jesus told the Pharisees in the book of Mathew that they shouldn't leave tithing undone. "Woe unto you, scribes and Pharisees, hypocrites! For ye pay tithe of mint and anise and cummin, and have omitted the weightier matters of the law, judgment, mercy, and faith: these ought ye to have done, and not to leave the other undone" (Matt. 23:23).

All Things in Common

If Christians don't pay for God's work to get done, then who will? We have already seen that God has ordained the church to do the work of God. Without the offerings of Christians, the work cannot be done. The devil will use this reluctance to tear down churches and the work of God. The reason you don't see the word *tithe* too many times in the early church is that they had all things in common. This means all the church members put all they had into the church kitty, and everyone received out of the kitty as he or she had need. This ensured that no one had more than he or she needed, and everyone had all he or she needed. I'm pretty sure most people who have a problem with the tithe would have a bigger problem with "all things in common."

I know "all things in common" sounds a lot like democratic socialism, but there is a difference. In this situation, all the people put in what they could afford, and all of them worked for a living. This only prevented some from working hard and still struggling to survive, while others didn't do anything and expected a free ride. Perhaps, however, the biggest difference is the fact that all these people were doing this voluntarily out of love for one another and not because the government was forcing them to do it for those who didn't deserve it. Even though this was all voluntary, we should notice in the following verses that it says distribution was made to every person according to his or her need. This means someone was put in charge and had the task of deciding who needed what and gave everyone just what they needed.

In our society, the government gives everyone a set amount regardless of what his or her actual needs are. You would be surprised to find out how many rich and dead people still receive government benefits of some sort. No one has a problem helping people who aren't capable of taking care of themselves, but most people don't want to help people who refuse to work, even though they could if they wanted to. Many times the government discourages people from working by paying them more to stay home than they would make if they went to work. I have seen this over and over with my own eyes. The government can convince good people to become dishonest.

And sold their possessions and goods, and parted them to all men, as every man had need. And they, continuing daily with one accord in the temple, and breaking bread from house to house, did eat their meat with gladness and singleness of heart, Praising God, and having favour with all the people. And the Lord added to the church daily such as should be saved. (Acts 2:45–47)

Neither was there any among them that lacked: for as many as were possessors of lands or houses sold them, and brought the prices of the things that were sold, And laid them down at the apostles' feet: and distribution was made unto every man according as he had need. (Acts 4:34–35)

Tithing Must Be Done by Faith in What God Says

This is how the tithe works: You cannot out-give God. Believe and receive. Doubt and do without. When you begin to give, you begin to live. God can make your food go farther, your tires last longer, your gas carry you farther, your clothes last longer, and all other things do better to sustain you. When you do what God tells you to do, He takes responsibility for your well-being, and God is your Father. He is the richest person I know, and He is our Father. "Give, and it shall be given unto you; good measure, pressed down, and shaken together, and running over, shall men give into your bosom. For with the same measure that ye mete withal it shall be measured to you again" (Luke 6:38).

I believe tithing should be done at your local church because the Bible says, "For where your treasure is there will your heart be also" (Matt. 6:21). Anything you give to others outside the church should be considered offerings and are above and beyond the tithe.

Notice It Says Men Give into Your Bosom

I think it should be noted here that this verse says that men will give unto you. God uses His people to take care of His people. Don't wait for the blessings from God to fall out of the sky. These blessings will come from other men; they may not even be Christians. If God makes a promise to bless you beyond measure, then you can believe what He says, but don't be surprised if it comes in an unconventional manner. Most people rob themselves of God's blessings because if you don't believe it will happen, then it won't. Most Christians receive only small blessings because they think small. We say that God, our Father, is the richest person there is, but we don't act like we believe that when we pray.

My wife and I recently started a new church, and we are currently using the conference room at the local airport where my business is located to hold Sunday services. Last week we had to cancel the service at the last minute because we couldn't get the door open to the building. My wife also has some very good ideas about starting a secondhand store/charity ministry, and we have been looking for a place to do both. Last week she and I drove around, hoping God would show us the place He would provide. We are praying about the situation and asking God to make it possible. I think maybe part of the problem is that we are limiting God's ability to provide what we need. Let me explain; we have been looking for an old building we can get cheap and maybe fix up because we aren't rich folks. A few days ago, during my routine morning prayers, God told me that I didn't need to be rich to get what I needed to do His work because He is rich, and He will give us what we need. I believe God has something extraordinary planned. I'm trying to think on His level and stay tuned to see the wondrous works of our Lord.

Be Careful What You Ask For

There was this certain church pastor; let's just call him Pastor Joe. One day before the Sunday morning service, Pastor Joe was out front, greeting his congregation as they entered the chapel. One of his regular Sunday morning worshippers, Mr. Roy Smith, approached him with his usual kind smile and welcoming attitude. His right hand was stretched out for the normal greeting. As their hands touched, Mr. Smith leaned in and told the pastor in a soft voice that he needed to speak to him about a private matter. Pastor Joe replied in the same whispering voice that Mr. Smith could come see him after the morning service.

The service took place without a hitch, and as soon as everyone had departed, there stood Mr. Smith, waiting for the pastor as though this was an urgent matter that needed immediate attention. Mr. Smith had been part of this congregation for many years, and he and Pastor Joe were well acquainted. Mr. Smith was a successful business owner, and even though he and the pastor had known each other for many years, they had seldom spoken other than the usual Sunday morning greeting. So Pastor Joe took Mr. Smith into his office and closed the door.

After the two men had sat down, the pastor asked, "So Mr. Smith, just what can I do for you?"

Mr. Smith began by saying, "Well, pastor, you know I have been in this church for many years now. When I first started my business, I didn't have anything. We were working out of our home and barely made enough to pay the bills, but with God's help, we survived. Now many years later, after God continued to bless us, my business has become very successful, as you know. If I continue to give 10 percent of my gross income to the church, it is going to make it difficult to continue to meet all of my other obligations. So I was wondering if I could just get a slight reduction in the amount I give each month."

The pastor looked at him and grinned. Then he replied, "The scriptures don't really offer too many options concerning this topic, so I think we should pray about it." So the two men bowed their heads, and the pastor began to pray. "Dear God, our Father in heaven, we come to You with a request. We thank You, Lord, for Mr. Smith and for the way You have blessed him and his business. We know, Lord, that Christians become successful due to Your blessings because we don't have anything that You didn't give us. Now I pray, Lord, that You would decrease Mr. Smith's income back to what it was when he began his business so he can once again afford to pay his tithe and meet all his other obligations without the possibility of losing Your blessings. Amen."

Who Should Receive My Tithe?

If you aren't currently a member of a local church, then you have no place to pay your tithe. There are numerous worthy Christian causes that could use the help, but my point is that the only standard God gives from His Word concerning your sacrificial offerings to His work is "all things in common" or at least 10 percent of your income (tithe). In my opinion, based on all the things we have discussed dealing with the benefits of church attendance, I think you should go to your church, find a local church to join, start a church, or allow the Lord to lead you to those who need and deserve your offerings. As I mentioned previously, I believe the tithe should be given to the church you attend if you are attending a church regularly. I believe this should be the case because Jesus said, "Where your treasure is, there will your heart be also"(Matt. 6:21); and if your heart isn't in the work your church is doing more than other places, then perhaps you should attend a different church. "Lay not up for yourselves treasures upon earth, where moth and rust doth corrupt, and where thieves break through and steal: But lay up for yourselves treasures in heaven, where neither moth nor rust doth corrupt, and where thieves do not break through nor steal: For where your treasure is, there will your heart be also" (Matt. 6:19–21).

I think I should also mention the fact that the apostle Paul says several times that he took nothing from anyone in his ministry because he didn't need to in order to survive, but he made it perfectly clear that the laborer is worthy of his hire. There aren't very many independently wealthy preachers out there. Most of the time preachers are either working another job so they will have what they need to be able to conduct their ministry without outside assistance or they are preaching full-time. These are men who have dedicated their lives to serving God and have taken on the responsibility of being intercessors between their congregations and God. The man who looks out for your spiritual well-being is worthy of being compensated for what he does.

> Let the elders that rule well be counted worthy of double honour, especially they who labour in the word and doctrine. For the scripture saith, Thou shalt not muzzle the ox that treadeth out the corn. And, The labourer is worthy of his reward. (1 Tim. 5:17–18)

> If we have sown unto you spiritual things, is it a great thing if we shall reap your carnal things? If others be partakers of this power over you, are not we rather? Nevertheless we have not used this power; but suffer all things, lest we should hinder the gospel of Christ. Do ye not know that they which minister about holy things live of the things of the temple? And they which wait at the altar are partakers with the altar? Even so hath the Lord ordained that they which preach the gospel should live of the gospel. But I have used none of these things: neither have I written these things, that it should be so done unto me: for it were better for me

> to die, than that any man should make my glorying
> void. (1 Cor. 9:11–15)

The Word of God doesn't tell us how much a preacher should be paid. Some say he should make a salary based on the average income of those in his congregation. I don't think he should be below average for certain, but I don't think he should be the wealthiest person in the church either. I can't tell you what "worthy of double honour" means, (1 Tim. 5:17-18) but I don't think your preacher should be poor.

The Great Commission

Jesus came to reconcile a lost people to God, their creator. The word *reconcile* means to restore. Jesus came to restore the lost relationship between God the Father and the people on earth. When He left the earth, He turned the task of reconciliation over to the apostles, who were the first church members. The task of reconciling the world to God was given to the church, the body of all born-again believers. Winning souls for Christ is the main objective of every Christian service. If you work in a church, it is for the ministry of reconciliation. If you are a missionary, it is for reconciliation. If you build churches or are a preacher or teacher in the church, you are doing so for the purpose of the reconciliation of lost souls to God. If you are a child of God, then you are called to the ministry of reconciliation.

If you are ever going to serve God in any capacity, it will be for the purpose of reconciling lost souls to God. For this reason, I believe every born-again Christian should know how to take his or her Bible and show someone how to be reconciled to God. I already shared the gospel with you in the first chapter of this book, as I do in all of my faith-based books, so I'm not going to do it again here; but you should write this information down and study it, memorize it, and learn how to use it to lead people to Christ. Make yourself a cheat sheet with the main points and references on a small piece of paper and leave it in your Bible. You should always be prepared to give an answer for the hope that is in you (1 Peter 3:15).This is sometimes referred to as "soul winning," but I prefer to call it "leading others to Christ" because we don't win souls; Jesus does that. We just show them how to ask Jesus for their salvation.

Reaching people for Christ should begin at home. God forbid that a man be saved and not be able to share this glorious gift of eternal life with his own wife and children. We saw how, through the lifestyle of the husband or wife, the lost partner in a mixed marriage can be saved. This makes it evident that God wants the members of your household to be saved (1 Cor. 7:16). I think all couples who are contemplating marriage should read this entire book and get some kind of idea of what God's plan for marriage actually is before they jump in.

I sure do wish I would have had some practical knowledge of what marriage should be like before I got married. I know there are several good books out there that cover different aspects of marriage, but many are based on worldly principles, not godly ones, and many of the Christian books just don't cover everything people need to know. I know there will be things I haven't covered as well, but I'm trying to be as comprehensive as possible.

So we can see that leading people to Christ or the ministry of reconciliation is one of the main responsibilities of the church. Many churches have what they call "soul-winning outreaches." No matter what you call it, this is a time set aside for church members to go out in the community and look for people to lead to Christ. I believe all churches and Christians should have some part in a soul-winning ministry.

> Therefore if any man be in Christ, he is a new creature: old things are passed away; behold, all things are become new. And all things are of God,

who hath reconciled us to himself by Jesus Christ, and hath given to us the ministry of reconciliation; To wit, that God was in Christ, reconciling the world unto himself, not imputing their trespasses unto them; and hath committed unto us the word of reconciliation. Now then we are ambassadors for Christ, as though God did beseech you by us: we pray you in Christ's stead, be ye reconciled to God. For he hath made him to be sin for us, who knew no sin; that we might be made the righteousness of God in him. (2Cor. 5:17–21)

The Thriving Church

One lady told me, "Soul winning isn't the only thing God tells us to do." I agree, but the other things we are commanded to do we should do and not leave this undone. The churches that have an outreach program of some sort are the ones that are growing, thriving, and seeing things accomplished for God, while those that don't seem to be standing still. Your purpose should be winning souls, but one of the benefits is a growing and thriving church. If your church doesn't place any emphasis on winning souls for Christ, if there is no soul-winning program of any sort, if the church hasn't seen any new converts, baptisms, or answers to God's call for service, then what is being accomplished? God in His wisdom has given us this mission of winning souls, leading people to Christ, and reconciling lost souls to Him. We can see here in these verses that we should take the place of Christ here on earth in telling people how they can restore their relationships with God. The following are the verses I spoke of concerning the Great Commission, as it is called.

Go ye therefore, and teach all nations, baptizing them in the name of the Father, and of the Son, and of the Holy Ghost: Teaching them to observe all things whatsoever I have commanded you: and, lo, I am with you alway, even unto the end of the world. Amen. (Matt. 28:19–20)

And he said unto them, Go ye into all the world, and preach the gospel to every creature. He that believeth and is baptized shall be saved; but he that believeth not shall be damned. (Mark 16:15–16)

And that repentance and remission of sins should be preached in his name among all nations, beginning at Jerusalem. (Luke 24:47)

Then said Jesus to them again, Peace be unto you: as my Father hath sent me, even so send I you. And when he had said this, he breathed on them, and saith unto them, Receive ye the Holy Ghost: Whose soever sins ye remit, they are remitted unto them; and whose soever sins ye retain, they are retained. (John 20:21–23)

But ye shall receive power, after that the Holy Ghost is come upon you: and ye shall be witnesses unto me both in Jerusalem, and in all Judaea, and in Samaria, and unto the uttermost part of the earth. (Acts 1:8)

The fruit of the righteous is a tree of life; and he that winneth souls is wise. (Prov. 11:30)

David Boudreaux

The Importance of Soul Winning

If your church doesn't put any emphasis on soul winning, then you might want to start looking for one that does. If you are looking for a church home, how do you know whether believers there are putting any emphasis on reconciling sinners? Is soul winning preached from the pulpit? Do they have an organized time for church-wide soul winning? Is the church seeing people saved or baptized regularly? If you aren't seeing these things, then there is probably not enough emphasis on this topic. I'm not talking about church visitation, although I think the pastor should regularly visit church members, depending on how much time he has. But I'm talking about the preacher and anyone else at the church who wants to see people saved; they should go out and try to find people to lead to Christ. "Jesus saith unto them, My meat is to do the will of him that sent me, and to finish his work. Say not ye, There are yet four months, and then cometh harvest? behold, I say unto you, Lift up your eyes, and look on the fields; for they are white already to harvest" (John 4:34–35).

I asked a friend a few weeks ago if he wanted to go flying with me. Recently, I have been flying my Cessna Sky Master. Anyhow, he answered, "No thank you. I am scared of heights." I explained to him that in my experience most people who are scared of heights are generally not scared when they fly in an airplane because they are in an enclosed area and don't feel exposed. I went on to say that since he was a Christian brother, he shouldn't be scared anyhow because Jesus told us that He will always be with us no matter where we are or what we are doing (Matt. 28:19–20). My friend corrected me and pointed out that this wasn't exactly what Jesus had said. He said that the verse says, "And lo I will be with you always." When you're in that airplane flying, you are not "low."

I know this has nothing to do with soul winning, but it does illustrate the practice of spending time fellowshipping with other Christians in your life and your church. Do you see other church members only during church events but spend most of your time with unsaved people? A Christian should be a Christian every minute of every day, and even though it's not possible for most people to spend all their time with saved people, if you don't desire that fellowship, then you may be too close to the world and worldly pleasures. Christianity is not an event; it is a way of life.

CHAPTER 8
Marital Intimacy

Marital Intimacy

We have already discussed some aspects of marriage, but in this chapter, we are going to look at it from a different perspective. Then we will move on to some other marital issues that come as a natural result of a normal relationship. You should understand by now that the normal, intimate life between a husband and wife is not adequately described by simply saying they have sex. We have seen that the consummation completes the bonding process between a man and a woman who have already made a lifelong commitment to one another, but it is still a lot more than that. It is a privilege and a joy. It is a responsibility and a normal part of a marriage. It is pure and clean in the sight of God, and it is the only kind of intimacy sanctioned by God. It is the means by which God chose to sustain human life on this earth. Only in the institution of marriage is it all that God intended it to be. It is a special closeness that can be shared only between a husband and wife.

You can have sex outside of marriage, but you cannot make love. Making love is the one act husbands and wives can share with one another that can bond them together more than any other. This bond doesn't form during sex; it forms between husbands and wives during lovemaking. If you don't understand what I'm talking about, then you are either still a virgin or you have never made love to a spouse, even though you may have experienced sex numerous times. Only when you are married can you make love without any regret, worry, shame, or guilt, and with a clear conscience. This is because it is the only kind of sex that isn't prohibited by God, and whether you know what the Word of God says about it or not, you have been trained in this concept one way or another. Only in a permanent, intentional, committed, loyal relationship can sexual intimacy reach its highest level of satisfaction because this is what our creator intended. Those who believe variety is the spice of life won't ever find the satisfaction they are looking for because variety isn't part of God's design or plan for humankind concerning intimate relationships.

You Don't Buy a Pair of Shoes without Trying Them On

It really irritates me when I hear people say, "I'm not going to buy a pair of shoes without trying them on first." I know you have all heard that; no one wants to admit he or she has friends who think or talk like that. My reply to that is this. I'm not going to marry a pair of shoes, and I plan to keep one wife for one life, not get a new one every year. This intimate relationship between a husband and wife has several purposes.

> And God blessed them, and God said unto them, Be fruitful, and multiply, and replenish the earth, and subdue it: and have dominion over the fish of the sea, and over the fowl of the air, and over every living thing that moveth upon the earth. (Gen. 1:28)

> And God blessed Noah and his sons, and said unto them, Be fruitful, and multiply, and replenish the earth. (Gen. 9:1)

And you, be ye fruitful, and multiply; bring forth
abundantly in the earth, and multiply therein.
(Gen. 9:7)

Lo, children are an heritage of the LORD: and the
fruit of the womb is his reward. As arrows are in the
hand of a mighty man; so are children of the youth.
Happy is the man that hath his quiver full of them:
they shall not be ashamed, but they shall speak with
the enemies in the gate. (Ps. 127:3–5)

Procreation

Obviously, God intended husbands and wives to have sexual relations
and produce children. Since it's a fact that sexual relations naturally
result in childbirth, that creates a tremendous responsibility to stay
together and raise them. This alone is reason enough for marriage to
be a lifetime commitment. Marital intimacy is a privilege because it
makes husbands and wives heirs together of the grace of life, as we
have already seen. (1 Peter 3:7).

Enjoyment

Sexual intimacy between a husband and wife is also intended to be
enjoyable. Some people talk about intimacy as if it is dirty and just
a duty for the wife to perform to keep her husband happy. This is
far from the truth. This act is intended to be very pleasurable for
both husband and wife. If it is not, then there is something wrong
physically, mentally, or emotionally. This intimacy isn't intended
only for reproduction; it is designed to consummate or complete the
bond between the husband and the wife and give them something to
enjoy between each other that cannot be achieved through any other
avenue. The pleasure of this union is mentioned in the first book

of the Bible. "Now Abraham and Sarah were old and well stricken in age; and it ceased to be with Sarah after the manner of women. Therefore Sarah laughed within herself, saying, After I am waxed old shall I have pleasure, my lord being old also?" (Gen. 18:11–12).

These verses also just happen to mention the fact that this intimacy between husband and wife can and should continue even after childbearing years are over. If it isn't for pleasure, then what would be the point? She is talking about sharing the same kind of pleasurable sexual intimacy she and her husband, Abraham, shared when they were younger.

To Prevent Incontinence

Sexual fulfillment is also a marital responsibility. After someone has lost his or her virginity, abstaining becomes more difficult. Therefore, when a couple gets married, they become responsible for each other's marital purity. Have you ever heard that if your wife or husband cheats on you, it is your fault because you are not giving your marriage partner what he or she needs? To a certain degree, this could be partially true. As we saw earlier in 1 Corinthians 7:1–5, the apostle Paul made it clear that the wife's body belongs to her husband and the husband's body belongs to his wife. In this regard, as a spouse, you do not have the right to tell your partner no when he or she is in need. If you do, this could lead to temptation from the devil and eventually the destruction of the marriage.

A man or woman should never use sex as a weapon or tool in marriage for leverage of any kind. People who do this are setting themselves up for a failed marriage. This doesn't mean either is the other person's sex slave, however. If either the husband or wife has a legitimate reason to abstain, such as prayer and fasting or injury or illness, the other partner should be patient and understanding. A wedding band isn't a license to rape, but if you have a husband or wife, you are entitled to certain expectations. If one of the partners continually says no without a legitimate reason, there is obviously something wrong. It may be physical, mental, or emotional, as I said before, but something isn't right because if the experience is pleasurable for both parties, there should be no reason to decline. If this is happening, perhaps some sort of marriage counseling is in order.

Christian Counseling

I'm not going to spend a lot of time on this point either because if you find yourself in this situation, you will have to use your spiritual judgment and discernment in determining the best avenue for counsel. I will say this: if you are in a Christian marriage, then it's best to seek Christian counsel. I mean no disrespect to those who have devoted their lives to trying to help people with marital issues from a secular standpoint. I know they are sincere and mean well. Here is the problem from my perspective.

1. First, they don't know or agree with the significance of the wedding vows and the marital relationship as it pictures the relationship of man with God.
2. Second, the promise we make to God when we get married to stay with our spouses for life means nothing to a worldly counselor who doesn't know God.
3. Third, they don't understand that when you get married, you become one flesh in the sight of God.
4. Fourth, they don't understand how devastating a divorce can be to a Christian when it may mean very little to an unbeliever.
5. Fifth, they won't understand the restrictions divorce will put on the Christian when it comes to future marital relations.

6. Sixth, they don't consider the guilt you will have to endure if you give up on a marriage before you have tried everything to fix it.
7. Seventh, they won't understand the harm a broken marriage can do to your relationship with God or your service to Him. The pastor is to be the husband of one wife. The widow the church cares for is to be the wife of one husband. These are just two examples. (This may be interpreted to mean just one wife or one husband at a time, but some believe it means being married only once during a lifetime.)
8. Divorce can cause severe trauma to any children involved. We will talk more about this later.

I'm going to admit here that I'm not the husband of one wife (married only once) as the scripture says a bishop should be according to most theologians. I have struggled with this fact for many years as I have tried to serve God. I didn't seek out this position, but I was asked to supply a need, and the Lord told me I should do what I needed to do to meet that need. Most of the Bible characters God used to do mighty works weren't really qualified according to God's Word or even by their own admission. A person who desires to fulfill God's will doesn't let excuses get in the way. I believe God can use anyone who is willing and can cleanse anyone who will ask for forgiveness. If you don't agree, then I'm sorry if my service offends you, and I pray that God can use you in a mightier way than He has used me.

It Takes Two to Make It Work

Personally, I don't think there is anything married couples can't overcome if they both dedicate themselves to making the marriage work and to serving God. The key word is *both*. It takes two to stay together, but it takes only one to tear the marriage apart. The worldly, unbelieving counselor won't comprehend this concept. Most pastors in most churches and most religions have had some training in marital counseling and are equipped to help others with their marital situations. They will be better prepared to deal with a Christian marriage than the unbelieving counselor who doesn't consider the influence of God. I think you should at least try your pastor first; and if he thinks you need more professional help, he will be able to recommend someone who is better prepared and also understands the significance of a Christian marriage.

As I said, it takes two to get married, and it takes two to stay married. Unfortunately, in most cases, one of the two partners has come to the point that he or she is no longer willing to try to fix the problem; and when this happens, no one can fix it. I think even the apostle Paul understood this when he said that if the unbelieving depart, let him or her depart (1 Cor. 7:15). No matter how hard you try or how spiritual you are, you cannot force the other person to stay with you. I realize this section is supposed to be about sexual relations between a husband and wife and not about divorce, but I believe these matters are related; and if you seek counsel concerning any portion of your marital relationship, you should consider your pastor first. If you are in a church that doesn't allow the pastor, bishop, priest, or whatever they call the leader of the church to be married, then this advice may not apply. Even if they have had training to deal with these situations there is no substitute for experience.

A Pastor Should Be Married

I think a pastor or bishop should be married because the Bible teaches that if he cannot rule over those in his own family (his wife and children), then how can he be expected to rule over the house of God? Not to mention that I think it could be a little uncomfortable for a couple to talk to anyone about their marital intimacy but especially to someone who has sworn an oath of celibacy. It is uncomfortable enough talking to a preacher about the issue, but at least if this preacher is married, he has some kind of idea about the topic.

> This is a true saying, If a man desire the office of a bishop, he desireth a good work. A bishop then must be blameless, the husband of one wife, vigilant, sober, of good behaviour, given to hospitality, apt to teach; Not given to wine, no striker, not greedy of filthy lucre; but patient, not a brawler, not covetous; One that ruleth well his own house, having his children in subjection with all gravity; (For if a man know not how to rule his own house, how shall he take care of the church of God?) Not a novice, lest being lifted up with pride he fall into the condemnation of the devil. Moreover he must have a good report of them which are without; lest he fall into reproach and the snare of the devil. (1 Tim. 3:1–7)

It plainly says in these verses that he is to be the husband of one wife, but it also says he should have his children in subjection. This would suggest to me that not only should the pastor or bishop be married but he should also have children. My dad used to say, "I'm going to be a bachelor and raise my kids to be just like me." He was just joshing, but seriously, I don't think a man who doesn't have a wife or children is qualified to be a pastor or give counsel to people who do.

This Doesn't Mean Married to the Church

I don't agree with those who say the pastor or bishop (priest) is married to the church and must remain single. I believe these verses also prevent the allowance of a woman pastor. Knowing what God's definition of marriage is (one man and one woman—Gen. 5:2; Mark 10:6), we understand it isn't possible for a woman to have a wife, (wife as described in the Bible is the female partner in a marital relationship) or for gay couples to produce children (Gen. 1:28).

Anyhow, for our purpose here, I'm just saying that if your pastor isn't married or doesn't have a biblical marriage, then you may be better off seeking out another religious leader who is married and has children for spiritual guidance concerning your marital relationship. I also find it difficult to understand how gay couples can be allowed to adopt children. As far as God is concerned, this is an abhorrent condition, therefore an adoption of this kind is a government-sanctioned placing of innocent children in the most sinful situation possible. (Rom. 1:26–27). Is there any wonder why our children are turning out confused, misguided, and sinful? We are placing them in the same kinds of conditions Noah's son Ham (Gen. 9:22–26) and Lot's daughters (Gen. 19:30–38) were in when they committed such grievous acts with their fathers that they altered the course of history.

Sometimes it is difficult to explain what God intended concerning His work when there are so many out there doing it in a way that is different from what God said. At the same time, I am told not to be critical of others who are doing their best to serve God in the way they think is right. Therefore, I am trying to tell you what the scriptures say about these issues without criticizing anyone else (1 Tim. 5:17; Heb. 13:17). I am all for anyone who is trying to serve God and doing so with a sincere heart and pure motives. I, above all sinners, have no right to judge others, especially those trying to serve our Lord. It's even more important, however, that our doctrine be based on the Word of God. (2 John 1:10).

Should I Have to Do, in the Bedroom, Anything My Spouse Wants Me to Do?

Now I think it is also important to know what is considered normal sexual activity in marriage. Does the husband or wife have the right to say no to some things? In this day and age of sexual promiscuity, it seems like anything goes inside or outside marriage. With a Christian, this isn't the case inside or outside the marriage, so let me explain why. We already know the Bible says marriage is honorable and that the bed of the married couple is undefiled. (Heb. 13:4).

The Marital Bed Is Undefiled with Three Qualifiers

This would suggest that anything a married couple does in their bedroom in private is all right with God. Personally, I agree with this statement except with three qualifying conditions.

1. First, this is true unless it is an act God has already told us is unacceptable under any conditions. (for example, bestiality).
2. Second, this is true provided it is with the consent of both partners.
3. Third, this is true provided that it doesn't violate what is considered the natural use of the body.

With Consent

I think this third qualification would include some things that are common practice today but used to be forbidden. Let your conscience be your guide. I believe this is evident by the verse in 1 Corinthians that says husbands and wives shouldn't say no to each other concerning sexual intimacy in the marriage except it be with consent. This leaves a great amount of freedom in the bedroom. "Let the husband render unto the wife due benevolence: and likewise also the wife unto the husband. The wife hath not power of her own body, but the husband: and likewise also the husband hath not power of his own body, but the wife. Defraud ye not one the other, except it be with *consent* for a time, that ye may give yourselves to fasting and prayer; and come together again, that Satan tempt you not for your incontinency" (1 Cor. 7:3–5 emphasis added).

Since the husband and wife shouldn't say no to each other concerning the offering of their bodies without consent of both parties, then it isn't a stretch to say that the acts of intimacy they share together with each other should also be with consent. I don't think it is okay for a husband or wife to force their mate to perform a sexual act he or she doesn't agree with. Personally, I don't see anything wrong with trying new things, such as different methods or role-playing (I mean dressing up, not fantasizing about being with someone else) or trying different things to enhance arousal. Your sex life in your marriage should stay exciting, new, and fresh. This will not be the case if you do only one thing all the time. Even intimate relations between a husband and wife can become routine and boring. I think anything the two of you can imagine to do with each other will help spice up your sex life so long as you both agree it is okay with God and that you can do so without having a guilty conscience. If you believe it is a sinful act, then for you it is, and your spouse shouldn't persist in the pursuit.

Be considerate and kind to one another. This is supposed to be pleasurable for both of you. I have already covered the things God has prohibited, so I won't go over them again. I am going to share with you some references that suggest sexual liberties within the marriage. In the book of Song of Solomon, there is a recorded love story between King Solomon and one of his wives. The book was considered so intimate that the Hebrews had to be at least twenty-one years old before they were allowed to read it. In this book Solomon confirms the fact that sexual intimacy is only for married couples. He also reaffirms that this sexual relationship was intended to be enjoyable and satisfying. The entire book reflects these facts and more, so I'm not going to quote the whole thing, but I will make it suggested reading for married couples. It may even be a good idea to read it together. Having seven hundred wives and three hundred concubines, Solomon may not be the best example of a faithful, monogamous marriage, but he was apparently a good lover.

The Natural Use of the Body

> Wherefore God also gave them up to uncleanness through the lusts of their own hearts, to dishonour their own bodies between themselves: Who changed the truth of God into a lie, and worshipped and served the creature more than the Creator, who is blessed forever. Amen. For this cause God gave them up unto vile affections: for even their women did change the natural use into that which is against nature: And likewise also the men, leaving the natural use of the woman, burned in their lust one toward another; men with men working that which is unseemly, and receiving in themselves that recompense of their error which was meet. (Rom. 1:24–27)

In these verses in Romans, it seems perfectly clear to me that God says the natural use of the woman's body is to please her husband. Likewise, the natural use of the man's body is to please his wife. Of course, we know it is for the purpose of reproduction, but now we also know it is for pleasing one's spouse as well. This becomes evident when we consider 1 Corinthians 7:4; the woman's body belongs to her husband and likewise. This is the definition of lovemaking. Anyone can have sex, but that isn't what God intended. If the man's or woman's body is used for anything other than this, God considers it unnatural and sinful. He specifically points out the examples of men with men and women with women.

I'm not prejudiced; I'm being honest with you about what the scriptures say. When it comes to lovemaking, I don't think the husband has done his part until his wife is satisfied, and the woman hasn't done her part until her husband is satisfied. A one-way street in the bedroom doesn't end well. It isn't uncommon for a husband and wife to have some difficulty perfecting the act of lovemaking in the beginning, but as their bodies become more adjusted to one another over time, the better the experience becomes. The experience between husband and wife should not become dull and dutiful; it should continue to get better and better. This is what God intended. This type of lovemaking cannot be accomplished through a casual playboy routine, friends with benefits, or one-night stands. These types of relationships cause more harm in the long run and seem to take away the value of a true lovemaking relationship when it finally comes.

When a man or woman gets used to having multiple partners (I mean one at a time) before he or she gets married, it is more difficult for this person to be content with just one partner after marriage. If this lovemaking relationship between the husband and wife isn't working like it should, this is generally because something else isn't right in the marriage. The most common problem is a priority error, meaning that at least one of the two people in this relationship doesn't have their priorities right. Both of them must have God before each other and each other before anyone else including the children. If they don't get this right, it will affect their marriage, their lovemaking, and their relationship with God.

Problems with Intimacy

If you are a man, you may not be able to control some things when it comes to your sexual abilities. Most men think, *This will never happen to me*, but for most men, I'm afraid it will. This can cause significant problems in a marriage, especially in today's society, because many couples get married at an older age due to the large number of divorces that take place every day. There are more older single people out in the market for a spouse now than ever before. I have heard that the single market today is mostly populated by people between the ages of forty and sixty. This alone presents a new dynamic in dating with new challenges.

I personally think that if someone develops a condition that prevents normal sexual activity soon after being married, it can cause some serious problems in the relationship. As a husband, you are expected to meet all your wife's needs, and her sexual fulfillment is certainly one of those needs. If you are a woman, part of your responsibility as a wife is also to meet your husband's needs.

Sexual dysfunction can be caused by a number of different mental, emotional, and physical factors. If it is determined that this condition is brought on by mental or emotional circumstances, some people are trained in counseling techniques to help couples with this. The majority of the time, however, with older gentlemen especially, the problem is usually physical. If a husband still gets excited when his wife attempts to seduce him but cannot get an erection, there is most likely a physical problem, not a mental or emotional one.

If a wife's attempts to arouse her husband just don't excite him at all, then this is most likely not a physical condition. In either case, some steps can be taken to remedy the situation. I know most of you are thinking of Viagra. Viagra is one possible remedy; however, it is very expensive, and many other medications can give the same results. You should consult your physician before deciding whether to try medications and, if so, which one. I don't recommend going to the local corner store and getting something off the shelf. This is a serious condition, and treatment should be conducted under the supervision of a medical professional. Even if you go to a doctor and receive a prescription, this doesn't mean the problem will be completely solved.

For a man, lacking the ability to perform is embarrassing and humiliating. It can affect his mental ability to perform in the future since he will worry about being humiliated again. The last thing a man wants to do is to fail at anything in front of his wife. On the other hand, the wife who cares about her husband will also be afraid to attempt intimate relations because she doesn't want her husband to feel humiliated if it should happen again. Some women may even feel like it is their fault because they no longer feel like they are attractive to their husbands. Ladies, I guarantee that this isn't your fault. He may be so excited that he feels like he is going to explode. He may even have a liquid release, but he's just not able to get an erection or maintain it.

Even if medication solves the problem, it still changes the sexual encounter. These medications aren't meant to be taken every day but only when an intimate encounter is anticipated. When lovemaking is no longer a spontaneous event, this too can cause it to become awkward and more like a task to be performed than a romantic response. Some couples learn to deal with it by planning a date night ahead of time. If it results in lovemaking, then the man has prepared himself ahead of time. Some couples just give up on the act of sexual encounters altogether and realize that a marital relationship is much more than just physical. If this is the case, then I think they should find other ways to enjoy each other's closeness. Sometimes just lying close to each other and feeling the warmth of each other's bodies, including soft and gentle caressing and hugs, can be all couples need.

Consider Having Children

"Likewise, ye husbands, dwell with them according to knowledge, giving honour unto the wife, as unto the weaker vessel, and as being heirs together of the grace of life; that your prayers be not hindered" (1 Peter 3:7).

What about the Use of Contraceptives?

In the normal course of a marital relationship, children will come. This brings me to another question many Christian couples seem to have. That is, what does God say about contraceptives? Some churches have been known to teach that sexual relations should be only for reproduction. If you believe this, then yes, any kind of contraception would prevent the natural course of things, and that would be wrong. I believe, however, as I have already shown you, that marital intimacy isn't just for reproduction but also for pleasure and bonding between a husband and wife. If this is true, then I see no harm in the use of some contraceptive methods. In my opinion, any type of contraceptive method that prevents fertilization of the egg from taking place is acceptable. Any method that destroys the egg after fertilization has taken place is murder. To say it plainly, the morning-after pill destroys the egg after it has already been fertilized; therefore, it is sometimes called the "abortion pill." This is murder just like any other type of abortion.

I think some couples want to spend some time getting to know each other better before they have children, and I certainly don't see anything wrong with that. Some say you should put children in God's hands, and if He doesn't want you to get pregnant right away, then you won't. For those who are in a position where they are capable of producing and supporting children, I can't argue with their position, but not everyone is that fortunate. I think God gave us common sense, and we shouldn't forget the laws of nature. If you jump off a building, the law of gravity says you are going to hit the ground. Even Jesus told the devil that He wouldn't cast Himself off a cliff because it was written, "Thou shalt not tempt the Lord thy God" (Matt. 4:7). This simply means, don't do something foolish and expect God to step in and prevent nature from taking its course. If you have sexual relations without protection, the laws of reproduction suggest that a child could very well be will conceived. I think using a contraceptive is better than having an unwanted pregnancy.

Does the Bible Teach That Discarding the Man's Seed Is Wrong?

Some people quote Genesis 38:9 to suggest that it's wrong for a man's seed to be wasted instead of being placed in the womb under all circumstances. I'm not going to say that this interpretation isn't one possibility, but I don't believe it is the correct one when we consider the context of the chapter. Under the laws of Moses, when an Israelite man died, leaving no children, it was the dead man's brother's duty to provide seed to his dead brother's widow until she bore a son to carry on the dead brother's seed. This was also done to provide a means of support for the widow when she got older. Her son would be responsible to support her. In this story, Judah, the son of Jacob, had a son named Er. Er took a wife named Tamar, but they had no children. Er was evil, and God killed him, leaving Tamar childless.

According to the law of Moses, which God gave to Moses, Er's brother, Onan, was required to provide seed to Er's wife, Tamar, to carry on his brother's namesake. Onan's father, Judah, told him to fulfill his duty, but he didn't want to. When he slept with Tamar, he decided to spill his seed on the ground instead of fulfilling his duty, allowing her to conceive. This act displeased the Lord, so the Lord also killed Onan. This passage is often referred to as grounds to say that the seed should always be used to allow conception.

I'll not deny that conception is the main purpose the seed is produced; therefore, this interpretation is consistent with the natural use of the body. But I don't believe this is the reason God was angry with Onan. Onan's sin, in my opinion, was breaking the law by refusing to fulfill his role in supplying seed to carry on his brother's name and support his widow. He was also disobeying his father's wishes and commands. I believe God killed him because of his rebellion and disobedience, not for spilling his seed. I can't fault someone for a different and even more conservative interpretation of these verses, but I don't personally believe this is what they are saying.

> And it came to pass at that time, that Judah went down from his brethren, and turned in to a certain Adullamite, whose name was Hirah. And Judah saw there a daughter of a certain Canaanite, whose name was Shuah; and he took her, and went in unto her. And she conceived, and bare a son; and he called his name Er. And she conceived again, and bare a son; and she called his name Onan. And she yet again conceived, and bare a son; and called his name Shelah: and he was at Chezib, when she bare him. And Judah took a wife for Er his firstborn, whose name was Tamar. And Er, Judah's firstborn, was wicked in the sight of the LORD; and the LORD slew him. And Judah said unto Onan, Go in unto thy brother's wife, and marry her, and raise up seed to thy brother. And Onan knew that the seed should not be his; and it came to pass, when he went in unto his brother's wife, that he spilled it on the ground, lest that he should give seed to his brother. And the thing which he did displeased the LORD: wherefore he slew him also. Then said Judah to Tamar his daughter in law, Remain a widow at thy father's house, till Shelah my son be grown: for he said, Lest peradventure he die also, as his brethren did. And Tamar went and dwelt in her father's house. (Gen. 38:1–11)

Many of you have probably heard someone quote a verse, saying, "It is better to plant thy seed in the belly of a harlot than to spill it on the ground." I believe this is also one interpretation of Genesis 38:9, which we just looked at. But that isn't what the verse says; in fact, there is no verse in any Bible translation that says that. That being said, 1 Corinthians does say that one of the reasons for marriage is to prevent sexual incontinence (uncontrolled fluid release). This does suggest that this release isn't what God intended. Numerous verses say that some men aren't capable of containing themselves; therefore, they should get married. Since there are good theological scholars on both sides of this debate, it seems clear to me that the Bible doesn't give definitive direction concerning this topic. Of course, it would be better to be married if you can't contain, but no scripture says it's better to sleep with a harlot than to self-satisfy. For a Christian, sleeping with a harlot is a sin against one's own body and defiles the temple of God, not to mention being fornication and adultery, which are also clearly labeled as sinful.

Here's what I think the scriptures are trying to show us. When our corrupt bodies crave something with such intensity that it causes us to lose control or have a lack of restraint, resulting in a physical reaction, this reaction is normally sinful. That being said, when two people are married and are having sanctioned intimate encounters with each other, they aren't reacting to the loss of control or lack of restraint; therefore, the use of contraceptives is useful in allowing them to enjoy one another without having to worry about having a child they are not prepared for. To me this isn't sinful; rather, it is using the modern technology and common sense God gave us to enhance our pleasure between each other. Fornication, adultery, and self-gratification are all results of our bodies craving something to the point that we lose control and the ability to restrain ourselves from indulging in the lust of the flesh. Still, this is only my opinion based on the fact that any significance given to a man's seed seems to be centered on the preservation of his namesake. The value doesn't appear to me to be found in the seed itself but rather in the heritage. If this is true, then each man is obligated to produce a male child to carry on the family name.

Today we say the family name is the surname (last name), but as we saw from the example above, back in biblical days, they were talking about the first name. Onan didn't want to provide seed for his brother because the child would be called the son of Er, not the son of Onan. This is why there are no surnames found in the Old

Testament. The twelve tribes of Israel were called the "sons of Jacob" or the "tribes of Israel," which is the name God gave Jacob. Jesus was called the "son of Joseph" by the people who didn't recognize Him as the Messiah. Jesus Christ isn't a first name and a surname the way we often think of them. Jesus means "Jehovah the savior," and Christ means "the anointed one." Jesus was also called many other names, such as the "son of David," the "son of man," and the "Messiah."

If all of this is true, then is it wrong for a person to have a medical procedure to prevent pregnancy? I think the same rules apply. If the person has met his or her obligation to carry on the namesake, then as far as scripture is concerned, his seed is no longer that valuable. Whether that means to carry on the first name as it did in scripture or the surname the way we use them today, I'll leave that up to the reader, but personally I think every man, provided he doesn't have a mental, physical, or emotional reason not to, should desire to carry on his bloodline, which is different from his brother's. The child would have been called the "son of Er" because the child would have been from the bloodline of Jacob and Tamar, Er's widow. This would have been different from the bloodline of Jacob and any other person Onan could have combined with. Though the woman could not carry on the name Tamar, she carried on her namesake because she was the wife of Er. This is because she became one with Er and, after his death, one with Onan, so her name was the same as his. I hope that didn't get too confusing. When a woman gets married, she takes her husband's name; therefore, when his name is preserved, so is hers because they are one.

Intimacy Isn't Just for Procreation

A census taker was walking around the neighborhood, going door to door. He stopped at one house and knocked on the door. A middle-aged woman answered the door, and the young man started his prepared speech. He said, "I am a census taker, and I am in the neighborhood, trying to get a count of how many people live in each home."He went on to say, "Do you live here alone?"

The woman replied, "No, I live here with my husband and children."

So he asked, "And just how many children do you have, and could I have their names and gender please?"

The woman replied, "Okay, well, let me think. There is Janet and Jane, then Jimmy and Johnny, then Timothy and Thomas."

It looked like she intended to continue, so the census taker interrupted her and said, "My goodness, did you and your husband have twins every time?"

She just stared at him for a moment with a look of confusion, then replied, "No, actually there were quite a few times when we didn't get anything."

Have Children at the Right Time and for the Right Reasons

I think every couple should consider the possibility of having children and discuss these issues even before they get married. If a woman already knows ahead of time that the one thing she wants more than anything is to be a mother one day and she ends up marrying a man who doesn't want children, she will never be completely satisfied and happy in her marriage. She will even eventually resent her husband because he doesn't want to help her fulfill her dreams. Personally, I think every married couple should experience motherhood and fatherhood; after all, this is one of the things God told us to do. He said to be fruitful and multiply (Gen. 1:28).This is one of the greatest things a married couple can share: the inherited ability to create life. (1 Pet 3:7)

On the other hand, many couples have children because they think it will hold their marriage together. That isn't a good reason to have children. Most of the time, having children for this reason ends up in disaster. Usually it doesn't work as for as keeping the family together or solving marital problems. In fact, it usually makes the situation worse. If you are having marital problems, make sure you take care of that situation first and then consider having children. Children are a gift and a blessing from God, but they also can add to an already-stressful situation if you're not ready for them.

I think it's amusing when people say a child was a mistake. If you have normal marital relations and don't take any steps to prevent pregnancy, getting pregnant isn't a mistake. It may have been a bad idea if the two of you aren't ready to have children, but it wasn't a mistake.

If you aren't ready for children when you first get married, then wait a while, but my advice is, don't wait too long. If you are waiting to see whether the marriage is going to work before you have children, then you shouldn't be in the marriage in the first place. You should never get married if you are still wondering whether it's going to work. Unfortunately, marriages today are more of an experiment than a commitment. It's exactly this attitude that generally results in unwanted pregnancies and abortions.

A man stood up in front of an audience the other day and proclaimed that he and his wife had discussed the matter of having children for an extended period of time. After considerable debate, they finally both agreed they didn't want to have children. So then the man said, "If any of you out there are interested, give us a call later so we can discuss a time and place to drop them off."

After a woman has conceived is the wrong time to discuss if you want children or not.

Who Should Make the Decision concerning Abortion?

As far as I am concerned, based on God's Word, abortion should never even be a consideration for a Christian couple at all. Yes, I said couple, since I don't believe this decision should be totally left up to the woman whether she is married or not. She didn't create this pregnancy by herself. I don't agree with those who say it is her body, so it is her decision. It is not her body; it is the body of another person who was created by two people. Those two people, I believe, should have equal say about what happens to their child. This is provided that this pregnancy is a result of two consenting adults having intimate relations.

God puts a significant amount of emphasis on the father. Under normal circumstances, the child would bear the father's name, not the mother's. It is the father's lineage that is carried on, not the mother's. It was the father who started the fertilization process, not the mother. It was the father who gave part of himself to the wife, not the mother giving part of herself to him. If the life was created under normal circumstances, the wife has become one with the husband, and she has his name. It's not the man who becomes one with the wife but the wife who becomes one with the husband. You might say isn't that the same thing, well, to God apparently it isn't.

When God breathed into Adam, man received life. When God put part of Adam into Eve, she received life. When God put part of Himself in Mary, Jesus received life in the flesh. When Christians get saved, they receive part of God (the Holy Spirit), and they receive spiritual life. When a man puts part of himself (through his seed) in his wife, they create life in a new child. On top of this, we all should know by now that it is the husband/father God holds responsible for the protection of the wife and child. In addition, both God and the government are more than willing to admit and enforce the fact that it is the husband's/father's responsibility to support the wife and child. The wife was created for the husband. (1 Cor. 11:9).

I think one of the most exciting things to happen in regard to Christianity today is the latest Supreme Court ruling on abortion that reversed *Roe v. Wade* on June 24, 2022. This law was the most horrific and disgusting one ever passed in the United States. Praise God that it is over, but the fight isn't. The reversing of Roe only puts the destiny of unborn children back in the hands of the individual states. Some of the states have very strict abortion laws, such as abortion being illegal after six weeks of pregnancy with the exception of cases involving rape and incest. Other states allow abortion under any circumstances up to the day of birth. Since these laws are now back in the hands of the states, I think its important for every Christian to know where and why he or she stands on this issue so each person will be ready for these battles in his or her state.

In Old Testament Times, Fathers and Judges Made These Decisions

In the following verse, God makes it clear that this decision concerning the unborn child and anyone who causes the child harm or causes harm to the wife during the pregnancy should involve the husband. According to scripture, it appears that the husband had more say-so than the wife. Here in this scripture, the husband and the judge decided. I believe in today's society both should have a say in the matter, since the child consist of both parents' DNA, but in any case the husband or father shouldn't be left out. The verse below is talking about a woman who gave birth prematurely because of two men accidentally causing harm to her during a confrontation between each other. Then it says, "if no mischief follow," meaning that she had the child early but that the child wasn't harmed. "If men strive, and hurt a woman with child, so that her fruit depart from her, and yet no mischief follow: he shall be surely punished, according as the woman's husband will lay upon him; and he shall pay as the judges determine" (Ex. 21:22).

Abortion Is Murder

I believe the Bible teaches that anyone who takes another person's life is guilty of murder, and an unborn child is another person. We can see how God viewed this issue in the Old Testament at Moses' birth. The Israelites were being held as slaves in the land of Egypt after Joseph had died, and they had been in captivity in Egypt over four hundred years. Pharaoh was concerned that there were too many Israelites and that they would take over the land from the Egyptians, so he ordered that all the male children born to the Israelites be put to death immediately after birth. They didn't have the means to put them to death before birth at the time, but this was the closest they could get to it. In our country today, several states have proposed legislation that would allow abortion up to the day of delivery. Anyhow, Pharaoh ordered the Hebrew midwives to kill the newborn baby boys, but the midwives knew this was murder in God's eyes, and they refused. I don't think abortion should be legal at any time but definitely not up until the time of birth. This should be considered murder in any society.

> And the king of Egypt spake to the Hebrew midwives, of which the name of the one was Shiphrah, and the name of the other Puah: And he said, When ye do the office of a midwife to the Hebrew women, and see them upon the stools; if it be a son, then ye shall kill him: but if it be a daughter, then she shall live. But the midwives feared God, and did not as the king of Egypt commanded them, but saved the men children alive. And the king of Egypt called for the midwives, and said unto them, Why have ye done this thing, and have saved the men children alive? And the midwives said unto Pharaoh, Because the Hebrew women are not as the Egyptian women; for they are lively, and are delivered ere the midwives come in unto them. Therefore God dealt well with the midwives: and the people multiplied, and waxed very mighty. And it came to pass, because the midwives feared God, that he made them houses. And Pharaoh charged all his people, saying, every

> son that is born ye shall cast into the river, and every
> daughter ye shall save alive. (Ex. 1:15–22)

Abortion Shouldn't Be an Option for God's People

The Bible says here that the midwives feared God; therefore, they chose to obey God rather than Pharaoh. Our government may have legalized abortion, but it isn't all right with God, and I believe one day America will pay dearly for this great sin. Every doctor, nurse, midwife, or anyone who participates in the delivery of children should absolutely refuse to have anything to do with this act of murder for fear of being punished by God. I'm not sure whether these midwives were God's chosen people or whether they were just the ones who helped the Israeli women deliver their children. In either case, even lost people should have enough moral integrity to understand just how awful and evil abortion is. These midwives were directly ordered to kill these babies by their government, but these women feared God more than breaking the law.

Christians Should Stand behind Anti-Abortion Legislation

Right now I am very proud of Governor Gregg Abbott of Texas for standing up for unborn babies. Our president is doing everything he can to overturn the new abortion laws in the great state of Texas, so what does this tell us about him? Joe Biden claims to be a Christian man, but when he was asked about how he could be a Christian and still be in favor of abortion, he said, "Well, my church [Catholic] teaches against abortion, but I can't let my religion get in the way of my governmental responsibilities." How can anyone who claims to be a Christian say such a thing? Mr. President, I respect the office, but because of you and some of your predecessors, our nation will pay for this great sin. In verses 17 and 20–21, we see that God rewarded these midwives for doing the right thing. Some people will say they understand that abortion should be a last resort, but what about cases of rape? Considering this question, I'd like to point out a few things concerning abortion:

1. It is a strange sort of justice that would kill an innocent child for the crime of his or her father.
2. Two wrongs never make a right; one violent act does not condone another.
3. It takes two to make a baby; no matter how the baby was conceived, at least half of its DNA comes from its mother.
4. If you found out tomorrow that you were the product of a rape, would you wish that your mother had aborted you?
5. All states have allowed (even before *Roe v. Wade* in 1973) immediate medical treatment to all rape victims. Such treatment can prevent conception in many cases.
6. Whatever the circumstances of his or her conception, the unborn child possesses an inalienable right to life.
7. The mother's lack of being responsible for the child's conception doesn't remove the child's right to life.
8. The unborn child isn't the attacker but is in fact a second innocent victim, who should not receive capital punishment for the father's crime. Even the rapist is spared the death penalty.
9. Good adoptive homes are still available in cases where a woman is unable to raise a child conceived by rape or incest.
10. Undergoing an abortion can pose a major physical health risk to the woman, both in terms of immediate and long-term complications, including the subsequent ability of a woman to bear children and have healthy children.
11. There are several reasons why a victim of forcible rape may not become pregnant:

    a. The woman may be on birth control.
    b. It may be during the unfertile days of her cycle.

    c.   She may be too young or old to conceive.

    d.   There can be disruptions in the ovulation cycle due to extreme emotional trauma.

12. In only a fraction of a percent of forcible rape cases does pregnancy occur—that is, less than 1 percent of all rapes.

Unborn Children Are Considered Very Much Alive to God

> And it came to pass, that, when Elisabeth heard the salutation of Mary, the babe leaped in her womb; and Elisabeth was filled with the Holy Ghost: And she spake out with a loud voice, and said, Blessed art thou among women, and blessed is the fruit of thy womb. And whence is this to me, that the mother of my Lord should come to me? For, lo, as soon as the voice of thy salutation sounded in mine ears, the babe leaped in my womb for joy. (Luke 1:41–44)

> And the children struggled together within her; and she said, If it be so, why am I thus? And she went to enquire of the LORD. (Gen. 25:22)

> For thou hast possessed my reins: thou hast covered me in my mother's womb. I will praise thee; for I am fearfully and wonderfully made: marvellous are thy works; and that my soul knoweth right well. My substance was not hid from thee, when I was made in secret, and curiously wrought in the lowest parts of the earth. Thine eyes did see my substance, yet being unperfect; and in thy book all my members were written, which in continuance were fashioned, when as yet there was none of them. (Ps. 139:13–16)

Then the word of the LORD came unto me, saying,
Before I formed thee in the belly I knew thee;
and before thou camest forth out of the womb I
sanctified thee, and I ordained thee a prophet unto
the nations. (Jer. 1:4–5)

Did not he that made me in the womb make him?
and did not one fashion us in the womb? (Job 31:15)

How Do You Feel about Abortion?

When I was in Bible College many moons ago, we had a time in
the middle of the class schedule when everyone came together for
a general assembly each day. Sometimes we had preaching sessions
from the staff or the preacher boy students. Sometimes the church
pastor gave a sermon. Sometimes skits were performed and so forth.
On some occasions, we were shown a spiritual movie of one sort or
another. On this one particular day, we were shown a movie on the
topic of abortions.

I learned a lot that day, a lot of things I wish I had never learned
or seen. I learned that abortions are used to make money, mostly
by selling baby body parts (greedy of filthy lucre, 1 Tim. 3:3). I
learned that many tools for the trade were developed just to crush
the baby's head or other large parts of their tiny bodies so they would
be easier to remove from the womb (inventors of evil things, Rom.
1:30). I learned that there are tools for cutting and tearing pieces of
the babies' bodies apart so they can be removed in smaller pieces.
I learned that they sometimes use ultrasound or even an X-ray to
locate the baby to facilitate its removal. I saw pictures of these babies
being torn apart and the pieces being pulled out of the womb one
at a time. I saw babies trying to get away from these instruments as
they struggled to avoid the inevitable.

At first, I just shrank in my chair in astonishment. Then I felt like I was going to throw up because what I was seeing made me sick. Then I just started crying uncontrollably at the horror. You can't tell me these babies aren't alive. I saw them trying to escape. I have never experienced anything that made me more ashamed, embarrassed, hurt, or disgusted. I think every woman who thinks she wants an abortion should have to sit and watch what I saw. If she can still let her baby be murdered after seeing that, then I wonder whether she is even capable of having any feelings at all. This was over thirty years ago, and I will never forget what I saw. It still makes me tear up when I think about it. There is no doubt that these babies are alive. This is the condition of the child only eight weeks after conception:

1. The heart can be heard on the ultrasonic stethoscope.
2. The heart has already been beating for one month.
3. An electrocardiogram can be done.
4. The brain waves were measurable two weeks ago.
5. The baby feels pain and responds to touch.
6. He or she sucks his or her thumb.
7. He or she can grasp an instrument placed in his or her hand.
8. He or she swims in the womb with a natural swimmer's stroke.
9. At two and a half months, the body is completely formed, even his or her fingerprints.
10. After three months, all the body parts are formed and functioning; there is only growth in size and maturity after this time.

What about Those Who Perform Abortions?

The Bible teaches that even if a woman gets injured accidentally while she is pregnant and it causes the baby to be born early, even if the baby is otherwise fine, the man who caused the accident should be punished. If the baby is injured or dies because of his actions, then he will have to pay an eye for an eye and so forth. There is no question about whether these babies are living souls. Look at these verses:

"If men strive, and hurt a woman with child, so that her fruit depart from her, and yet no mischief follow: he shall be surely punished, according as the woman's husband will lay upon him; and he shall pay as the judges determine. And if any mischief follow, then thou shalt give life for life, Eye for eye, tooth for tooth, hand for hand, foot for foot, Burning for burning, wound for wound, stripe for stripe" (Ex. 21:22–25).

The person who had caused this accident to happen was to be punished or killed. I should also point out that it says here that the man should have to pay according to what the woman's husband demanded. I think that tells us that the father should definitely have some say as to what happens to his unborn children as well as the mother, like I previously pointed out. Today women are allowed to get abortions without even telling their husbands or the baby's father (whoever he is). I don't believe this should be allowed and most definitely not without the mother and father's consent. I know what you are thinking. I'm living in a fantasy world where all mothers and fathers are willing to take responsibility for their actions. I'm not naïve, and I know some fathers don't want to have anything to do with their children—some mothers don't either, for that matter. I think that is a shame, but what I'm trying to say is that they should at least have the opportunity to say whether they intend to participate in the child's future. Yes, I said "future" because I am talking about the child as if he or she were already born.

Guess what? To God the child already lives. It is too late to make that decision. You can't have the privilege of fatherhood without the responsibility of it. This includes the provision, protection, guidance, nurturing, and admonition of the child as previously discussed. If the father doesn't intend to support the child, then he doesn't have the right to the privileges either. This doesn't change the fact that the child has a right to life whether the father intends to participate in it or not. I believe the woman's father should take the responsibility to help raise this child if the father doesn't. His daughter and what she does are his responsibility until she marries; at that point, her husband should take over the privilege and responsibility.

What Does Science Say about the Creation of Life?

While I was preparing this lesson, it dawned on me that I should consider the scientific aspect of motherhood and fatherhood as well. Somehow the governments in the majority of societies on earth today seem to think that fathers have little to do with reproduction; therefore, the mother should have all the say about what happens to her body.

First, I think I should make it perfectly clear that according to God, this baby inside her is not part of her body. When a person gets injured and needs temporary help breathing from a respirator, we don't consider this person to be dead, and the respirator doesn't become part of the person's body. This baby is a new separate, independent life form that just needs a little life support until it is finished being developed. When a pilot flies above eleven thousand feet in his non-pressurized aircraft, he or she is required to have supplemental oxygen to breathe because of the oxygen molecules' density at that elevation. Does that mean the pilot is no longer a living soul? Does that mean the oxygen mask is now part of the pilot's body?

Anyhow, I want to share with you what I discovered from science when I investigated this topic of life development. We all know that physically speaking, life begins with the fertilization of the egg supplied by the mother with the sperm supplied by the father. The result is ultimately that each parent supplies half of the child's DNA. This alone should be sufficient to say that half of the decision of what happens to the child should come from the father. Here is what I didn't know; the mother does not produce the egg. Every egg a woman supplies during her entire reproductive lifetime is an egg she was born with. This suggests that at least half of the egg-producing process comes from the father and that the mother isn't capable of producing them on her own since she is born with all these eggs, and they have to be placed in storage in the mother's body until it's time to present them for their turn to be fertilized.

An average reproductive lifetime for the human female is around forty years. During that time she will deliver one egg per lunar month; that means thirteen eggs a year, since a lunar month is twenty-eight-and-a-half days. So during her lifetime, she will supply around five hundred eggs. This is why they have sperm banks, not egg banks. Every woman has eggs she is born with; not every man is capable of producing healthy sperm.

Basically what I am saying is that though the woman has a very important and essential role in this process, she doesn't produce the eggs from which life comes. She takes them out of storage and delivers them to a perfect environment for the fertilization process to take place. Then she provides the ideal place for incubation during the child's development, and she provides all the temporary life support required to keep the child alive until his or her birth. I should also mention that even though the woman doesn't manufacture this egg, it does come from her body, and it does contain her DNA. It consists of half of her mother's DNA and half of her father's DNA. I should also mention that in many ways the eggs are neutral, in that it is the father who determines many of the features the child will have, such as gender. The father, on the other hand, actually produces millions of sperm cells every day after he reaches puberty and throughout the remainder of his life.

I'm not trying to take away the significance of the mother's role here. I'm simply trying to emphasize the significance of the father's role. All things considered, to say the least, the father should have at least as much right to the child as the mother scientifically speaking. Nature itself also illustrates this principle by the fact that every egg that doesn't get fertilized is considered lifeless waste material, and the woman's body naturally discards it each month.

David Boudreaux

Adoption as an Option

Adoption Is God's Solution for an Unplanned Pregnancy

Now we shall discuss adoption as God's choice as an alternative to abortion (murder). God is definitely against abortion as we have seen, but on the other hand, not only is adoption a viable option, but God has used this alternative Himself. We Christians are adopted into the family of God. In addition, the scriptures talk about Moses being adopted into Pharaoh's family. Let's look at some other scriptures concerning adoption.

> For ye have not received the spirit of bondage again to fear; but ye have received the Spirit of adoption, whereby we cry, Abba, Father. The Spirit itself beareth witness with our spirit, that we are the children of God: And if children, then heirs; heirs of God, and joint-heirs with Christ; if so be that we suffer with him, that we may be also glorified together. (Rom. 8:15–17)

> For I could wish that myself were accursed from Christ for my brethren, my kinsmen according to the flesh: Who are Israelites; to whom pertaineth the adoption, and the glory, and the covenants, and the giving of the law, and the service of God, and the promises; Whose are the fathers, and of whom as concerning the flesh Christ came, who is over all, God blessed forever. Amen. Not as though the word of God hath taken none effect. For they are not all Israel, which are of Israel. (Rom. 9:3–6)

Having predestinated us unto the adoption of children by Jesus Christ to himself, according to the good pleasure of his will. (Eph. 1:5)

But when the fullness of the time was come, God sent forth his Son, made of a woman, made under the law, To redeem them that were under the law, that we might receive the adoption of sons. And because ye are sons, God hath sent forth the Spirit of his Son into your hearts, crying, Abba, Father. Wherefore thou art no more a servant, but a son; and if a son, then an heir of God through Christ. (Gal. 4:4–7)

Misconceptions about Adoption

There are a lot of myths and misconceptions out there about adoption. Let me give you some facts. These numbers were accumulated a few years back, but the statistics haven't changed much.

1. In one year, less than 10 percent of women who give birth to babies out of wedlock decide on adoption.
2. At least two million American couples and qualified singles would like to adopt regularly.
3. On average, adopted children actually develop a stronger sense of identity than other children.
4. There are three options for a single Christian woman with a crisis pregnancy: be a single parent, get married to the father, or pursue adoption. These are the only acceptable choices in God's eyes.
5. Only about fifty thousand women put infants up for adoption, while over 1.6 million lives are aborted each year.

6. Since 1978, abortion has terminated approximately 40 percent of all teenage pregnancies.

7. It has been estimated that in 1985 alone, over two million infertile couples sought to adopt healthy newborns, but only twenty-five thousand were successful.[1]

Facts about Rape Victims and Abortions

1. Fewer than 1 percent of all abortions take place because rape or incest was involved in creating the pregnancy.

2. Up to 85 percent of the women who become pregnant through rape or incest choose to have their children.

3. The national rape-related pregnancy rate is 5.0 percent per rape among victims of reproductive age.

4. About thirty-two thousand pregnancies result from sexual assaults or rape every year in the United States.

5. The majority of rape-related pregnancies occurred among adolescents and resulted from assault by a known, often-related perpetrator.

6. Only 11.7 percent of these adolescents who were raped by a known, often-related predator received immediate medical attention after the assault.

7. 32.4 percent of victims didn't discover they were pregnant until they had already entered the second trimester.

8. In a 1996 study of rape victims and pregnancy, 11.8 percent of pregnancies resulted in a spontaneous abortion. Only about 6 percent of mothers chose to have the child and then give it up for adoption.

---

[1] Information on premarital sex, rape, incest, and adoption provided by Jean Lutchfield, c/o Trinity Lutheran Church 600 Water St., Edwardsville, IL 62025.

9. An Elliot Institute study on rape-related pregnancies found that nearly 80 percent of the women who aborted said that abortion was the wrong solution.

10. 43 percent of women said they felt pressure to abort from family members or health workers.

11. 95 percent of those who mentioned rape or incest as a reason for an abortion also named other reasons for deciding to abort.

12. The number of abortions that occur in the United States (based on statistics) because of rape or incest is twelve thousand per year.

13. When the Pennsylvania legislature modified the law to say it covered only rape or incest reported to law enforcement authorities, the number of publicly funded abortions dropped from thirty-five a month to three.

14. Almost 70 percent of sexual assaults go unreported to law enforcement officials.

15. The number of states who currently pay for abortions for poor women who have been the victims of rape or incest is eight.

16. Another twelve states finance abortions for poor women with broader circumstances.

17. On the other end of the spectrum, 90 percent of children who are battered in the USA were wanted pregnancies.

18. In 2008, the Supreme Court of California upheld that pregnancy resulting from rape constitutes great bodily injury.

Many laws introduced to restrict access to abortion even exclude pregnancies that are caused by sexual assault. Although there has been a steady decline in abortion rates since 1980, there are still about 1.2 million abortions in the United States every year, a figure that leads the world in per capita abortions. [2]

---

[2] The above statistics are provided by Healthresearchfunding.org.

David Boudreaux

Although Abortion Is Not an Option for
Christians, There Are Several Alternatives

I hope that between the scriptures I have shared with you and the
statistics we just looked at, at least some of you will look at having
and raising children as a blessing from God. This is true even if the
child was a so-called accident or mistake or even in cases of rape
or incest. God knows what you are going through. If you are in a
position where you just absolutely cannot take care of a child, then
you should first turn to family for help. If they can't help you or you
have no family, then consider adoption. Please don't forget to include
the father in these decisions because the child is just as much his
as it is the mother's. Maybe the father or the father's family will be
able to take care of the child. They should at least have the option.

The decision to have the child is already made and not up to
the father or the mother. Numerous programs are available to help
single women in this situation. Adoption agencies are also normally
in a position to offer help. For a Christian woman, abortion is not
an option, and it shouldn't be an option for an unsaved person
either. Murder shouldn't be a legal option in any country, and no
matter what you feel or think, according to God's Word, abortion
is murder. I know this may be hard for some people to accept, and
maybe you won't be judged for this according to the government,
but one day you will be judged before God.

As the Biological Mother, You Still Have Choices to Make

One other thing to consider if you are a mother who is putting your
child up for adoption if you will be able to choose a proper home for
the child. If the adoption agency isn't giving you any choices, then
you should find another agency. This is important because many of
the families being approved by these agencies aren't qualified to raise
a child according to God. Best case scenario, you will find a man and

woman who are married and saved. God says this is the best chance of raising a godly seed (Mal. 2:15). At the very least, it should be a couple with one man and one woman, since this is God's definition of marriage (Eph. 5:31).

All Can Be Forgiven

For those who have already been through an abortion, I know you must be suffering the consequences already. Just remember that God can forgive you for anything. All you have to do is admit that you made a terrible mistake and that you are remorseful for your actions. Ask God to forgive you. You will still have to live with the scars sin leaves, but you will be forgiven.

My sister-in-law, Tanya, just shared with me yesterday an illustration that depicts this concept in a very real way. If you take a perfectly flat sheet of paper, it represents our lives before we do anything to defile it. When we commit sins, they cause the paper to get wrinkled. The more sins we commit, the more wrinkled it gets until eventually the paper is just a wrinkled ball. Then we get saved, or for someone who is already saved, we ask for forgiveness. When we do, God forgives the sins and straightens the paper back out. However, even after the paper is straightened, and even though it may be flat again, you can still see in the paper the creases caused by the wrinkles. Even though the sin is gone and we have a clean slate, our lives will still reflect the scars the sin caused. Thank you for this illustration, Tanya.[3]

---

[3] Information pertaining to premarital sex, rape, incest, and adoption was provided by Jean Luchtefeld, C/O Trinity Lutheran Church, Edwardsville, IL 62025. Information on venereal disease was provided by Birth Choice, PO Box 94553, Oklahoma City, OK.

CHAPTER 9
Raising Children

God Gave Mankind the Privilege of Creating Life

God gave the privilege of having children to the husband and wife (1 Peter 3:7); as it says, they are heirs together of the grace of life. I don't think there is a greater honor or privilege God has given the husband and wife together than the ability to create life just like God Himself has. God the Father is the giver of physical life, and husbands and wives inherited the ability to create life from Him. God the Son, Jesus Christ, is the giver of spiritual life. When we receive that spiritual life, we become Christians or part of the body of Christ; therefore, we inherit the ability to give spiritual life when we lead others to Christ.

The Bible also teaches that having children is a gift from God. Unfortunately, they don't come with instruction manuals, and for most parents, the learning process can be difficult and frustrating as well as new and exciting. Learning how to adjust to having children can be as difficult as learning to live with a new husband or wife, and many times children come before a couple is done with the first adjustment to each other.

When my wife and I had our first child, we were scared, unsettled, and nervous. We had no idea what we were doing. When we were getting ready to leave the hospital, a nurse helped us get ready to go. My wife and I asked this nurse a lot of questions, and I guess it was pretty obvious that we were nervous about what to do with a new baby. Finally, my wife just came right out and said to the nurse, "I'm really nervous about taking this baby home. I have no idea what I'm doing."

At that moment, I heard the best advice I have ever heard. The nurse stopped what she was doing, looked at my wife, and said, "Just take him home and love him." I have pondered this statement over and over in my mind, and I still believe there is nothing she could have said that would have been any more simplistic or more profound at the same time. "Just take him home and love him" is all you need to know. If you love your child, you will do anything and everything imaginable to care for, provide for, and protect him or her. As a parent, this is your responsibility.

"Likewise, ye husbands, dwell with them according to knowledge, giving honour unto the wife, as unto the weaker vessel, and as being heirs together of the grace of life; that your prayers be not hindered"(1 Peter 3:7).The difference between grace and mercy is this: Mercy is God withholding something we deserve, such as punishment for our sins. Grace is God giving us something we don't deserve, such as salvation. This verse says that God has given us something we don't deserve, and that is the gift of the ability to create life. This is a great privilege and also a great responsibility. It is a gift from God He first gave to Adam and Eve; then it was passed down to us through an inheritance from them. That is why we are heirs to the gift of life. But this ability to create life extends only to the ability to create a living body and soul.

Our children inherit their bodies and souls from their parents, but there is still an element missing. Children are born with a body and soul but not a spirit. This is why they aren't breathing when they are born. The words *breath* and *spirit* come from the same word in the original language of the Bible. So the body and soul come from the parents, but the spirit or breath comes from God at the time of birth. Yet the baby is alive even before he or she receives the spirit or breath because that breath is provided by the mother until the child receives his or her own. We know that the life of the flesh is in the blood, so the flesh is alive from the time of conception, but the immaterial part of man receives life from the spirit, which happens at birth. The fact that this child isn't part of the mother's body can also be verified by the fact that even in the womb, the baby's blood and DNA are not the same as the mother's.

"And the LORD God formed man of the dust of the ground, and breathed into his nostrils the breath of life; and man became a living soul" (Gen. 2:7). Since Adam was formed from the dust of the ground, he had no life in him until God put breath in him. I guess you could say that Adam and Eve were conceived when God breathed life into them since they were never in the womb. The word *conceive* means to begin or to start. This is when life began for them. When a woman conceives therefore that is when the baby's life inside her begins or starts. Throughout history we as humans have proved over and over again that we don't deserve this awesome privilege of the ability to create life because of the way we have failed at this task. Children are born to single moms. Children are exposed to drugs and dangerous surroundings. Fathers and mothers neglect and abuse their children. There are also abortions and improper marriages or home lifestyles. Children aren't cherished, loved, protected, and raised the way God intended because He gave us this privilege; and we don't take the responsibility to do so the way He tells us to.

Children, Obey Your Parents

I believe that ultimately it is the father's responsibility to have his household in order and in subjection. I say this because this is plainly what the Bible teaches. Keep in mind that the husband or father is an overseer more or less since he is the one who answers to God for the guidance, well-being, provision, and protection of the entire family. I don't think this means the wife doesn't have her part. The scriptures teach that children should obey their parents, not just their father. In fact, children are told that if they will honor their parents, they will live long and have prosperous lives. This is the first commandment with a promise, if it is followed.

The First Commandment with the Promise of a Long and Prosperous life (Spock Verse: "Live Long and Prosper")

"Children, obey your parents in the Lord: for this is right. Honour thy father and mother; which is the first commandment with promise; That it may be well with thee, and thou mayest live long on the earth. And, ye fathers, provoke not your children to wrath: but bring them up in the nurture and admonition of the Lord" (Eph. 6:1–4). These verses also tell us the father should bring up his children in the nurture and admonition of the Lord. The "nurture … of the Lord" refers to proper disciplining, chastening, correcting, and instructing. I believe this point can best be illustrated by these verses in the book of Hebrews.

Don't Despise God's Punishment

> And ye have forgotten the exhortation which speaketh unto you as unto children, My son, despise not thou the chastening of the Lord, nor faint when thou art rebuked of him: *For whom the Lord loveth he chasteneth,* and scourgeth every son whom he receiveth. If ye endure chastening, God dealeth with you as with sons; for what son is he whom the father chasteneth not? *But if ye be without chastisement, whereof all are partakers, then are ye bastards, and not sons.* Furthermore we have had fathers of our flesh which corrected us, and we gave them reverence: shall we not much rather be in subjection unto

the Father of spirits, and live? For they verily for a few days chastened us after their own pleasure; *but he for our profit,* that *we might be partakers of his holiness.* Now no chastening for the present seemeth to be joyous, but grievous: nevertheless *afterward it yieldeth the peaceable fruit of righteousness* unto them which are exercised thereby. (Heb. 12:5–11 emphasis added)

1. Discipline is evidence that God loves us: "Whom the Lord loveth he chasteneth."
2. It proves we are God's legitimate (not illegitimate) children.
3. He disciplines us for our profit. It is for our good, not God's.
4. So we can be partakers of His holiness. We will remain separated and pure.
5. No chastening or discipline is fun while it's happening, but it yields good fruit.
6. Discipline yields forth the fruits of the Spirit: peace and righteousness.

Discipline of the Wife Isn't the Husband's Job

We know God is our Father spiritually speaking, and in this scenario, the child in the family looks at his father the same way we are supposed to look at God, our Father. Our Father, God, is in charge of disciplinary action, so it stands to reason that in our earthly families, God expects the father to be primarily responsible for the discipline of the children. I think I should mention here that it isn't the father's job to discipline the wife. We should remember that when a woman and man are married, they are one flesh. A husband doesn't punish himself, and since the wife is one with the husband, it is not for him to punish her either. Both are subject to the punishment of God the Father. Just because I said the father is ultimately responsible for the discipline of the children, that doesn't mean the wife doesn't have a role in this also. Again, the wife and husband are one flesh, and both are held accountable for the proper upbringing of their children. We already saw where the scriptures say children should obey their mothers and fathers. Therefore, while I believe it's primarily the father's responsibility, the father isn't always there, and the rules still need to be enforced.

Discipline Is Primarily the Father's Responsibility

I can remember when I was around fifteen or so, I made my mom angry about something, and most of the time my dad did the punishing, but this time he was at work. My mom got a belt and started to whip me, and I couldn't help myself. I just stood there and laughed at her. My response made her even angrier, but no matter what she did, she wasn't hurting me. Finally, she just gave up, looked at me, and said, "You think it's funny? Wait till your daddy gets home." Trust me, when Daddy got home, it wasn't funny anymore. I'm not going to say my dad was abusive. I'll just say that people don't do now what he did back in those days. After that day, every time my mom decided to whip me, I screamed like she was killing me. I may not have been very smart, but I didn't fall off the cabbage truck yesterday. So why do I say the father is primarily responsible for discipline?

1. Because he is the authoritative figure of the home (must rule over his own house)
2. Because he is intimidating (often intimidation is sufficient for correction)
3. Because he symbolizes God's authority (God the Father punishes His children)
4. Fathers need to discipline with love and compassion (Moms can really help with this)

My dad worked at the Comet rice mill near Houston, Texas, during what seems like a hundred years ago. He was a welder and a pipe fitter. He had this leather strap that was part of a discarded conveyor belt from the mill. It was about eight feet long, one-eighth inch thick, and about one and a quarter inches wide. He doubled that thing up in his hand and hit us with both ends of it at the same time. I remember nursing welts and bruises on numerous occasions. I also remember going out of my way to hide that thing. I could tell you some stories that would curl your toe nails backward, but I think you get the picture.

I will tell you I do believe in whippings, spankings, paddling, corporal punishment, or whatever you want to call it. I believe in it because God said so but also because I'm a living testament to the fact that it works. However, I also believe if it's not done correctly, it is and should be considered abuse. The fact is, you don't have to use corporal punishment to be abusive. There are all sorts of abuse, and we will talk about these things as well.

In any case, if you are going to use this type of punishment for discipline, you must learn to do it out of love and not out of anger. It is far better for a child to be punished when he or she is young than for him or her to learn that there are no consequences for disobeying authority. *This is a lesson that must be taught at a young age; therefore, it is the parents' job to do so. A child who won't obey his or her parents won't obey teachers, law enforcement, government, or rules. This person will rebel against all authority including the authority of God. We are the children of God, and He punishes us for our own good. We should punish our children for their own good as well.* I can remember my dad saying to me, "Son, this hurts me more than it does you." That didn't make sense to me at the time, but I get it now. No parent should enjoy disciplining his or her child, but it must be done if the parent expects the child to turn out to be respectful to God and his or her neighbors.

The Rewards of Discipline

1. Discipline proves we love our children.

   "My son, despise not the chastening of the LORD; neither be weary of his correction: For whom the LORD loveth he correcteth; even as a father the son in whom he delighteth" (Prov. 3:11–12).
2. Discipline proves we won't give up on them.

   "He that spareth his rod hateth his son: but he that loveth him chasteneth him betimes" (Prov. 13:24).
3. Discipline proves we have high hopes for their future.

   "Chasten thy son while there is hope, and let not thy soul spare for his crying" (Prov. 19:18).
4. Discipline proves we are concerned about their souls.

   "Withhold not correction from the child: for if thou beatest him with the rod, he shall not die. Thou shalt beat him with the rod, and shalt deliver his soul from hell" (Prov. 23:13–14).
5. Discipline proves we want them to be delightful people.

   "Correct thy son, and he shall give thee rest; yea, he shall give delight unto thy soul" (Prov. 29:17).

Proper Discipline Isn't Child Abuse, Abuse Is the Result of the Loss of Control

1. Child abuse is caused by anger.
2. Child abuse can be the result of substance abuse.
3. Child abuse can be caused by jealousy, which turns to anger.

I most certainly do not condone any sort of child abuse. Child abuse normally occurs under one of two circumstances. *First is being under the influence of anger.* The Bible says to be angry and sin not (Eph. 4:26). This is being angry and sinning. The first rule of discipline should be, do not discipline your child while you are angry. If you think he or she is too young to remember what he or she is being disciplined for an hour later, then the child is probably too young to discipline with corporal punishment in the first place.

Second, is being under the influence of drugs or alcohol. Again this is a loss of control, which is also sinful. You shouldn't allow anything to cause you to lose control. Sin is always a result of the loss of control if you are a child of God. The second rule of discipline is that you should never discipline your child if you are under the influence of alcohol or drugs.

Discipline Must Be Administered Appropriately

1. Discipline while out of control is physical abuse.
2. Discipline withheld is mental abuse.
3. Discipline must fit the child.
4. Discipline must fit the crime.
5. Discipline must be done while in the right frame of mind.
6. Discipline must be administered with consistency.

Too Much or Too Little Can be Bad

There are numerous ways to discipline. We have been talking about corporal punishment because it seems to be what is most frowned upon in our modern society. I think the reason for this is that most people do it incorrectly. *They either overdo it, and therefore cause it to become a form of physical abuse, or they underdo it by avoiding physical punishment altogether. In the long game, both methods can result in mental abuse. Both are wrong, and one can cause just as much harm to the child as the other.*

David Boudreaux

It Must Fit the Child

Each child is different as well. Some children, like my little granddaughter, Eliza, have such a soft heart and tender spirit that corporal punishment is almost never needed. She is so sensitive that a harsh word will cut her to the bone. A person who feels like this doesn't need physical punishment to understand he or she did wrong and become remorseful for his or her actions. But I have some grandsons who are so hard headed that they would rather rebel, tell a lie, and get in trouble, than tell the truth and be rewarded. This is the result of pure and simple rebellion to authority.

This rebellion must be dealt with, and sometimes it requires more physical methods. In this example, it is the girl who is tender and the boy who is hard headed; but sometimes it's the other way around. *Every child is different and has to be dealt with individually. The punishment shouldn't be greater or lesser than the offense calls for to correct.* Even the laws by the government don't require the death penalty for stealing candy from the local corner store, but there should be a small penalty for a small infraction. Otherwise no punishment teaches no consequences for doing wrong. Even if the punishment is just a stern verbal rebuke, then the lesson is taught.

Discipline Must Be Administered Consistently While in the Right Frame of Mind

Here are some other forms of discipline that can be effective, but *keep in mind that all forms of discipline should be done while one is in the right frame of mind. The key to administering any effective discipline is consistency.* The person cannot be punished for doing something one time and then not be punished when he or she does the same thing again the second time. It would be better not to be punished either time. If you aren't consistent, then the child thinks he or she

246

is being punished because of the mood the parent is in rather than for the offense he or she committed.

1. Grounding (removing certain privileges for a specific time and sticking to it)
2. Restricting the use of a certain item related to the offense, such as cell phone privileges
3. A time-out is usually effective when one child misbehaves in a group. It is appropriate to separate him or her from the group for a set amount of time. (You must stick with the set time, or this method is ineffective.)
4. Standing in the corner or putting his or her nose in a circle. This is difficult for a child to do because he or she can't stand still for long, but I don't think it should be done around other children because it can also be humiliating. Humiliation results in bitterness, not submission.
5. Sending the child to his or her room. This method is effective only if the child is missing something he or she could do outside the room that he or she can't do inside the room.
6. Having the child do some sort of physical activity. This may not only serve as a punishment but also burn off some extra adrenaline that can cause aggressive behavior. (Examples could be holding books in outstretched arms or doing push-ups.)

One effective method is predetermined punishment because it:

1. eliminates parental disagreement;
2. creates an atmosphere of consistency;
3. serves as a warning for the child (like the justice system penal code); and
4. is always appropriate and fair.

For some, it might be a good idea to make a list of offenses along with a list of consequential punishments. This works well *for parents who may not always agree on what punishment is appropriate for which offense. This creates consistency, which the child needs, and eliminates disagreement between the parents concerning appropriate punishment. It also provides a predetermined warning to the child as to what will be the consequences of his or her actions if a violation occurs.* This list should be prepared and agreed upon by both parents before introducing it to the child. I believe it's important for the child to know that parents are going to support each other in enforcing this agreement.

Discipline Should Never Include Angry Outbursts

Discipline should not include yelling at the child over and over to do the same thing, especially if the yelling includes a threat. Tell them once, and if they don't respond to it, then tell them a second time followed by a distinct action on your part that ensures compliance. If you repeat the same command over and over without requiring compliance, you are teaching them they don't have to do anything until you get mad. If you threaten them without following through, then you are teaching them that your words don't mean anything. Most people teach their own children the bad habits they have developed.

Discipline Should Never Include the Removal of Entitlements

Discipline shouldn't include the withholding of things they are entitled to as your children such as a roof over their heads or food in their bellies. Removing the necessities for basic life could be considered abusive and isn't needed to make a point. This type of discipline can lead to resentment, hatred, or other ill feelings. Children should be disciplined in such a way that they have no doubt you are doing it for them because you love them and want to protect them. When God punishes us, we know it is because we did something wrong and had it coming. We don't blame God because it's our fault. We reap what we sow (Gal. 6:7–8). When we punish our children, they should know that it's not our fault they are being punished, but rather it is because of their actions. Just like God punishes us because He loves us, we should punish our children because we love them too.

Discipline Should Never Include an Argument between Mom and Dad

If the mom and dad disagree on a certain disciplinary action taken by the other parent on a child, they shouldn't confront the other parent in front of the child. It should always appear to the child that they are in agreement with each other concerning these actions. If one of the parents disagrees, they should talk about it away from the child; and once they have reached an agreement, the one who administered the original disciplinary action should be the one to amend it as required. Most of the time it's best to let the discipline stand as administered on this occasion and perhaps adjust the discipline as agreed for future offenses. There are many good books on how to rear children by Christian authors. I think you should be using Christian methods, so I don't recommend non-Christian books, counseling, or advice.

Mothers Are Most Effective with Daughters and Dads with Sons

The second part of this verse talks about the admonition of the Lord (Eph. 6:4). *Admonition* means a mild rebuke or warning. This is talking about training a child to be an adult. While this command is given to fathers, because the man of the house is held accountable to God for the guidance, protection, and provision in the home, I believe this applies to a mom and dad. We know that the older women are commanded to teach the younger women and to have rule over or guide the household. Like I said before, guiding the home and raising the children are part of the woman's responsibilities. I don't think you have to be a genius to understand that men are probably better equipped to train boys to be godly men and women are better equipped to train girls to be godly women.

> I will therefore that the younger women marry, bear children, guide the house, give none occasion to the adversary to speak reproachfully. (1 Tim. 5:14)

> The aged women likewise, that they be in behaviour as becometh holiness, not false accusers, not given to much wine, teachers of good things; That they may teach the young women to be sober, to love their husbands, to love their children, To be discreet, chaste, keepers at home, good, obedient to their own husbands, that the word of God be not blasphemed. (Titus 2:3–5)

All Training Should Be Bible Based

1. Object lessons should be from Bible stories.
2. Godly principles should be based on God's Word.
3. Morals such as the Ten Commandments should be promoted.
4. All instructions should lead to their eventual conversion to Christianity.
5. All doctrine should be based on God's Word. (Don't trust anyone if he or she can't show it to you from God's Word.)

Easier to Teach Children at a Young Age

Of course, all the *children's training should be Bible based*. Children are most impressionable at the youngest ages, and they also retain knowledge better. *Teach your children Bible stories and godly principles and morals.* Teach them about Jesus. They aren't ready to understand the plan of salvation until they reach the age of reason or age of accountability. That is when they are old enough to understand that we are all sinners and in need of a savior. This age differs with each individual, and no one can tell you when that right time is for your children. If you communicate with them regularly, as you should, then you will know when they understand. I don't think you should try to push it too early to gain bragging rights. *If you have children go through the motions without understanding what they are doing, you may actually cause more harm than good.* This could give children a false sense of security, even though they don't understand what they did. They may have placed their trust in you and not in God. I have found in my personal dealings with children that it is best to wait until they come to you and ask how to be saved. Of course, without them being trained in the Word of God, that will never happen. This is your responsibility as a parent.

Don't Trust Your Child's Salvation to a Stranger

Salvation is the most important decision your child will ever make in his or her entire life, and this will happen under your watch. Most parents today don't understand this; if they did, they wouldn't just ignore God altogether, and they wouldn't send their kids off to a church without having any idea of what they are being taught there. I'm sorry to say that some churches, even though they may mean well, are misguided; and it would be better for your children not to go anywhere than to go someplace where they hear false doctrine.

"But continue thou in the things which thou hast learned and hast been assured of, knowing of whom thou hast learned them; And that from a child thou hast known the holy scriptures, which are able to make thee wise unto salvation through faith which is in Christ Jesus. All scripture is given by inspiration of God, and is profitable for doctrine, for reproof, for correction, for instruction in righteousness: That the man of God may be perfect, throughly furnished unto all good works" (2Tim. 3:14–17).

The Importance of Family Structure

Obviously, it's best for children to have both parents when they are growing up. I was discussing this issue with a friend of mine a couple of days ago, and he reminded me of a fact. Most gay men come from homes of single mothers or mothers who make and enforce the rules at home, while the fathers don't show any authority. Generally speaking, girls raised by single mothers don't learn to be submissive to authority. Boys raised by single moms tend to be effeminate. Girls raised by single dads don't learn how to be ladies. Boys raised by single dads don't learn how to respect women. It's obvious throughout the scriptures that raising children was intended to be a married couple's job. The book of Malachi teaches that the family is important and that there should be one wife (woman) per one husband (man). We know this because God made only one wife for Adam, and He very well could have made as many as He wanted. It also says the reason for this was to produce a godly seed. Raising godly children becomes more complicated when the family is split up (Mal. 2:14–15).

1. God's plan is one wife for one life.
     The following verses refer to a bishop (pastor) and his family, but we know the bishop is supposed to be setting an example for families in the church.
     "This is a true saying, If a man desire the office of a

bishop, he desireth a good work. A bishop then must be blameless, the husband of one wife, vigilant, sober, of good behaviour, given to hospitality, apt to teach; Not given to wine, no striker, not greedy of filthy lucre; but patient, not a brawler, not covetous; One that ruleth well his own house, having his children in subjection with all gravity; (For if a man know not how to rule his own house, how shall he take care of the church of God?)" (1 Tim. 3:1–5).

2. Follow instructions from Mom and Dad.

"My son, hear the instruction of thy father, and forsake not the law of thy mother: For they shall be an ornament of grace unto thy head, and chains about thy neck. My son, if sinners entice thee, consent thou not" (Prov. 1:8–10).

I think this verse is illuminating because it depicts the father as the trainer of the child (instructions) and the mother as the rule maker (law of thy mother). To me these verses suggest that the mother is the rule maker and the father is the enforcer.

3. Teach them while they are young.

"Train up a child in the way he should go: and when he is old, he will not depart from it" (Prov. 22:6).

4. Rebellion against parents will bring failure.

"The eye that mocketh at his father, and despiseth to obey his mother, the ravens of the valley shall pick it out, and the young eagles shall eat it" (Prov. 30:17).

It may seem a bit extreme, but the verse is telling us that children who don't listen to their parents will bring about their own destruction. Ephesians 6:4 talks about admonition from the father; admonition is a warning, and I think this is a good one.

5. It pleases God when children are obedient.

"Wives, submit yourselves unto your own husbands, as it is fit in the Lord. Husbands, love your wives, and be not bitter against them. Children, obey your parents in all things for this is well pleasing unto the Lord. *Fathers, provoke not your children to anger,* lest they be discouraged" (Col. 3:18–21 emphasis added).

6. Train them in the ways of God through the Word.

"And, ye fathers, *provoke not your children to wrath:* but bring them up in the nurture and admonition of the Lord" (Eph. 6:4 emphasis added).

Nurture means to train up, and *admonition* means to warn. Maybe Dad is warning about either following mom's rules or suffering the consequences.

Provoke Not Your Children to Wrath

I would also like to point out that God says twice in the verses above that fathers should be careful not to provoke their children to wrath or anger (Eph. 6:4; Col. 3:21). There are several ways fathers can do this. I find it interesting that God intentionally addressed fathers in these instructions because I seldom ever see any mothers doing this. Fathers should train and discipline but not provoke to wrath. How do fathers provoke their children to wrath? How would you feel if God, your Father, did these things to you?

1. Punishing a child for no reason (because you are angry, you punished the wrong child, or one child did something wrong but all of them were punished for it)
2. Punishing severely for a minor infraction (If children get the same punishment for everything they may do wrong, they will become frustrated and feel as though they cannot please their fathers no matter what they do.)
3. Punishing a child for something he or she is not guilty of
4. Using the same type of punishment for every offense

5. Punishing to the point that the spirit is broken. The goal is to break the child's will to rebel, not to break the spirit. The spirit is what drives a child to succeed. The will is what drives him or her to rebel.

6. Name calling, criticizing, belittling, embarrassing, insulting, telling the child he or she embarrasses you or that you are ashamed of him or her. Your goal isn't to make the child feel useless or worthless, or to humiliate him or her. Your goal is to make the child better so he or she will have productive and successful lives.

7. Picking on your child for no reason, intentionally making him or her angry, or doing things you know the child hates for no reason. If you know your child hates doing a certain thing when one of the other children likes doing it, don't make him or her do it just because you want to see the child get angry. I have seen so many fathers do this, and I don't understand why. No, this method doesn't build character. If one child hates taking out the trash and the other hates washing dishes, don't force them to do chores they hate just to be mean.

8. Making the child feel as though he or she can never do anything right. It is a good idea to point out something the child did right, even when he or she was being punished for something else he or she did wrong. Praise is a much more effective motivator. Teach your child to be persistent and not to quit. Making mistakes and learning from them are part of the formula for success. Consistently telling a child where he or she failed and never pointing out what the child did right makes him or her feel like a failure.

9. Making the child feel that your failures, whether it be in your marriage or other issues in your life, are his or her fault. Kids tend to blame themselves when their parents argue in the first place. This is why parents shouldn't argue in front of their kids.

10. Punishing without love. "I love you, and I don't want to have to punish you, but there are certain things we have to do. This is how you learn."

11. Punishing without guidance. If a child gets punished for doing something wrong, he or she should first know what he or she did wrong and second how he or she should have done it.

12. Punishment that results in physical harm. (Any type of punishment that results in the need for medical attention is wrong and sinful.)

13. Punishing a whole group of children for the actions of one

Discipline with Purpose

All discipline should have a specific purpose, and that is to correct a sinful action the child committed. This cannot be accomplished by punishing a child without direction. The child must know what he or she is being punished for and how to correct the problem. If you, as the parent, do not know how to correct it, then how do you expect him or her to know how to correct it? The child is naturally looking to you for guidance. The offense should be explained to the child as well as the means of correction by using the Word of God as a guide. Then it would be appropriate to include a prayer, asking God for forgiveness for the offense as well as thankfulness for the correctional instructions and power from the Holy Spirit to do right in the future.

Every disciplinary process should also be a learning process. This is how you discipline with love and purpose. This doesn't mean you have to explain every command to your child when you give it to him or her. Your child should learn to trust that what you are telling him or her is for the child's own good. I am talking about once an offense has been committed; you are instructing your child on how to correct the situation. Here are the steps:

1. Correct sinful behavior.
2. Explain what he or she did wrong.
3. Explain how to fix the problem.
4. Use the Bible as a guide.
5. Include prayer (teach our child to pray at a young age).

   a. Ask for forgiveness.
   b. Thank the Lord for corrective instructions.
   c. Pray for strength to resist the temptation.

6. End with a summary to ensure the lesson was understood.

   "If you beat him with a rod he shall not die" (Prov. 23:13).

I feel as though I should elaborate somewhat on the terminology concerning the words *beating* and *rod* since these terms could be interpreted as being abusive. That is not what they mean, so I will illustrate this for you. The word *beat* is translated from the Hebrew word *nakah* (naw-kaw), which means to smite or strike. I know in English we think of beating as excessive hitting or bashing; this is not what is being said here. The word *rod* comes from the Hebrew word *shebet* (shay-bet), which means a stick or a board used for discipline.

1. Use an instrument designed for this purpose.
   I believe what this means is a board designed to be used to administer punishment. Punishment is not abusive; therefore, the instrument used to punish shouldn't cause damage to the body. Discipline is slightly painful and uncomfortable but not harmful or torturous. Discipline is meant to be used for correction, not retribution. Based on this premise, the instrument or rod should be designed to accomplish this goal. My own design consists of a board; it

is around sixteen inches in length by five inches in width. It has a handle at one end, which is approximately six inches long and one and one-half inches wide. In the large part of the board, there are holes, approximately one-half inch in diameter, that are around three inches apart from one end to the other. The holes are designed to let the air escape when the rod strikes the target. This causes the rod to distribute the strike across a wide, even area; it results in a sting to the area but no damage to the body. Using these dimensions creates a fairly wide area and so the board appears to be too big but the larger the area of contact the less likely it is to cause injury.

2. Remember the best target for discipline.

I believe the rear end is the best target because it is designed with a significant amount of cushion. My daddy used to make us grab our ankles; this is probably a good idea. First, it helps to provide a clearly defined target since you don't want to strike the child on the legs or back. Second, the time necessary for the child to assume the position gives the parent a moment to regain a proper attitude and climate for proper discipline. It also tightens the clothes around the target, making the strike more effective. If done properly, this technique results in correction, not abuse. The way corporal punishment is depicted in today's society it is not even comfortable to talk about it but according to God's Word it is needed.

3. Avoid inappropriate instruments.

In my opinion, a narrow board, limb, or switch is an inappropriate instrument for this task because it can break blood vessels and result in damage to the body, such as bruises, welts, and cuts. Any other instruments that have these same negative results are also inappropriate; these would include ropes, extension cords, wires, hoses, fishing rods, and narrow leather straps and belts. If it causes physical harm to the body, it doesn't result in what we are trying to accomplish, and it should be considered abuse.

I would also like to add that using your hand is not the best idea either. This is because you can cause physical harm to your hand and the child, if you're not careful; it also causes the child to associate you, the parent, with the punishment. If your child is close to you, does he or she act like he or she is about to be attacked when you raise your hand? If so, this is because you or someone else has used a hand to administer punishment. You don't want your child to associate you with discipline. You don't want your child to be scared of you. You can see this type of reaction from women and children who have come out of abusive relationships as well as any animal that has been abused. Your child should respect you but not fear you.

4. Use discipline for the right reason.

Remember, we want children to understand that they are being punished because of their actions, not because Mom or Dad is mad at them. The whole idea is to teach them that sinful behavior results in punishment. This is true with parents, police, judges, government authorities, and God.

5. Avoid disciplining other people's children.

The last thing I want to mention about discipline is that you should never use corporal punishment on other people's children, even if you have the parents' permission. No two people administer this type of discipline the same way, and this situation could end up causing you to lose a friend or something worse. Children also don't always tell the truth about what happened, and parents may take their word over yours.

David Boudreaux

The Leather Rear

By the time I went to high school, I had been disciplined by corporal punishment so often that I had a leather posterior. In my freshman year, I enrolled in a class called Future Farmers of America, often referred to as the FFA. When you join this organization for the first year, you are called a greenhorn. When I was a greenhorn, I had to go through certain traditional treatments or tests by the upper classmen, called "initiation." One of those traditions was taking swats on the rear from each of the upper classmen. It didn't take any time at all for me to gain the reputation of having a leather rear, although that's not exactly how they said it.

Anyhow, once the president of the local chapter heard about my reputation, he decided he had to break me. So he took it upon himself to prove that nobody was tough enough to take the swats he could deliver. He was a huge guy and very muscular, so even though I had received all the preconditioning for the task at hand that anyone could have, he was a bit intimidating. As the most daunting task approached, I believe the anticipation was worse than the event. When he finally got me out in the woods with all my other classmates, everyone knew this would be the ideal time for the testing of the leather rear end.

He had me grab my ankles; that was funny because it was just how my dad always did it. Then he reared back and took his best shot. I think I probably came off the ground and landed about three feet forward from where I had been. I turned around, looked at him, and said something like, "Wow, you must have slipped or something. I know a big guy like you can do better than that. Are you sure you don't want another shot?"

My response surprised him, and he took it as another even more severe challenge than before. So I resumed the position and bit my lip. This time I think he wound up like a baseball pitcher at the World Series. When that paddle made contact with my leather rear, it sounded to me like it could have been heard throughout the

260

state of Texas. I flew even farther. After I regained my balance and composure, I turned, looked at him, smiled, and said, "Seriously? Is that all you got?" At that point, the tears were on the edge of my eyes, but I wasn't about to give in now.

He grinned back at me and said, "Okay, I give up. You do indeed have a leather rear, and I think you must be the toughest person I've ever met. From now on, no one touches this guy; if they do and I hear about it, they will have to answer to me." He and I became best friends after that day.

Celebrating Holidays Using Pagan Traditions

There is one other area I would like to discuss. That is the celebration of holidays and traditions. I think honesty is always the best policy, but I find little harm in celebrating holidays in a traditional fashion. Regardless of what I say about these traditions, most people won't totally agree. Funny thing is, some will say I am too liberal with this topic, while others will say I'm too conservative. I'm not trying to present absolutes in this discussion; I'm simply telling you how I feel about it.

1. ChristmasTrees

    We know that the Christmas tree came from a heathen form of worship; the tree represented the heavens, and the globes and lights represented the planets and the stars to be worshipped. If we still looked at the tree that way, it would still be false worship and therefore be sinful, but I have never been in a home at Christmas time where the family worshipped the Christmas tree. This is merely a traditional part of the Christmas celebration and has nothing to do with worship. It's important for you as a parent to make sure your children worship our Savior, and that is what Christmas is for.

Hear ye the word which the LORD speaketh unto you, O house of Israel: Thus saith the LORD, Learn not the way of the heathen, and be not dismayed at the signs of heaven; for the heathen are dismayed at them. For the customs of the people are vain: for one cutteth a tree out of the forest, the work of the hands of the workman, with the axe. They deck it with silver and with gold; they fasten it with nails and with hammers, that it move not. They are upright as the palm tree, but speak not: they must needs be borne, because they cannot go. Be not afraid of them; for they cannot do evil, neither also is it in them to do good. Forasmuch as there is none like unto thee, O LORD; thou art great, and thy name is great in might. (Jer. 10:1–6)

Even though this verse clearly says we shouldn't do what the heathens do with trees, I think God is saying not to use them as items of worship. A tree is nothing spiritually speaking. Pay no attention to the signs from the heavens (astrology?). They make it stand upright, but it can't speak. They have to be carried because they can't walk. Don't be afraid of them because they aren't capable of doing good or evil. An idol is nothing unless you choose to worship it; then it becomes a tool of the devil.

2. Easter

We know that the symbols found around the celebration of Easter, the egg and the rabbit, are simply symbols of fertility originally used in the worship of the goddess of fertility. Yet again, I have never been in a home where these symbols represented anything concerning worship. They are just traditional representations of the Easter holiday, which celebrates the resurrection of our Lord Jesus. I have heard some Catholics explain these symbols by saying they represent Jesus breaking out of the tomb like a newborn chick breaks out of an egg. That may be how some view it, but that doesn't explain the rabbit. The only explanation concerning a rabbit is they are one of the most fertile animals in the world. I have heard others say they represent new life such as the spiritual life one receives at salvation. That may be a good way to express it to your children.

3. Halloween

Then there is Halloween. This holiday's origins also stem from heathen worship practices, but today it's just a way for children to go out and have fun. I don't see people teaching their children to worship the devil, skeletons, or witches because of this tradition. It's up to the parents to teach their children about these holidays and what they are about. If Halloween is being used to teach about false gods or idolatry, then it is obviously wrong. If your pastor preaches against these things, I can't say he is wrong, but if your children are hearing one thing at church and another at home, you may have to answer some questions. I believe that if you are going to let your children participate in these types of events, you should explain to them about spirits and witches when they are old enough to comprehend. The forces of evil are real and if you believe in good spirits then you must believe in evil spirits as well. Teach your children that evil spirits and witches are from the devil. Even the so-called white witch is from Satan.

4. Santa Claus

Now, what about Santa Clause? Again, I think it's best to tell the truth from the beginning by telling your child that gifts come from God.

He sees you when you're sleeping
He knows when you're awake
He knows if you've been bad or good

Doesn't this sound like God? On the other hand, as long as children learn about Jesus and what Christmas is for, I don't see a problem with Santa. I have been known to dress up as Santa a few times myself. It is for the kids to have fun and has nothing to do with worship. Sometimes there isn't a right answer. Some will tell you that you shouldn't let your kids participate in any of these traditions. I can't fault them for their stand, but for me it is a preference and not a conviction as long as we're not teaching our children false worship or idolatry. If you don't want them to understand about Santa then you are going to have a hard time explaining it to them when Santa is everywhere at Christmas time every year. Yes I know if you move the letters around Santa spells Satan and he could represent that if you let him but as a parent you have the responsibility to teach your children about the truth.

5. Trick-or-Treating

Should you allow your children to go trick-or-treating? I think if they have an alternative such as church event, that would be a better choice. This is not only because this is a celebration of a pagan event (All Souls Day) but also because the world is full of evil people who cannot be trusted. People use these events to kidnap children, poison candy, or put razor blades in it. We still live in an evil world that gets worse every year.

Is trick-or-treating a sin? I will leave that up to your conscience to decide. If you can't participate in it with a clear conscience then it is wrong for you. I will tell you that some of my fondest memories as a child are celebrating holidays such as Thanksgiving and Christmas, when all my dad's relatives came over. We had more food than we could eat and more kids to play with. I also remember Halloween and the old couple who lived down the street and made candy apples every year. They had these two wiener dogs that were so fat that they looked like sausages with four tiny toothpicks sticking out of the bottom. They didn't walk like normal dogs; they waddled.

I'm glad I have those memories, which have nothing to do with idolatry. I would hate for my children and grandchildren to miss experiences because of silly superstitions, but I don't want them to be in any situation where they are influenced to do evil or are in danger.

6. Mardi Gras

This holiday is a whole new kind of creature to deal with. It isn't even really a holiday. If you know anything about this French tradition, you won't want you or your kids anywhere near it. Mardi Gras is straight out of the Catholic faith and began in the medieval times in Italy and France. The words *Mardi Gras* are French for "Fat Tuesday." Mardi Gras refers to the ritualistic eating and celebration of all the things that aren't good for you in preparation for the forty days of fasting during Lent. In some places, this event is also known as "Shrove Tuesday" or "Pancake Day."

As I said, this tradition started with the celebration or feasting leading up to the forty days of fasting before Ash Wednesday. Today it's just a place to go drink too much alcohol, throw beads, and seek out the opportunity to misbehave and see nudity. It's strange how what started as a so-called Christian tradition before religious periods of sanctification has become so perverted. This is a tool the devil uses to misguide people who are seeking God. Be careful concerning religious traditions and holidays.

Follow Your Conscience

"To him that knoweth to do good and doeth it not, to him it is sin" (James 4:17).

If celebrating these holidays in this fashion makes you have a guilty conscience before God, then you shouldn't celebrate them, and you shouldn't let your children do so. If celebrating these holidays doesn't make you feel guilty, then it's up to you. Many churches are now offering alternatives to some of the traditional celebrations, especially Halloween. I think this is a good idea. It gives the kids a good way to celebrate the holiday so they don't feel left out, and it provides them with an opportunity to spend more time with fellow Christians.

Many good Christian books are out there on how to raise and discipline children. I have just given you a few tips here, but if you need help in these areas, please consider the following resources: *Dare to Discipline* and *The Strong-Willed Child* by Dr. James Dobson of the organization Focus on the Family. I also recommend *How to Rear Children* by the late Dr. Jack Hyles of the First Baptist Church in Hammond, Indiana.

CHAPTER 10

Marriage and Substance Abuse

One of the Most Common Causes of Marital Disputes

There is obviously no way I can think of every possibility that can go wrong in a marriage, but I can cover some of the most common situations and hopefully give some scriptural advice concerning them. One of the most common causes of marital problems in today's society is the same as what also causes problems among single people. That makes sense because most marital problems begin with one of the partners in the marriage doing something or getting involved in something that either is unacceptable to the other partner under any circumstances or grows into something that becomes excessive.

I think I've mentioned before that one definition of sin could be the loss of control. The Bible teaches that Christians shouldn't allow anything to control them. Even though we Christians have been delivered from the condemnation of the law, which makes all things legal for us, it doesn't make all things beneficial for us, and we shouldn't allow them to control our behavior. When you abandon this primary principle, it generally ends up in sin. Most of you have probably already figured out where I'm going with this. "And such were some of you: but ye are washed, but ye are sanctified, but ye are justified in the name of the Lord Jesus, and by the Spirit of our God.

All things are lawful unto me, but all things are not expedient: all things are lawful for me, but I will not be brought under the power of any" (1 Cor. 6:11–12).

Drug and Alcohol Abuse

The first situation I want to talk about is drug and alcohol abuse. Today more than ever before, drugs and alcohol are having a tremendous effect on our everyday lives. Just yesterday I heard that overdose related deaths are now the number one cause of death in young Americans. It has even exceeded the deaths caused by car accidents for the first time in history. Since alcohol is a drug and the Bible speaks mostly about alcohol, we will treat them the same. Keep in mind that drugs, for the most part, are illegal, but alcohol is not. Whether it should or shouldn't be is another discussion for another time, but for now, drugs are illegal, and that is another reason to abstain. We are taught as Christians that we should obey the laws of the land. After studying the Word of God extensively concerning the use of alcohol, I believe it can essentially be divided into four major categories: celebration, degradation, dedication, and separation. We will also briefly discuss two additional minor subtopics, medication and explanation. Whether God requires complete abstinence depends on which of these categories you place yourself in.

Celebration

The first category is celebration. In the Old Testament, the word *wine* is the Hebrew word *yayin* (yah'-yin), which means effervesce or fermented fruit of the vine. In the New Testament, the equivalent word in the Greek is *oinos* (oy'-nos). Contrary to what I have heard some say, this is fermented wine, not just grape juice. This is the word used to describe the water Jesus turned into wine at the wedding party.

And when they wanted wine, the mother of Jesus saith unto him, They have no wine. Jesus saith unto her, Woman, what have I to do with thee? mine hour is not yet come. His mother saith unto the servants, Whatsoever he saith unto you, do it. And there were set there six waterpots of stone, after the manner of the purifying of the Jews, containing two or three firkins apiece. Jesus saith unto them, Fill the waterpots with water. And they filled them up to the brim. And he saith unto them, Draw out now, and bear unto the governor of the feast. And they bare it. When the ruler of the feast had tasted the water that was made wine, and knew not whence it was: (but the servants which drew the water knew;) the governor of the feast called the bridegroom, And saith unto him, Every man at the beginning doth set forth good wine; and when men have well drunk, then that which is worse: but thou hast kept the good wine until now. This beginning of miracles did Jesus in Cana of Galilee, and manifested forth his glory; and his disciples believed on him. (John 2:3–11)

The wine was used to celebrate the wedding. It was symbolic of God's blessings, prosperity, and approval. The fact that this was Jesus' first miracle alone tells me there is nothing wrong with the growth of grapes, including the processing and the distribution of alcohol in itself. If used properly, it is acceptable to God.

What was the purpose of recording this event in the Bible? Jesus had only recently selected His apostles, and at the time they had no physical way to know He was the Son of God. They had proved their faith by dropping everything and following Him blindly, and now Jesus was going to show them proof. This was when He manifested (showed them) His glory (deity), and this was when they believed in Him totally.

When Jacob (Israel) Gave His Blessing to Judah

> Judah, thou art he whom thy brethren shall praise: thy hand shall be in the neck of thine enemies; thy father's children shall bow down before thee. Judah is a lion's whelp: from the prey, my son, thou art gone up: he stooped down, he couched as a lion, and as an old lion; who shall rouse him up? The sceptre shall not depart from Judah, nor a lawgiver from between his feet, until Shiloh come; and unto him shall the gathering of the people be. Binding his foal unto the vine, and his ass's colt unto the choice vine; he washed his garments in wine, and his clothes in the blood of grapes: His eyes shall be red with wine, and his teeth white with milk. (Gen. 49:8–12)

The children of Israel were to tithe ten percent of their blessings or increase from God; this included the tithe of the wine, which was considered a blessing or gift from God.

> And thou shalt eat before the LORD thy God, in the place which he shall choose to place his name there, the tithe of thy corn, of thy wine, and of thine oil, and the firstlings of thy herds and of thy flocks; that thou mayest learn to fear the LORD thy God always. And if the way be too long for thee, so that thou art not able to carry it; or if the place be too far from thee, which the LORD thy God shall choose to set his name there, when the LORD thy God hath blessed thee: Then shalt thou

turn it into money, and bind up the money in thine hand, and shalt go unto the place which the LORD thy God shall choose: And thou shalt bestow that money for whatsoever thy soul lusteth after, for oxen, or for sheep, or for wine, or for strong drink, or for whatsoever thy soul desireth: and thou shalt eat there before the LORD thy God, and thou shalt rejoice, thou, and thine household, (Deut. 14:23–26)

God is given credit here for actually being the One who produces wine to make man have a glad heart. "He causeth the grass to grow for the cattle, and herb for the service of man: that he may bring forth food out of the earth; And wine that maketh glad the heart of man, and oil to make his face to shine, and bread which strengtheneth man's heart" (Ps. 104:14–15).

See these additional references: 2 Samuel 13:28; Esther 1:10; Psalm 4:7; Proverbs 3:10.

All these verses indicate that God intended humankind to use alcohol to celebrate how God had blessed them. I will have to say that this isn't what I expected to find when I began my personal study concerning the use of alcohol. I have seen so many people, marriages, and families destroyed by alcohol that I thought I would find definitive, conclusive evidence in God's Word that men shouldn't ever partake in its consumption, but that isn't what I found. Even though alcohol in itself is obviously not condemned by God, the terms and conditions of its use are clearly defined in the categories that follow.

Alcohol Abuse Leads to Loss

Many years ago before I started my own business, I worked for a company that repaired aircraft components in a shop. When I was there, I knew a man who was very fond of his drink; and on numerous occasions, it seemed to cause problems for him and his family. He had a grown son I knew who had the same problem. Both of these men were my friends, and we spent a lot of time together.

One weekend the son decided he wanted to attend a gathering with me. There was plenty of social drinking going on, but the young man, just like his father, had trouble knowing when he needed to stop. When I began to see there was going to be a problem, I asked him for the keys to his car, and he gave them to me. Later in the evening, he became out of control. He made a very snide remark to one of the ladies there that irritated her husband. Her husband was a great guy, but he was big, strong, and not someone you wanted angry at you.

The young man was too drunk to know what he was doing, but it was obvious to everyone else there. He continued to stir up trouble, and the big guy was really getting angry. I told the young man he needed to stop talking before he got himself in a jam, but he got mad and demanded his keys. This put me in a precarious situation because this was my friend's son, but I refused to give him the keys, and he became furious. He came at me, declaring that he would take his keys away from me no matter what it took, so I slapped him across the face. He sat back down in his chair and remained quiet until he fell asleep.

I had solved the current crisis, but I was concerned about what would happen when he told his dad what I had done. I waited for the shoe to drop the whole following week, but life went on as normal like nothing had ever happened. After about a week, I found an opportunity when I was alone with the father. I asked him whether his son had said anything to him about what had happened over that weekend. He said no; he hadn't said anything. Then he asked me what had happened. I told him the whole story and waited for a bad reaction. This is what he said: "It's about time somebody put that boy in his place." None of us ever mentioned the event again.

I could tell many other stories like this as I'm sure most of you can as well. Alcohol and drug abuse are very large issues in America, and the problem is getting bigger every day. This shouldn't be the case among Christians. I'm not criticizing these individuals who have fallen into this snare of the devil. They are victims. But this is such an easy trap to fall into, and many people are genetically more susceptible to the addiction than others. If you are one of those people who are susceptible to this snare, then you should take proper precautions to avoid it.

Degradation

1. Alcohol provided the occasion to allow sin.

   The misuse of alcohol has very early beginnings in the Bible and has resulted in the degradation of moral character and personal standards or prohibitions since the beginning. In this first example, we will look at Noah, whom we all know as a great man of God. He was used in an amazing way to save all mankind when God destroyed all life with the flood. Yet through the use of alcohol, Noah became an instrument of sin. After God blessed him following the flood, He used the blessings as an occasion to celebrate by drinking wine. We saw in the verses we just looked at that drinking to celebrate God's blessings to the point of having a glad heart is not a sin. Noah went too far with the wine, however, and got drunk and passed out.

   Because of this drunkenness, he was unaware of his surroundings and was passed out drunk on his bed. This situation allowed his son Ham to see his nakedness, which resulted in the curse on Canaan. (In the Bible, the words "to uncover one's nakedness" normally means there was a sexual sin committed.) In this situation, alcohol didn't directly cause the sin, which Ham committed, but it did cause the conditions leading to the sin. The alcohol made Noah vulnerable.

I believe this is an illustration to us that if we go to a celebration, even with no ill intent, and allow ourselves to go too far with strong drink, we may open an opportunity for sin to be the end result. When a husband or wife starts out with a small drink to celebrate or relax, it may be all innocent at first. But if they aren't able to stop with just a drink or two, it often ends up turning into spousal abuse or worse. Ladies, when you go out and celebrate with your friends and allow yourselves to go too far with alcohol, you put yourselves in a position of vulnerability. The definition of *vulnerable* is susceptible to physical or emotional attack or harm.

And the sons of Noah, that went forth of the ark, were Shem, and Ham, and Japheth: and Ham is the father of Canaan. These are the three sons of Noah: and of them was the whole earth overspread. And Noah began to be an husbandman, and he planted a vineyard: And he drank of the wine, and was drunken; and he was uncovered within his tent. And Ham, the father of Canaan, saw the nakedness of his father, and told his two brethren without. And Shem and Japheth took a garment, and laid it upon both their shoulders, and went backward, and covered the nakedness of their father; and their faces were backward, and they saw not their father's nakedness. And Noah awoke from his wine, and knew what his younger son had done unto him. And he said, Cursed be Canaan; a servant of

servants shall he be unto his brethren. And he said,
Blessed be the LORD God of Shem; and Canaan
shall be his servant. (Gen. 9:18–26)

2. Alcohol was used to intentionally deceive Lot, resulting
    in sin.

    The second example involves the daughters of Lot,
    Abraham's brother's son, who was also a God-fearing
    man and was saved from the destruction of Sodom and
    Gomorrah along with his two daughters. He was also
    deceived by alcohol. In this example, however, alcohol
    was used specifically for this purpose. The daughters of
    Lot, believing their father's bloodline would end with his
    passing, devised a plan to get their father drunk and take
    advantage of him to get pregnant. Being a man of God, Lot
    would never have gone along with this plan, but apparently
    the daughters didn't care about that. This was the use of
    alcohol with the intent of taking advantage of someone.
    This is the same as using what they call a date rape drug or
    intentionally getting someone drunk with the intentions of
    taking advantage of them.

    I believe in both of these cases that the persons who
    became drunk were the victims. One caused himself to
    become vulnerable by abusing the alcohol on his own,
    and the other became vulnerable by putting himself in a
    position where someone else could take advantage of him.
    I'm not suggesting in any way that when someone gets taken
    advantage of that he or she brought it upon themselves. I'm
    just pointing out the fact that we should be aware of our
    surroundings and be careful of what situations we allow
    ourselves to be put in and what kind of people we hang
    out with. But most of all, we should be aware of how much
    alcohol or other drugs we allow to influence us.

    If you have enough alcohol in your system that it makes

you unaware of your surroundings, makes you lower your moral standards, or causes you to allow people to influence you to do what you normally wouldn't do, then you have exceeded what is considered acceptable to God. If so, then you went too far. As for drugs, they are used in the same way. The main difference between drugs and alcohol is the fact that several drinks are needed to get in this condition, but it may take only a very small amount of drugs to have the same effect. Incidentally, this verse also proves that it's possible for a man to be raped. Many people think it's impossible for a man to be raped, but that isn't true.

This is just a side note, but I mentioned that this happened after Sodom and Gomorrah were destroyed due to their immorality. Could it be that Lot's daughters had been influenced toward evil thinking because of the place where they grew up and the people they had been exposed to? It's also interesting to note that Ham, Noah's son, took advantage of him right after God destroyed every living thing off the face of the earth because of sin and corruption. Incidental? I don't think so! Just saying.

And Lot went up out of Zoar, and dwelt in the mountain, and his two daughters with him; for he feared to dwell in Zoar: and he dwelt in a cave, he and his two daughters. And the firstborn said unto the younger, Our father is old, and there is not a man in the earth to come in unto us after the manner of all the earth: Come, let us make our father drink wine, and we will lie with him, that we may preserve seed of our father. And they made their father drink wine that night: and the firstborn went in, and lay with her father; and he perceived not when she lay down, nor when she arose. And it came to pass on the morrow, that the firstborn said unto the younger, Behold, I lay yesternight with my father: let us make him drink wine this night also; and go thou in, and lie with him, that we may preserve seed of our father. And they made their father drink wine that night also: and the younger arose, and lay with him; and he perceived not when she lay down, nor when she arose. Thus were both the daughters of Lot with child by their father. And the first born bare a son, and called his name Moab: the same is the father of the Moabites unto this day. And the younger, she also bare a son, and called his name Benammi: the same is the father of the children of Ammon unto this day. (Gen. 19:30–38)

3. Alcohol was used to steal what rightfully belonged to someone else.

In Genesis 27:23–29, Jacob used alcohol to deceive his father Isaac, so he could steal his brother's blessing. In Proverbs 4:14–17, alcohol is associated with evil and violence. In Proverbs 20:1, alcohol is described as a deceiver (mocker) and being unwise. In Isaiah 28:7, it is associated with poor judgment. In Isaiah 5:11–17, it is associated with destruction.

Who hath woe? who hath sorrow? who hath contentions? who hath babbling? who hath wounds without cause? who hath redness of eyes? They that tarry long at the wine; they that go to seek mixed wine. Look not thou upon the wine when it is red, when it giveth his colour in the cup, when it moveth itself aright. At the last it biteth like a serpent, and stingeth like an adder. Thine eyes shall behold strange women, and thine heart shall utter perverse things. Yea, thou shalt be as he that lieth down in

the midst of the sea, or as he that lieth upon the top
of a mast. They have stricken me, shalt thou say,
and I was not sick; they have beaten me, and I felt
it not: when shall I awake? I will seek it yet again.
(Prov. 23:29–35)

Have you ever seen a better description of an alcoholic?
Who ends up sorrowful? Who starts conflicts? Who says
things that don't make sense? Who gets hurt all the time
for no reason? Who gets lured by the harlot? Who utters
vulgarity? Who placed himself or herself in harm's way?
Who feels sick when there is nothing wrong with him or
her? Who takes a beating and feels no pain? Who after all
that, when he or she wakes up, even knowing what is going
to happen, seeks it yet again?

4. Alcohol was used to medically treat someone (medication).

In the following verses, alcohol could be considered a
use of medication due to the dire circumstances described.
I don't believe this qualifies as a major category, however,
because, especially today, there are other resources available
to assist people in these areas. What most people fail to
recognize is the fact that alcohol is a depressant. It may
make you have a merry heart for a short time, but the result
leaves you worse off than when you started. "It is not for
kings, O Lemuel, it is not for kings to drink wine; nor
for princes strong drink: Lest they drink, and forget the
law, and pervert the judgment of any of the afflicted. Give
strong drink unto him that is ready to perish, and wine unto
those that be of heavy hearts. Let him drink, and forget his
poverty, and remember his misery no more" (Prov. 31:4–7).

I used to object to the use of drugs in any sort of way, but in light
of what the scripture says here, perhaps it does have its proper use.
According to these verses, the legal use of drugs to treat people for

depression could be considered legitimate. I think this would need to be clinically diagnosed depression and the drugs would need to be prescribed by a doctor with specific terms of use. It is a fact that the recreational use of marijuana usually leads to other more addictive drug use. This verse describes these people as being ready to perish. (This is someone who is depressed to the point of being suicidal or perhaps terminally ill and ready to die.) It also says for those who are of a heavy heart. (This could be someone who suffered a major loss in his or her life and desperately needed some relief from mental anguish.) This can be caused by the death of a loved one or maybe even a great loss during a divorce. Finally, it refers to those who suffer from excessive poverty or misery. This could be someone who is starving to death, and there is no one to help him or her survive or someone who is in misery for some other reason.

Alcohol and or other drugs can help people in certain situations, but these situations should be considered necessary medical treatments, with alcohol or drugs being properly distributed and monitored. Alcohol and drugs, like most other things in life, can be used for good. Unfortunately, they can also be abused, and that is when they cause sinful behavior. In any case, though anyone can fall victim to these adverse situations, hopefully this doesn't describe the physical or mental condition of most Christians. I think it's interesting that the verse says those who are "ready to perish." To perish means to suffer everlasting death or cease to exist in the presence of God. Christians, according to God's Word, don't perish. They are asleep in Christ until the resurrection.

Dedication

The third category I will talk about concerning wine is the abstinence of it altogether for those who want to serve God to the fullest of their potential. In reality, this isn't a category of the use of wine but rather a condition for those who have chosen a life dedicated to serving

God. These people were to abstain from strong drink either for the length of their commitment or for their entire lives if they were dedicated to God for life. At the very least, they weren't allowed to be under the influence of it while performing the duties of God.

"And the LORD spake unto Aaron, saying, Do not drink wine nor strong drink, thou, nor thy sons with thee, when ye go into the tabernacle of the congregation, lest ye die: it shall be a statute for ever throughout your generations: And that ye may put difference between holy and unholy, and between unclean and clean; And that ye may teach the children of Israel all the statutes which the LORD hath spoken unto them by the hand of Moses" (Lev. 10:8–11).

1. Alcohol distorts sound judgment.

    At the very least, this verse is saying two things. One, you shouldn't use alcohol when doing God's work. Two, the use of alcohol distorts and often perverts sound judgment. Some would go on to say that this verse is saying that alcohol is unholy and unclean.
2. Alcohol was forbidden for those dedicated to God's work.

    The vow of a Nazarite included the abstinence of alcohol or strong drink altogether.

    And the LORD spake unto Moses, saying, Speak unto the children of Israel, and say unto them, When either man or woman shall separate themselves to vow a vow of a Nazarite, to separate themselves unto the LORD: He shall separate himself from wine and strong drink, and shall drink no vinegar of wine, or vinegar of strong drink, neither shall he drink any liquor of grapes, nor eat moist grapes, or dried. All the days of his separation shall he eat nothing that is made of the vine tree, from the kernels even to the husk. All the days of the vow of his separation there shall no razor come upon his head: until the days be fulfilled, in the which he separateth himself unto the LORD, he shall be holy, and shall let the locks of the hair of his head grow. All the days that he separateth himself unto the LORD he shall come at no dead body. He shall not make himself unclean for his father, or for his mother, for his brother, or for his sister, when they die: because the consecration of his God is upon his head. All the days of his separation he is holy unto the LORD. (Num. 6:1–8; see additional references: Judg. 13:1–5; 1 Sam. 1:11–18)

3. John the Baptist was filled with the Holy Spirit and forbidden to drink wine.

Even though we are never told that John the Baptist was a Nazarite, he was separated to do God's work from the womb; therefore, he was never to drink wine or strong drink.

"But the angel said unto him, Fear not, Zacharias: for thy prayer is heard; and thy wife Elisabeth shall bear thee a son, and thou shalt call his name John. And thou shalt have joy and gladness; and many shall rejoice at his birth. For he shall be great in the sight of the Lord, and shall drink neither wine nor strong drink; and he shall be filled with the Holy Ghost, even from his mother's womb" (Luke 1:13–15).

4. There is a difference between *filled* and *indwelt*.

The word *filled* in this last verse, which is talking about John the Baptist being filled with the Holy Spirit, is the Greek word *ple-tho* (play-tho). which means imbue, influence, supply, or furnish. On more than one occasion, we are told the influence of alcohol should be replaced by the influence of the Holy Spirit. The Holy Spirit not only influences our behavior as Christians but also supplies or furnishes the Christian with the gifts or abilities he or she needs to accomplish the things God tells him or her to do. The obvious conclusion then is that God cannot use you if you are being controlled by alcohol instead of by the Spirit, and it seems to suggest you cannot be controlled by both at the same time.

It isn't possible to serve God without being influenced by the Holy Spirit, so where does that leave us? We need to understand that being filled with the Holy Spirit isn't the same thing as being indwelt by the Holy Spirit. The Holy Spirit didn't indwell (live inside) Christians until after the ascension of Jesus Christ into heaven. Before the ascension, Jesus' followers and the Old Testament saints were filled (influenced) with the Holy Spirit without being indwelt by the Holy Spirit. Likewise, we can be indwelt by the Holy Spirit and not be filled or influenced by Him. Yes, I am saying we can be indwelt by the Holy Spirit and still be under the influence of the devil. We cannot be possessed by the devil if we are saved, but we can be oppressed by him. This is because the Holy Spirit doesn't control the believer. We must submit to His influence as I have mentioned before. "The spirit of the prophets are subject to the prophets" (1 Cor. 14:32).

5. The use of wine is associated with a lack of wisdom.

    "Wherefore be ye not unwise, but understanding what the will of the Lord is. And be not drunk with wine, wherein is excess; but be filled with the Spirit" (Eph. 5:17–18).

These verses point to a clear contrast between wine and the lack of wisdom as opposed to the Holy Spirit and knowing the will of God. Which do you prefer to have in your life?

Separation

The final category is that of separation or sanctification. God says, "Be ye Holy for I AM Holy" (1 Peter 1:16).We are told that as Christians we should abstain from all appearance of evil, and some people obviously believe Christians shouldn't drink.

1. Be ye holy (it is a command).

    "Wherefore gird up the loins of your mind, be sober, and hope to the end for the grace that is to be brought unto you at the revelation of Jesus Christ; As obedient children, not fashioning yourselves according to the former lusts in your ignorance: But as he which hath called you is holy, so be ye holy in all manner of conversation; Because it is written, Be ye holy; for I am holy" (1 Peter 1:13–16).

    "In all manner of conversation" means in all areas of your life. *Holy* means separated from sin, pure.

2. Abstain from all appearance of evil.

    "Prove all things; hold fast that which is good. Abstain from all appearance of evil. And the very God of peace sanctify you wholly; and I pray God your whole spirit and soul and body be preserved blameless unto the coming of our Lord Jesus Christ" (1Thess. 5:21–23).

3. Don't do anything that would offend a brother.

    We are also told that we shouldn't do anything that would cause a weaker brother to stumble. Even if we think or know there is nothing unclean for a Christian, it may not be a wise thing to do.

I know, and am persuaded by the Lord Jesus, that there is nothing unclean of itself: but to him that esteemeth any thing to be unclean, to him it is unclean. But if thy brother be grieved with thy meat, now walkest thou not charitably. Destroy not him with thy meat, for whom Christ died. Let not then your good be evil spoken of: For the kingdom of God is not meat and drink; but righteousness, and peace, and joy in the Holy Ghost. For he that in these things serveth Christ is acceptable to God, and approved of men. Let us therefore follow after the things which make for peace, and things wherewith one may edify another. For meat destroy not the work of God. All things indeed are pure; but it is evil for that man who eateth with offence. It is good neither to eat flesh, nor to drink wine, nor any thing whereby thy brother stumbleth, or is offended, or is made weak. (Rom. 14:14–21)

While I have a hard time finding any scripture that completely demands the abstinence of alcohol use in the New Testament, it does seem to agree with the Old Testament, in that the circumstances where it is allowed seem to be extremely limited. It is also obvious to me at this point that Christian service and alcohol don't mix. The scriptures make it clear that we shouldn't be under the influence of anything except the Holy Spirit; therefore, getting drunk is out of the question. That being said, while it may take a significant amount of alcohol to be influenced by it (by "influenced" I mean allowing it to alter our behavior), it normally takes only a small amount of other drugs to have the same effect.

I find it interesting that un-prescribed drug use is against federal law, but many states are passing state laws to legalize drugs, and no one does anything about it. On the other hand, the state of Texas passed a law to restrict abortions to save lives, which is contrary to federal law, and President Biden and his State Department filed a lawsuit against the state for breaking federal law. It seems to me that this is someone who isn't as much interested in righteousness as in popularity. Thank God that all this has backfired and resulted in the overturning of *Roe v. Wade*. We will talk about this more later.

A Bishop Shouldn't Be Given to Wine

Now I want to be specific about alcohol use among the clergy because this is where the Bible gets specific about it. In 1 Timothy the Bible teaches that a bishop (pastor) should "not be given to wine." Most theologians believe this means addicted to wine or that they shouldn't be alcoholics. I'm not sure that I totally agree with this translation because just a few verses later it says, in the same chapter, that a deacon should "not be given to much wine."

> A bishop then must be blameless, the husband of one wife, vigilant, sober, of good behaviour, given to hospitality, apt to teach; *Not given to wine*, no striker, not greedy of filthy lucre; but patient, not a brawler, not covetous; One that ruleth well his own house, having his children in subjection with all gravity; (For if a man know not how to rule his own house, how shall he take care of the church of God?) Not a novice, lest being lifted up with pride he fall into the condemnation of the devil. Moreover he must have a good report of them which are without; lest he fall into reproach and the snare of the devil. Likewise must the deacons be grave, not doubletongued, *not given to much wine*, not greedy of filthy lucre. (1 Tim. 3:2–8 emphasis added)

If "not given to wine" means not an alcoholic, then what does "not given to much wine" mean? At first, I thought there was no difference between the one statement and the other and that both are saying these men shouldn't be addicted to alcohol, but then I saw the same wording applied again in a different scripture, which leads me to believe that it doesn't mean the same thing. In the book of Titus, the Word of God says bishops should "not be given to wine" and aged women should "not be given to much wine."

> For a bishop must be blameless, as the steward of God; not selfwilled, not soon angry, *not given to wine*, no striker, not given to filthy lucre. (Titus 1:7 emphasis added)

> The aged women likewise, that they be in behaviour as becometh holiness, not false accusers, *not given to much wine*, teachers of good things. (Titus 2:3 emphasis added)

Now I may not be a great theologian with more degrees than a thermometer behind my name, but I do believe, "All scripture is given by inspiration of God, and is profitable for doctrine, for reproof, for correction, for instruction in righteousness:" (2 Tim. 3:16). Therefore, I don't believe this wording is coincidental. I believe it's saying in both instances that the pastor or bishop should be the one setting the example and has dedicated himself to God's service; therefore, God has a higher standard for him than for others. The pastor shouldn't drink alcohol at all. In these verses, the other two groups of people are the deacons in the church and the elderly women. Both of these groups are people whom others in the congregation may be looking up to, so they shouldn't allow alcohol to ever have enough influence over them to alter their behavior (get drunk), but they are not told to abstain altogether. By the way, in the verses above, the words "filthy lucre" simply mean dirty money.

Explanation

I'd like to address one other topic just briefly because I have heard other people use these verses to say God doesn't think there is anything wrong with drinking alcohol because He did it Himself. These following verses seem to suggest that even though John the Baptist didn't drink wine, apparently Jesus did. They say this for the following reasons:

1. Because He was called a glutton and a drunk

   "For John came neither eating nor drinking, and *they say*, He hath a devil. The Son of man came eating and drinking, and *they say*, Behold a man *gluttonous*, and a *winebibber*, a friend of publicans and sinners. But wisdom is justified of her children" (Matt. 11:18–19 emphasis added).

   I believe it becomes necessary here to point out that the scripture says that "they say." It was the scribes and Pharisees who said Jesus was a *winebibber and a glutton.* Since both of these terms suggest an overindulgence, or out-of-control eating and drinking, then we know this isn't true because one definition of sin is loss of control. This means the entire statement isn't true. We know Jesus was tempted in all areas just like we are, but He remained sinless (Heb. 4:15).They also accused Jesus of casting out devils by the power of Satan. That wasn't true either. This doesn't prove Jesus ever drank alcohol.

Then was brought unto him one possessed with a devil, blind, and dumb: and he healed him, insomuch that the blind and dumb both spake and saw. And all the people were amazed, and said, Is not this the son of David? But when the Pharisees heard it, they said, This fellow doth not cast out devils, but by Beelzebub the prince of the devils.

And Jesus knew their thoughts, and said unto them, Every kingdom divided against itself is brought to desolation; and every city or house divided against itself shall not stand: And if Satan cast out Satan, he is divided against himself; how shall then his kingdom stand? And if I by Beelzebub cast out devils, by whom do your children cast them out? therefore they shall be your judges. But if I cast out devils by the Spirit of God, then the kingdom of God is come unto you. (Matt. 12:22–28)

2. Because He turned water into wine and drank wine at the wedding

His mother saith unto the servants, Whatsoever he saith unto you, do it. And there were set there six waterpots of stone, after the manner of the purifying of the Jews, containing two or three firkins apiece. Jesus saith unto them, Fill the waterpots with water. And they filled them up to the brim. And he saith unto them, Draw out now, and bear unto the governor of the feast. And they bare it. When the ruler of the feast had tasted the water that was made wine, and knew not whence it was: (but the servants which drew the water knew;) the governor of the feast called the bridegroom, And saith unto him, Every man at the beginning doth set forth good wine; and when men have well drunk, then that which is worse: but thou hast kept the good wine until now. This beginning of miracles did Jesus in Cana of Galilee, and manifested forth his glory; and his disciples believed on him. (John 2:5–11)

I would admit that these verses seem to indicate that Jesus didn't have a problem with people drinking alcoholic beverages to celebrate special events. I don't disagree with this. I wouldn't go as far as to say that this proves Jesus consumed alcohol. The verses say He changed the water into wine and then had the servants take the wine to the governor of the feast. It doesn't say anywhere in these scriptures that Jesus drank wine. This would coincide with what we have already seen concerning anyone who desires to be filled with the Holy Spirit and used by God; he or she shouldn't drink at all. That doesn't mean he or she cannot be around anyone who does.

3. Because He drank wine at the Last Supper

"And he took the cup, and gave thanks, and gave it to them, saying, Drink ye all of it; For this is my blood of the new testament, which is shed for many for the remission of sins. But I say unto you, I will not drink henceforth of this fruit of the vine, until that day when I drink it new with you in my Father's kingdom" (Matt. 26:27–29).

At the Last Supper, Jesus offered the wine or "fruit of the vine" to His disciples and told them to drink it. First, "fruit of the vine" comes from Greek words that are interpreted to mean "offspring" or "product of." The offspring or product of the grape vine are grapes or grape juice in the unfermented state. Fermented wine is a different Greek word. Second, it says Jesus poured the fruit of the vine into the cup, gave it to His disciples, and told them to drink it. It doesn't say Jesus Himself drank it. Then, just to make it clear, He said He wouldn't drink the fruit of the vine (grape juice) until He was together with His disciples in the kingdom of God.

Again this scripture is telling us that Jesus didn't drink alcohol while here on earth, even though He didn't forbid it and didn't seem to have any problem being around those who did as long they didn't abuse it. When He said, "I will not drink henceforth," "henceforth" means at this time or after this time. I believe Jesus made it clear here that drinking alcohol was for special celebratory occasions and that He wouldn't be ready to celebrate until His disciples were with Him in His Father's kingdom, referring to the millennial reign or heaven. It will truly be a great day to celebrate when our Lord and Savior calls us home.

I think I should mention a couple of side points here. First, Catholics believe they actually change the wine (fermented drink) into the blood of Jesus Christ. They call it "transubstantiation." The Protestant religions use grape juice (fruit of the vine) and believe it is only symbolic of Jesus' blood.

4. Would it have been a sin if He had drank wine?

In conclusion, the Word of God teaches that Christians shouldn't drink alcohol in excess. "For the time past of our life may suffice us to have wrought the will of the Gentiles, when we walked in lasciviousness, lusts, excess of wine, revellings, banquetings, and abominable idolatries" (1 Peter 4:3).

This is the Greek word *oinophlugia* (oy-nof-loog-ee'-ah), which means overflow, surplus, or drunkenness. Now here is the answer to the question everyone wants to know the answer to. Since Jesus' first miracle was turning water into wine and the Pharisees called Him a glutton and a drunk, did Jesus ever drink alcohol? The Bible never says Jesus drank alcohol as far as I can see. The Pharisees called Him a lot of things because they were looking for reasons to condemn Him, and since His ministry was to the lost, those are whom He spent most of His time with. I do believe He turned water into an alcoholic beverage, but He didn't drink any of it. Would it have been a sin if He had? I guess that depends on each individual to decide for him or herself, and that is exactly why I don't think He did. As we saw in the verses above, He told His disciples He wouldn't drink of the fruit of the vine until they were with Him in heaven. He didn't say, "I will not drink of it *again*" until then. This leads me to believe He didn't drink it while He was here with us either.

Personally, because of my desire to be used by God in a significant way and the fact that I want to be influenced by the Holy Spirit rather than by the devil, I choose abstinence for myself. I do not, however, judge others who choose differently. Whatever is not of faith is sin, so if you can drink alcohol with a clear conscience, which is between you and God, just keep in mind that a Christian should never be under the influence of any alcohol or drugs unless it is for medical use, and then it should be done only legally.

I have included some statistics and facts concerning drug and alcohol use in the USA from an article by American Addiction Centers. "Alcoholism is an extremely serious problem in our world today that leads to approximately 88,000 deaths each year in the United States alone. Alcohol-related deaths are the fourth-leading preventable cause of death in the United States. So understanding the dangers and warning signs of addiction could make a big difference in reducing the risk of harm. It is also important that those addicted to alcohol and the ones who love them recognize the short- and long-term health effects associated with alcoholism." Following are some of the statistics from this article:[4]

---

[4] American Addiction Centers.

David Boudreaux

The Cost of Alcohol Addiction

In 2013, almost half of the 72,559 liver disease deaths, including those resulting specifically from cirrhosis of the liver, involved alcohol.

Excessive alcohol use results each year in approximately 2.5 million years of potential life lost or an average loss of thirty years for each fatality.

In 2010, more than 2.6 million hospitalizations were related to alcohol.

About one-third of deaths resulting from alcohol problems take the form of suicides and such accidents as head injuries, drowning incidents, and motor vehicle crashes.

About 20 percent of suicide victims in the United States involve people with alcohol problems.

In 2014, 30 percent of the country's fatal traffic incidents were related to alcohol-impaired driving.

Among youth, underage drinking is responsible for more than forty-three hundred deaths each year and one hundred eighty-nine thousand emergency room visits for alcohol-related injuries and other conditions.

Excessive drinking was responsible for one in ten deaths among adults between twenty and sixty-four years of age.

In 2010, the economic impact of excessive alcohol use in the United States approached an estimated $249 billion.

Alcoholism and Alcohol Abuse: Men vs. Women

Studies consistently demonstrate that more men than women struggle with alcoholism and alcohol abuse. While 5.7 million women are affected by an alcohol use disorder in the United States, nearly twice as many men—about 10.6 million—are affected. With a little less than 6 million women struggling with alcoholism, this gender discrepancy obviously shouldn't be taken to suggest that women are in the clear. Women may in fact need to be relatively more careful about their alcohol consumption because, due to gender differences in body structure and chemistry, which result in them effectively absorbing more alcohol from their drinks, women can become intoxicated more quickly than men when drinking comparable amounts of alcohol. In addition, women are more likely than men to experience problems related to alcohol, such as abusive relationships, unwanted sexual advances, and depression.

Health problems related to alcohol addiction and alcoholism vary, but they are of great concern because of their severity. For example, a Harvard School of Public Health study showed that having two or more drinks per day increases the risk of developing breast cancer. Heavy alcohol use directly affects brain function and has been shown to induce mental disorders such as mood, anxiety, psychotic, sleep, and dementia disorders.

In addition to mood and behavior changes, alcohol can affect thought, memory, and coordination. Excessive alcohol use can affect other organs such as the heart, liver, and pancreas, contributing to cardiomyopathy, irregular heartbeat, stroke, and high blood pressure.

Liver cirrhosis can occur from heavy drinking as can alcohol hepatitis and liver fibrosis.

Alcohol causes inflammation and swelling of the pancreas (pancreatitis), which can be painful and debilitating, and it can prevent proper digestion.

Alcohol abuse increases the risk of developing certain cancers of the mouth, esophagus, throat, liver, and breast as well as weakening the immune system, making the body more susceptible to various diseases like pneumonia and tuberculosis.

Aside from injury, violence, alcohol poisoning, susceptibility to certain diseases, and mental health problems, alcohol dependence or alcoholism can develop from long-term use and result in social problems, such as job loss, family issues, and lost productivity to name a few.

Pregnant women who drink are at risk for miscarriage, stillbirth, or fetal alcohol spectrum disorders.

Alcohol use can interact with certain medications, increasing the risk of additional health problems or even death.

In adolescents, alcohol use can interfere with brain development.

Excessive underage drinking has many consequences that affect college students across the United States, whether they choose to drink, including the following:

Consequences of Excessive Underage Drinking

Academic problems: Approximately 25 percent of college students reported falling behind, missing class, doing poorly on papers and exams, and receiving low grades as a result of drinking.

Alcohol abuse and dependence: About 20 percent of students meet the criteria for an alcohol use disorder.

Assault: About 696,000 students aged eighteen to twenty-four became victims of assault; the perpetrators in these cases were other students who had been drinking.

Death: About 1,825 college students aged eighteen to twenty-four die from unintentional injuries related to alcohol.

Drunk driving: About 85 percent of alcohol-impaired driving is associated with binge drinking.

Alcohol poisoning: Each year thousands of college students are transported to the emergency room because of alcohol poisoning, which can result in permanent brain damage or even death.

Health problems and suicide attempts: Suicide attempts are significantly higher in those who drink heavily compared with those who do not drink. Liver and other organ damage can result from long-term excessive drinking.

Injury: An estimated 10 percent of college students are injured because of drinking.

Police involvement: An estimated one hundred twelve thousand students were arrested for an alcohol-related offense in a single year.

Property damage and vandalism: Many colleges in the United States have major or moderate problems with property damage resulting from alcohol use; making these claims are more than 50 percent of administrators from colleges with high drinking levels among students and more than 25 percent of administrators from colleges with low student drinking levels.

Sexual abuse: Approximately ninety-seven thousand students aged eighteen to twenty-four reported experiencing sexual assault or date rape as a result of alcohol use.

Unsafe sex: An estimated 8 percent of college students had unprotected sex as a result of their drinking.

Given some of these consequences, it's clear that there is a strong relationship between crime and alcohol use. About three million violent crimes occur annually in the United States, and alcohol plays a role in 40 percent of them. Two-thirds of victims who have suffered domestic or partner violence reported there had been alcohol involved, and among cases of spousal violence, three out of four incidents involved an offender who had been under the influence of alcohol.

What Are the Effects of Drug Abuse and Addiction?

The consequences of drug abuse can be severe, destructive, and sometimes irreparable. Drug abuse and addiction can affect your life on every possible level, including socially, financially, occupationally, and health wise. A few reasons for this are that feeding a drug habit requires a lot of money, and being under the influence of drugs makes it difficult to honor your work obligations. The unrelenting cycle of high drug costs and incapacitation can lead to stealing, lying, or cheating to support your addiction.

Personal problems drug addiction sometimes lead to, may include the following:

1. Crime
2. Difficulty keeping a job and having other work-related problems
3. Homelessness
4. Contracting a disease(s)
5. Degeneration of physical and mental health
6. Conflicted relationships with loved ones
7. Isolation
8. Death

Certain drug abuse impacts your judgment and reaction time because these substances slow down your cognitive and motor functioning through various biological actions. Slow reaction time and impaired judgment can lead to a plethora of social and behavioral problems due to an inability to make rational decisions, including the following:

1. Physical violence
2. Risky sexual behaviors
3. Child abuse and neglect
4. Driving under the influence
5. Crime such as theft and prostitution
6. The spread of infectious diseases

One of the biggest problems drug addiction can cause is in your relationships with friends and family. Once you're in the grips of an unrelenting addiction, your personality changes because you believe the drug is an integral part of your survival. You make decisions while addicted that you would have never even entertained the thought of before your addiction.

If you have children, problems can include the following:

1. Forgetting to feed, wash, and dress your children
2. Exposing your children to harmful environments or people
3. Not paying rent, electric, water, and other essential bills
4. Abusing or neglecting your children's physical, emotional, and medical needs
5. Exposing your children to fights and conflict
6. Being unable to protect your children from accidents and other harm
7. Increasing the likelihood that your children will have a drug problem
8. Possibly having your children removed from your care by Child Protective Services

Statistics on Heroin Addiction and Abuse

An irreversible problem caused by opioid abuse is death by overdose, as evident in these statistics:

1. The number of heroin-overdose deaths has nearly tripled since 2010.
2. Heroin-overdose deaths were highest among adults between the ages of twenty-five and forty-four from 2000 to 2013.
3. In 2013, the rate of heroin overdose was four times higher in men than in women.
4. Between 2000 and 2013, the rate of overdose deaths involving heroin rose in each area across the country, with the Midwest experiencing the largest increase.

How Drug Addiction Affects Your Health

Provided you avoid an accidental overdose, you will most likely experience other health-related issues as a result of your drug abuse. Certain drugs can cause specific types of health problems, given

297

their chemical makeup and the way they are ingested or metabolized in the body. For example, methamphetamine can cause serious dental issues, while inhalants can destroy cells in the peripheral nervous system and brain.

Other diseases can result from the intravenous use of opioids, crack, and crystal meth, such as the following:

1. HIV
2. Hepatitis C (a liver virus that causes inflammation)
3. Cellulitis (a skin infection)
4. Endocarditis (an infection of the heart valves)

Drug addiction can also affect the health of those around you. Secondhand smoke has been well researched related to tobacco and is just the beginning in regard to illicit substances people commonly smoke. Presently, one study found that nonsmoking subjects exposed for an hour to high-THC marijuana in an unventilated space reported mild drug effects, and an additional study showed positive urine screens in subjects in the hours immediately after being exposed.

Also, engaging in unprotected sex after drug use exposes your partner to the infections listed above, and being under the influence of drugs makes it more likely that you will engage in risky sexual behaviors due to your impaired judgment.

If you're pregnant, drug use during pregnancy can cause your baby to be born with an addiction. This can lead to your baby experiencing severe withdrawal symptoms, known as neonatal abstinence syndrome (NAS), after he or she is born. Symptoms of NAS vary depending on what you used during pregnancy. Common symptoms can include seizures, restlessness, tremors, and difficulty eating and sleeping.

Along with physical health issues, your mental health can also be jeopardized by drug abuse. Many people who abuse substances also have a mental health disorder, such as depression or anxiety, and using drugs or alcohol can exacerbate the symptoms associated with these disorders. In some cases, substance abuse can be the cause of mental health issues.[5]

Is It Worth What It Costs You Spiritually?

Based on the scriptures we have studied in this chapter, I don't believe God disallows alcohol consumption altogether; however, the circumstances in which it is acceptable seem to paint a grim picture for the most part. It seems like alcohol may be acceptable for some celebratory activities but should be limited to the point that it doesn't affect our behavior. Personally, I believe most people drink to affect their behavior. Then there is the medical application, in which it can be used for those who need to be comforted or relieved of physical or mental anguish and those who are ready to die.

Finally, it shouldn't be used by anyone serious about serving God. When I combine that with the statistics concerning the effects being felt by our nation concerning alcohol and drug abuse, I have decided that it is simply not worth the price or chance. In addition, I would suggest that if anyone knows he or she has a problem with alcohol in these two following areas, it would be wise to refrain altogether.

The first area is the lack of self-control when intoxicated. I know too much alcohol can affect anyone, but some always become aggressive and violent when they drink. If this describes you, then you shouldn't drink.

Second, is the person who lacks the ability to drink only one or two and then stop. This is the type of person who, once he or she starts drinking, won't stop until it is all gone or he or she passes out. These are the two types of people who can cause serious problems even during small celebrations or social events.

---

[5] The previous statistics on alcohol and drug use in the US were provided by American Addiction Centers, Project Know.com. Written by Lauren Brande and edited by Meredith Watkins. Last updated October 19, 2021. 24/7 Hot line: (888) 830-7624

CHAPTER 11

Hindrances to a Happy Marriage

Jealousy Is Not a Joke

I'm sure most of you know what the green-eyed monster is; that would be the monster of jealousy. It is called that for a very good reason. Jealousy can be a huge monster in your relationship whether it is with your boyfriend, girlfriend, fiancé, or spouse. This is something everyone should be looking out for. Some people treat it like it is some sort of joke. I can tell you from firsthand experience that jealousy can be a deal breaker, a relationship killer, and a marriage destroyer. I wish I could tell you I learned about these things from a classroom instead of real-life experiences, but that wouldn't be true. I have faced every heartache relationships can provide, but who is better to warn you about these things than someone who has been there?

Suffice it to say that when it comes to relationships, I have probably made every mistake possible. They say fools learn from their mistakes and wise people learn from a fool's mistakes. I have played the fool, and therefore I'm hoping I can help you be wise. In the interest of full disclosure, I will tell you that some of the methods of recognition and remedies I am going to share with you I picked up in a class I voluntarily attended over thirty years ago. I have combined some of these methods with personal experiences and

David Boudreaux

Christian principles to come up with the information I am going to provide to you here.

If you think it is funny when you make your partner jealous, you need to pay attention to what I'm going to tell you. If you tend to flirt with the opposite sex, especially when your spouse is around, you are playing with fire. Jealousy breeds bitterness (James 3:5–6). Believe me when I tell you it is true that hell hath no fury like a woman scorned. You may think it is humorous when your wife gets upset because she catches you looking at another woman. But trust me, this isn't funny. Some women will try to play it down for a while and even point other women out to you just to see how you react, but inside she is building a flame (James 3:14–18).

I have seen so much destruction caused by this beast that I tend not to show any kind of jealousy at all, and sometimes my wife expresses to me that it doesn't appear that I care much about her. Actually, the truth is quite the opposite. I care enough that I refuse to allow jealousy to become a problem for us. You must be able to trust the person you are with enough that you don't allow any doubt or anxiety to influence your behavior toward him or her. I trust her wholeheartedly, and I don't fear losing her. I have no desire to be anywhere else or be with anyone else, and I hope she knows that. I also hope she believes and feels the same way about me.

Jealousy Is the Rage of a Man

The Bible tells us that jealousy is the rage of a man (Prov. 6:34). It is a man's job to provide, protect, and guide his wife; and it is true that her body belongs to him just as his body belongs to her. This makes it only natural for feelings of insecurity to creep in for some men when another man is checking her out. Personally, I have enough faith in my wife and her moral standards that it doesn't bother me when other men look at her or tell me how nice she looks. It makes me appreciate her natural beauty, character, loyalty, and how God has blessed me with her. How much jealousy is appropriate to let her or him know that you care about him or her but not so much that it causes insecurities in the relationship? That is sometimes a difficult balance to achieve, and every case is different. With my wife, it isn't hard to detect in her reactions if I'm going too far in either direction.

Jealousy Can Control You

When under the influence of excessive jealousy, both men and women may do irrational things they later remember with much embarrassment, regret, or even shame. They may behave as if they are totally possessed with these jealousy fears. A man who takes a day off work to spy on his wife or lets the air out of the tires on her car to keep her at home when he is not there may later wonder what on earth would ever make him do such a thing. This is likely to be the same man who eventually becomes physically abusive in his relationship and still wonders what in the world he was thinking. He feels like something else is controlling him, like it is out of his control.

Jealousy is a feeling (emotion), and there are many ways in which these feelings can be expressed. Jealous feelings usually start small and grow just as feelings of anger do. Because they start out small, the person may feel like they are nothing to be concerned about. This is the perfect time to deal with it before it turns into the monster we talked about. If not dealt with in these early stages, it may continue to grow and develop into jealousy fantasies. The person may become completely overcome with these jealous thoughts to the point of losing touch with reality. Eventually, he or she will decide that he or she will have to do something drastic to ensure that these jealousy fantasies don't play out in real life.

This person, though he or she doesn't realize it, has choices to make at each step along the way. The person can intimidate or threaten his or her partner without revealing the source of his or her anger, or the person can express his or her feelings directly to the spouse. The person can keep these jealous thoughts to him or herself and let them fester, or the person can talk about this issue with someone, preferably a pastor or a good spiritual friend. This should be someone who will keep the problem confidential and yet try to help him or her get it out in the open between the person and their spouse so it can be dealt with.

Jealousy Is about the Fear of Personal Loss

Jealousy is about the fear of personal loss. This may be actual loss or only imagined loss. Jealousy fears reflect many different kinds of loss or potential loss. If a man's wife or future wife has physical relations with another man, this would cause him to feel the loss of that sacred bond of trust and the sense of special importance and security that can exist only in marriage. He may develop feelings of embarrassment or inadequacy. He may feel he isn't a sufficient protector or provider. All these losses tend to produce the strongest emotions in the area of sexual jealousy, but these same feelings of jealousy can arise even if his wife is spending a lot of time with other women. Of course, I'm obviously talking about these things from a man's perspective, but women can experience these same types of feelings. When this jealousy reaches the point where it shows itself when the spouse is spending time with anyone other than his or her partner, it is past time for it to be dealt with. These are the signs of a codependent relationship and could eventually culminate into a disaster. If the way you feel about yourself depends on the mood or actions of your spouse, then this could be about you. Obviously, if my wife is in a bad mood, I'm not going to be happy about it, but I will try to cheer her up and not also get in a bad mood with her.

Jealousy Can Be a Sign of Codependency

If you are totally dependent on your wife or she is totally dependent on you, if you feel somehow that she is necessary for your survival, then it is difficult to react calmly to the threat of losing her. An imagined loss can sometimes even stir up your emotions more than a real one. Those stirred-up emotions are likely to interpret her actions in the worst possible way. Her smile at another man, in your mind, means she is considering having an affair. To you her wanting to get a job to help out with expenses could mean she doesn't consider you an adequate provider.

This is the negative effect of jealousy. When jealousy, like violence, becomes a tool a person uses to control the actions of his or her spouse, then it is harmful. If the spouse yields to these control tactics, then the controller may feel somewhat reassured, at least for a short time. But in reality, the controller has just pushed the spouse even further away. Understand that because men are usually the more aggressive and stronger gender, they are usually the ones who use these controlling tactics, but that isn't always the case. Some women use these and other tactics to control their husbands as well.

Jealousy Can Be Used as a Type of Punishment

Some partners may also use jealousy as a means of punishing their spouses. It may become an avenue for the release of built-up anger about something or some way they feel like they have been treated wrong or unfairly (or will be). Possibly, they could be using this control tactic to punish their partner for something another person has done to them in the past, such as an ex-wife or husband, and they fear it will happen again.

The final result of all this is the fact that jealousy destroys trust and creates resentment in both the man and woman in these types of relationships. If a man or woman has a problem with insecurity in his or her marriage, it will end up causing jealousy, deceitfulness, and mistrust; and it will eventually destroy the marriage if it isn't dealt with. I believe it's natural for a man to be head over his wife, just as God says he should be, but it isn't natural or normal for him to be obsessed with feelings of jealousy to the point that he becomes controlling. If he feels he needs to watch her every move throughout the day or always needs to know where she is and what she is doing, if he is afraid to let her leave the house without him or have her own friends or have her own transportation, this is controlling jealousy. This behavior will eventually drive his wife away.

A marital relationship must be built on mutual trust and respect for one another. A man of God should never have this kind of jealousy concerning his wife because his dependence on existence should be on God and not on his wife. The wife should feel the same way about her husband. Even though God has given the husband the responsibility of protecting and providing for his wife, it is ultimately God who provides these things through her husband. If he is not doing his job, it's better for her to talk to God about it and let Him deal with the husband. However, if a man or woman gets his or her priorities wrong, then this jealousy thing becomes a significant threat. Therefore, jealousy is a product of wrong priorities. Men, your ultimate strength for survival should be from God, not from your wife; and ladies, your ultimate strength for survival should be from God, not from your husbands.

Jealousy Can Be Controlled

Both husbands and wives should seek to please God in their relationships with one another. If this is the case, then both will have a relationship that is codependent on God and not on each other. If you are in a marriage where you or your spouse is codependent, a problem that manifests itself in jealousy and anger issues, then someone doesn't have God where He belongs in the relationship. If pleasing your wife is more important than what God tells you to do, then your relationships with God and your wife are both in trouble. If pleasing your husband is more important to you than pleasing God, then your relationship is in trouble. If you think your wife should put you ahead of serving God or if she thinks you should put her ahead of serving God, then your marriage is headed for trouble. Satan wants an opportunity to let jealousy destroy your marriage and your relationship with God.

I have already showed you that your relationship with God won't be what it should be if you're not in a good place in your life with your spouse (1 Peter 3:7). You can see in the following verses that jealousy and anger work hand in hand with one another; this is usually the result of a cheating spouse or the fear of having one. Most of the time, these feelings of fear, jealousy, and anger aren't justified and are the result of insecurities. If you are in a relationship where these types of actions (controlling behavior) are taking place, then it is time to get professional help. Your pastor should be able to help you deal with this situation or guide you to someone who can.

> But whoso committeth adultery with a woman lacketh understanding: he that doeth it destroyeth his own soul. A wound and dishonour shall he get; and his reproach shall not be wiped away. For jealousy is the rage of a man: therefore he will not spare in the day of vengeance. He will not regard any ransom; neither will he rest content, though thou givest many gifts. (Prov. 6:32–35)

> Wrath is cruel, and anger is outrageous; but who is able to stand before envy? (Prov. 27:4)

> Set me as a seal upon thine heart, as a seal upon thine arm for love is strong as death; jealousy is cruel

as the grave the coals thereof are coals of fire, which hath a most vehement flame. (Song of Solomon 8:6)

But if ye have bitter envying and strife in your hearts, glory not, and lie not against the truth. This wisdom descendeth not from above, but is earthly, sensual, devilish. For where envying and strife is, there is confusion and every evil work. But the wisdom that is from above is first pure, then peaceable, gentle, and easy to be intreated, full of mercy and good fruits, without partiality, and without hypocrisy. And the fruit of righteousness is sown in peace of them that make peace. (James 3:14–18)

Neither shalt thou desire thy neighbour's wife, neither shalt thou covet thy neighbour's house, his field, or his manservant, or his maidservant, his ox, or his ass, or anything that is thy neighbour's. (Deut. 5:21)

He that is slow to wrath is of great understanding: but he that is hasty of spirit exalteth folly. A sound heart is the life of the flesh: but envy the rottenness of the bones. (Prov. 14:29–30)

Before we move to the next point, I want to share a few observations from these verses. In Proverbs 6:32–35, we learn that once a man has been consumed by jealousy, there is no way to pacify him. Offering gifts, money, apologies, or anything else won't work. Proverbs 27:4 says anger can result in cruel treatment and outrageous behavior, but jealousy can become incurable. In Song of Solomon 8:6, jealousy is as cruel as the grave; it is like burning coals that can't be extinguished and will turn into an uncontrollable, raging fire. In James 3:14–18, bitterness, jealousy, and conflict come from the devil and are fleshly and worldly. They result in confusion and every evil work. It goes on to tell us that the fruit of righteousness, in other words, the things that come from God, results in peace and is the work of the righteous peacemaker.

In the Beatitudes, Jesus said happy are the peacemakers. A peacemaker is someone who will walk away from a fight. When I was young, I was taught that a man should stand up and fight, and there are times when that may be needed. But for the most part, it takes a much bigger man to walk away, especially if he is avoiding or preventing a fight with his spouse. In Proverbs 14:29–30, we learn that he who is quick to anger stirs up mischief, and he who is slow to anger has great understanding. Jealousy is like rottenness in the bones.

Codependent Relationships Should Be Avoided

A man who displays symptoms or signs of jealousy or controlling behavior and uncontrollable anger doesn't treat his wife properly and isn't dwelling with her according to knowledge. If this conversation seems strange to you and you don't understand why anyone would treat their wife or husband poorly and your spouse feels the same way, then this is probably not a concern for you. However, if you, a husband or wife, feel I am talking to you about your or your spouse, then maybe you should investigate this issue a bit further or talk to your pastor about it. I think both partners should read this and decide whether they need to look into it further because a husband or wife may see something in his or her spouse, even if the spouse has no idea it is there.

If you are dating someone who shows signs of controlling behavior, even before the relationship is serious, *run*. The woman in a relationship is generally the one who realizes a problem has developed or is developing before the man does. I think this is because God made women more emotional and sensitive, for the most part, which makes them able to pick up on issues like this one sooner than most men do. If you are a man and your wife believes this is or can be an issue, you should listen to her. The first step to stopping a codependent relationship from developing further is to recognize there is a problem developing and talk about it. Following I have listed ten typical signs that you may be in an abusive relationship:

Embarrassment

Humiliation is a type of abuse that generally begins with little pokes or criticisms of your character or behavior in private that eventually migrate into blown out shouting matches in public before you know what happened. The abuser will become angry at the drop of a hat and will try to make everyone think it is your fault. It is intended to make you surrender to their control over you.

Verbal Abuse

Name calling should never be part of a conversation between you and your spouse. Bad language and name calling are tools of the devil used to destroy your self-worth and it is easily recognized by the attacks on your looks, intelligence or character. This behavior is intended for the purpose destroying self reliance so you become totally reliant upon your spouse.

Physical Abuse

When we were talking about disciplining children I mentioned that you should never punish your child with your hand. It causes them to be scared of the parent. Physical abuse doesn't usually start out with physical contact. A first sign may be when your spouse grabs your arm to keep you from walking away or a teasingly kind of punch in the arm are a push with the shoulder to cause intimidation. If you don't notice this for what it is, it could evolve in to slaps, choke holds or harmful punches.

Efforts to Control You

This is when your spouse makes every effort to keep you away from everyone else that you know. This is so your friends or family won't see how they are treating you. Their goal in this behavior is to have you become totally dependent on them for everything. This is a warning sign of the abusive, obsessive control tactics that normally follows.

Abrupt Mood Swings

If your spouse has sudden mood swings that seem consistently out of the ordinary, especially when it is just you and them alone, they are probably displaying signs of controlling behavior. It would not be unusual for them to go from being cuddly and gentle to angry and aggressive in a moment.

Pointing Out Your Imperfections

If your spouse makes a habit of pointing out your imperfections and treats you more like you are their child than their spouse this is not normal. Do they act like they are trying to correct you or discipline you? I have made it clear already that it is not the husband's job to discipline his wife. As a married couple the two of you have become one flesh and the husband doesn't punish himself.

Isolating You From Your Friends and Family

The abuser will not want their spouse to have the outside support from anyone else even friends and family. They will try to persuade you that your friends and family don't value you or appreciate you like they should. If you allow this to go unchecked soon you will be isolated from everyone except the abuser. This in turn gives them freedom they are seeking to put you under their complete control.

Pointing Fingers

You may as well plan on being blamed for every bad thing that happens to the abuser if you decide to stand by them in this relationship as it is. They will never accept blame for anything that happens. Anytime you try to point out something is wrong they will turn it around and make it look like it all is your fault.

Deceptive Control

The abuser has perfected the skill of convincing their spouse that whenever they lose control it is the spouses fault. They are acting that way because of something the spouse did to them first and they will actually convince the spouse that this is true, it isn't. The reason they do this is to make their spouse doubt their self-worth. This usually results in the spouse excusing or forgiving the abuser because he or she makes them feel like they caused it.

Anger Tantrums

Once it has progressed to this point you have probably noticed that they only throw their fits and yell at you and blame you when the two of you are alone. They will tell you that they have no control over their fits but the fact that they never do it in front of others proves that this isn't true at all.

Anger is a Learned Behavior

The devil is using anger to destroy homes, and it is very effective. If there is a jealousy problem in the home, the person should confess it as sin and ask God to forgive him or her and help the person get past it. Jealousy isn't a disease or condition that cannot be corrected. It's an emotion that, if not controlled, can result in sinful behavior. Even God gets angry at times, but with repentance comes forgiveness, and joy comes in the morning. "Sing unto the LORD, O ye saints of his, and give thanks at the remembrance of his holiness. For his anger endureth but a moment; in his favour is life: weeping may endure for a night, but joy cometh in the morning" (Ps. 30:4–5).

This behavior is most often learned as a child. I don't like to admit it, but I had an unhealthy dose of this behavioral condition in my life many years ago. It is something you can get over by admitting that you have a problem with it and learning how to change your behavior. Anger is generally the end result of jealousy, and it can be controlled. We will talk more about anger and how to deal with it in a moment.

If you have a problem with jealousy, you should seek counsel from your pastor or another spiritual person who has been trained to deal with this issue. If you don't get a handle on it, it will destroy your marriage. The best time to deal with it is before it gets to the violent behavior stage. This isn't one of the reasons God gives to allow divorce, but that is usually where it leads. This is a behavioral disorder that can and should be overcome rather than result in divorce. I will say that this may be a good reason to separate, at least temporarily, if that is necessary to correct the situation. Physical, mental, or verbal abuse in a marriage isn't acceptable under any circumstances. In some more severe situations, not only might separation be required, but it may also be necessary to file an order of restraint or even assault charges. This happens more often than anyone wants to admit. Divorce isn't God's will for your marriage, but neither is abuse.

A preacher was walking along the side of the road when he heard shouting and cursing off in the distance. He stopped walking and looked around. Out in the field, he saw a rancher yelling at his mule, slapping it, and calling it names. The preacher yelled at the man and said, "Hey! What are you doing?"

The rancher replied, "I can't get this stubborn old mule to do anything I tell it to do."

The preacher yelled back, "Well, that's not the way to do it. You have to talk nicely to him."

The rancher thought, *What does a preacher know about mules?* So he told the preacher, "Oh yeah? Then why don't you just come over here and show me."

So the preacher wiggled his way through the fence and walked toward the rancher and the mule. He picked up a pine knot piece of wood on the way. As soon as he reached where they were, he struck the mule between the eyes with the pine knot club, nearly knocking the mule to its knees.

The rancher said, "Hey, what are you doing? I thought you said you had to talk nice to him."

The preacher replied, "Yes, I did, but you have to get his attention first."

If you are in an abusive situation and have tried talking to the abuser but the problem keeps happening over and over, then something has to change. You may have to take those drastic steps (restraint order or assault charges) to get the person's attention before he or she is willing to admit that they have a problem and needs help dealing with it. This is not being mean or cruel to the person; this is doing what has to be done to get the person to see that he or she needs help.

Anger in Itself Isn't a Sin Either

Jealousy is one condition that results in anger, but it certainly isn't the only one. In my experience, anger more often appears as part of a character trait than a physical condition. Some people are just angry all the time. I believe this is also a learned behavioral or mental reaction. The Bible says to be angry and sin not, so it is obvious that being angry in itself isn't sinful. This is called "righteous indignation." Even Jesus got angry when the merchants had changed God's holy temple into a den of thieves.

> Be ye angry, and sin not: let not the sun go down upon your wrath. (Eph. 4:26)

> And Jesus went into the temple of God, and cast out all them that sold and bought in the temple, and overthrew the tables of the moneychangers, and the seats of them that sold doves, And said unto them, It is written, My house shall be called the house of prayer; but ye have made it a den of thieves. (Matt. 21:12–13)

Apparently, then, that anger isn't the problem but rather the reaction to the anger. Yet even though it's normal for people to get angry when certain things happen that are out of their control, what is important is how they respond or react to this anger. The Bible teaches that it rains on the good and evil alike, so what really matters is how you look at the rain. Is it a blessing or curse? Is your glass half full or half empty?

"Ye have heard that it hath been said, Thou shalt love thy neighbour, and hate thine enemy. But I say unto you, Love your enemies, bless them that curse you, do good to them that hate you, and pray for them which despitefully use you, and persecute you; That ye may be the children of your Father which is in heaven: for he maketh his sun to rise on the evil and on the good, and sendeth rain on the just and on the unjust" (Matt. 5:43–45).

Anger Must Be Kept under Control

I just finished writing a book called *Lord Jesus, Please Help Me Find My Happy*. It was published through WestBow Publishing and is now available everywhere. Anyhow, this new book explains that one of the main secrets to being a happy Christian is to learn to be content with whatever God sends our way. We can do this because we know all things work together for good for those who love God.

> Not that I speak in respect of want: for I have learned, in whatsoever state I am, therewith to be content. (Phil. 4:11)

> And we know that all things work together for good to them that love God, to them who are the called according to his purpose. (Rom. 8:28)

Happiness is a state of mind, and as such it influences behavior the same way anger does. I believe God wants His people to be happy, and even though anger isn't a sin, it can often lead to improper behavior, which is sin. Therefore God suggests not only that we try to be slow to anger, as He is, but also that we not hang out with people who get angry too often or too quickly.

> For his anger endureth but a moment; in his favour is life: weeping may endure for a night, but joy cometh in the morning. (Ps. 30:5)

> Wherefore, my beloved brethren, let every man be swift to hear, slow to speak, slow to wrath: For

the wrath of man worketh not the righteousness of
God. (James 1:19–20)

Be not hasty in thy spirit to be angry: for anger
resteth in the bosom of fools. (Eccl. 7:9)

He that is soon angry dealeth foolishly: and a man
of wicked devices is hated. (Prov. 14:17)

A soft answer turneth away wrath: but grievous
words stir up anger. (Prov. 15:1)

A wrathful man stirreth up strife: but he that is slow
to anger appeaseth strife. (Prov. 15:18)

He that is slow to anger is better than the mighty;
and he that ruleth his spirit than he that taketh a
city. (Prov. 16:32)

It is better to dwell in the wilderness, than with a
contentious and an angry woman. (Prov. 21:19)

An angry man stirreth up strife, and a furious man
aboundeth in transgression. (Prov. 29:22)

Let all bitterness, and wrath, and anger, and
clamour, and evil speaking, be put away from you,
with all malice: (Eph. 4:31)

Out-of-Control Anger Is a Learned Behavior

"Make no friendship with an angry man; and with a furious man
thou shalt not go: Lest thou learn his ways, and get a snare to thy
soul" (Prov. 22:24–25). From this verse, we can see that uncontrolled

anger is a behavior usually learned from a bad example. The point is, if it can be learned to have uncontrollable anger, then it can also be learned to have controlled anger. It isn't jealousy or even anger that is the sin; it is the way people respond to it. We are conditioned as male children to believe a strong man will stand his ground and not be afraid to fight. I'm not saying this is totally wrong, but this should happen only when you are trying to defend your family. You shouldn't be fighting with your spouse. As I said before, it takes a much stronger, bigger man to control his anger and avoid a fight than it does to lose control and lash out.

What we as humankind need to do then is control how we respond to these emotions, and that isn't hard to do. I have listed a few suggestions to get you started.

Be Slow to Wrath

As the verses say, "Be slow to wrath."Be aware of your emotional state. It isn't difficult to know when you start feeling your emotional anger growing. Be aware of your emotional state, and if you feel the buildup, then change the situation causing it. If it's an argument with your spouse, then stop the argument. Some people suggest taking a deep breath and counting to ten. If you catch this emotional rise in its earliest stages, stopping it is much easier. What should you be looking for?

1. A red face
2. An increased heart rate
3. An uneasy feeling in your gut
4. A change in your breathing
5. Hot flashes
6. An urge to act, fidgeting
7. Nervousness

Decide What Issues Are Worth Fighting Over

There are convictions in life, and then there are preferences. If I have a conviction about something like stealing, cheating, or lying, then that is something worth arguing over. If I have a preference, such as I prefer my wife to be home when I get off work in the evening, then this is something I'm not going to fight about. If someone tries to get you to go against God's words when you have vowed to God that you won't do so, then this is a conviction you must stand up to. If you don't stand for something, you will fall for anything, as the song goes. If someone asks you to do something morally neutral, then just choose based on what you desire. This is a preference.

Learn to Walk Away from a Fight

If you know you're getting angry about something and counting to ten didn't do the trick, then excuse yourself and walk away. It's better to delay the conversation until both parties have thought about their positions and had a chance to calm down.

Learn to Let Others Walk Away from a Fight

Sometimes you may not be the one who is getting angry but the other person you are dealing with is. An argument will never be settled peacefully when one of the persons involved is angry. Give the person some space and let him or her cool off. Nothing is so important that it can't wait a few minutes or even a day. If they try to walk away, don't follow the person around while continuing to make snide remarks and throwing jabs.

Learn to Bite Your Tongue

When you start getting angry, the first thing to let go is the tongue. Unfortunately, the tongue is the one thing that can cause the most damage in a relationship in the shortest amount of time. If your wife is like mine, then you know one slip of the tongue on your part is something you will continue to hear about for the next twenty years. Women are emotional creatures and they have a memory like an elephant. Don't say something in anger you will regret. Bite your tongue and walk away. Don't kindle a flame that will turn into a raging inferno.

An emotional buildup is growing adrenaline or extra energy, which always results in aggressive behavior. Try to find something aggressive and constructive to do with the extra energy rather than using it to lash out. If you will take a brisk walk or sprint, go work out, find a punching bag, or do anything that will burn excess energy in a short period, you will be surprised by how much different you will feel afterward. The activity will give you a clear mind. If you don't find a constructive way to release this excess energy, it will come out in a destructive way.

Consider the Consequences

If you are having a problem with this, then this probably isn't your first time. It may be the first time it happened when you were equipped to recognize it and deal with it in an appropriate manner. Stopping for a moment to think about it will do two things. First, it will most likely make you realize it just really isn't that important. Second, it will give you a moment to cool off. It's better to choose your fights with a clear mind.

My wife and I always agree on everything now since we have been at it so long. I have learned to say, "I'm sorry. It was my fault," and she always agrees. (Just kidding.)

Do Not Address Items of Conflict While You Are Using Alcohol or Drug-Related Products

These products will only cause you to lose your ability to keep the situation under control. Most violent behavior in relationships takes place when one or both partners have been indulging in these products. Some people are prone to argumentation when drinking.

Do Not Resort to Criticism, Insults, or Name-Calling

When the conversation heads in this direction, there is no longer anything constructive going to come from it, and the situation will only escalate from there.

Do Not Resort to Destructive Behavior

You may think there is no harm in putting your fist through a wall, but it isn't the wall that is the problem. These acts of violence are only a means of taking control by using violent scare tactics. Violence never helps any situation with your partner. Do you really want your partner to be scared to talk to you or be around you? Once you have started this type of behavior, this is the beginning of the end. Don't go down that road.

Don't Hold on to Your Anger

Don't allow jealousy, anger, or violence to destroy your marriage. This isn't what God wants for you or your spouse, but this is where it will go if you don't learn to change this behavior. Consider these last two verses, and we will move on to another topic. "Husbands, love your wives, and be not bitter against them" (Col. 3:19).

Don't Hold a Grudge

One of the most important things you will ever learn to do is forgive and not hold a grudge, especially with your wife. A grudge is simply a lack of forgiveness. When you forgive your wife or husband, you forgive yourself because you and your spouse are one. Refusing to forgive your spouse is self-destructive behavior. You aren't perfect, and neither is your partner. Get over it and press forward. "Be ye angry, and sin not: let not the sun go down upon your wrath" (Eph. 4:26).

Don't Go to Bed Angry

This may sound contradictory because I just told you it is better to walk away from a heated discussion than to have one while you are angry, yet here I am telling you not to go to bed while angry with each other. This isn't a contradiction. Of course, it would be better if the argument could be settled before bedtime, but that may not always happen. What can always happen is preventing the conversation from making you angry. If you allow yourself to go to bed angry, you will just stew in it all night, and it will be worse the next day. If you stop the conversation before someone gets angry, then you can get a good night's rest and attempt to deal with it in the morning when everyone involved is rested and feeling better. This also allows any other influences, such as alcohol or drugs, to get out of the system. Let's face it—when you stay angry with your wife or husband for any length of time, it is because you are being stubborn and trying to prove a point. Remember, he or she loves you, and you don't need to prove anything to him or her. The two of you are one, and to be angry, hold a grudge, or be jealous or bitter against yourself is a tremendous waste of energy.

The other day my wife and I decided we aren't going to go to bed angry with each other ever again. So far, neither of us has had any sleep for three days. Just kidding. "Laughter doeth the heart good like a medicine" (Prov. 17:2).

CHAPTER 12

The Proper Way to Treat Your Wife

The Cost of Divorce

I'm not sure that it is always the wife who gets mistreated the most, but I am sure it is the wife who usually pays the higher price. A lot of the verses I am going to use here in this section are the same ones that have already been used, but many times one verse may cover a lot of different areas. I think the reason she suffers the most is multifold.

1. She loses the things she was promised and is entitled to.
    First, she is the one who suffers the most emotionally when she is abandoned. She is the one who loses the provision, protection, and guidance God intended her to have as long as she was here on this earth. Marriage is intended for life, and it is the husband's job to provide these things for his wife.
2. Women usually suffer more emotionally than men.
    It is also a known fact that, for the most part, women are more sensitive and more emotional creatures than most men. This isn't a weakness or fault; this is just the way God created them, and because of that fact, they have a much

greater perception and intuition than men, but this also usually makes them more vulnerable.

3. Women usually end up with the children.

Another reason is that women are usually the ones who end up with the children. I know it's difficult to lose your children like most men do during divorce proceedings, but at the same time, it's much easier to survive when you're providing for only one. I'm not talking about monetarily since many men do pay their support to assist in that area, but there is a lot of other stress involved in raising children alone.

4. The woman is the weaker vessel.

The final reason I will give here is that, generally speaking, the woman is the weaker vessel. I believe this refers only to physical strength; this isn't meant as a derogatory remark in any sense of the word. Divorce is never a positive thing in my opinion.

5. Divorce should happen only as a last resort.

Sometimes it's a means for people to get out of a bad position or circumstance, but personally I believe there is always another way unless, of course, we are talking about a cheating spouse or a saved person trying to live with an unsaved person who doesn't want to change. Nevertheless, this section is about how we should treat a wife, and if we do this well, we won't have to worry about divorce.

6. If your spouse has divorced you, God hears your cries.

If you are a woman whose husband has divorced you, God hears your cries. In the following verses, God is angry with Israel because of all the women who have been divorced by their husbands and treated treacherously by them. This means to deal with deceitfully, pillage, be unfaithful; to offend or transgress against. The altar of God is covered with the tears of the divorced. God hears and sees your cries, and they anger Him.

These verses refer to the tears of men who have divorced their wives; because of this, God ignores their prayers (1 Peter 3:7). As I read this passage, however, God also speaks to me concerning the tears of those who have been put away (dealt with treacherously) by their spouses, both husbands and wives. While there may be only one precise translation of scripture, there can be numerous appropriate applications. When we get to the chapter on man's divorce, we will look at these scriptures more closely for an accurate translation.

And this have ye done again, covering the altar of the LORD with tears, with weeping, and with crying out, insomuch that he regardeth not the offering any more, or receiveth it with good will at your hand. Yet ye say, Wherefore? Because the LORD hath been witness between thee and the wife of thy youth, against whom thou hast dealt treacherously: yet is she thy companion, and the wife of thy covenant. And did not he make one? Yet had he the residue of the spirit. And wherefore one? That he might seek a godly seed. Therefore take heed to your spirit, and let none deal treacherously against the wife of his youth. For the LORD, the God of Israel, saith that he hateth putting away: for one covereth violence with his garment, saith the LORD of hosts: therefore take heed to your spirit, that ye deal not treacherously. (Mal. 2:13–16)

7. God says here that he hates "putting away" or divorce.

God says here that He hates divorce because marriage is a sacred institution that pictures His relationship with His children and because it causes intense suffering among all those involved. Therefore, I would conclude this first point by saying that the first task in treating your wife the way you should as a Christian, is to never even consider a divorce. This causes intense grief to the family, including the wife, children, and husband. There is almost always another answer to whatever the problem is. Whether to stay with a spouse is a decision that should be made before the wedding, not after it.

The next scripture I want to bring to your attention concerns how men should treat their wives (Eph. 5:25–31). There are several things to discuss here.

God Will Hold You Accountable for Her Sanctification

For the husband is the head of the wife, even as Christ is the head of the church: and he is the saviour of the body. (Eph. 5:23)

Therefore as the church is subject unto Christ, so let the wives be to their own husbands in everything. (Eph. 5:24)

Okay, fellows, I'm not pointing out these verses for you to show your wife that you are the man of the house. Trust me, if she is a Christian woman, she already knows that God placed man as head of the household. This isn't about her responsibility (we will get to that), but this is about yours. What I want to point out is the reason why God made you the head, and that is because "he is the saviour of the body." In a normal Christian home, where both the husband and the wife are saved, the man is given the responsibility of being the spiritual leader in the home. As the spiritual leader, it is his job to sanctify the family. That means to train them in the things of God. He is supposed to make sure his family is separated from the world and worldly things, and serves God. This is also the reason for the next verse, which says the wife should be subject to him because God won't hold the husband responsible for a wife who is worldly if she won't follow his lead.

On the other hand, if she is subject to him, God will hold him responsible for her spirituality or lack of it, because she is doing what God told her to do through her husband's guidance. This is one way in which the wife is protected by the husband. So how should we treat our wives? We should guide and protect them and accept the responsibility for them from God. This is a tremendous privilege and responsibility. Are you spiritual enough in God's eyes (and in your wife's) for her to trust you with this sacred task? If not, then maybe that is why she has a hard time being obedient to you because your leadership doesn't bring her closer to God, and that is your job. Personally, I think if you do the job God gave you to do with your wife, she will not have any trouble doing her part.

Love Her More Than You Love Yourself

"Husbands, love your wives, even as Christ also loved the church, and gave himself for it" (Eph. 5:25).This next verse gives us another task. It says men should love their wives enough that they are willing to give their lives to save them just like Jesus gave His life to save His body (the church). Men, we already know we should love our wives as we love ourselves, but this verse says we should love them more than we love ourselves. If you love someone so much that you are willing to die for them, that suggests that the person's life is worth more to you than your own. So I ask this: how do you treat someone you love more than you love yourself? Jesus said, "Greater love hath no man than this, that a man lay down his life for his friends". Do you think that if you loved her that much that you would do anything to hurt her? Does she think you love her enough that you would die for her? "This is my commandment, That ye love one another, as I have loved you. Greater love hath no man than this, that a man lay down his life for his friends. Ye are my friends, if ye do whatsoever I command you" (John 15:12–14).

I had to have a medical procedure done last week, and the anesthesiologist told the doctor that he needed to tell me a joke before he put me to sleep. I'm not sure why he said that, but the Holy Spirit has been providing material for this book from all sorts of sources, so I thought it would go well here.

He said there was a group of men who got together every month, and they all went to a ball game or some other event together. Their wives were talking one day and decided they should get together and do something as well. So they all planned on meeting up and catching a bus to Galveston to spend a day at the beach. The women were on the bus when they were hit head-on by an eighteen-wheeler, and they all died in the crash.

All the husbands mourned the loss of their wives for a time, but eventually they slowly began to get it together and move on. One man, however, didn't seem to be recovering from the loss, and several months later, he still broke down and cried when he ran into any of the other husbands.

One day one husband approached him when he started to break down, and he asked him, "I understand the devastation of your loss, but the rest of us have come to the point where we are accepting what happened and are moving on. Why are you having such a hard time getting past this grieving process?"

The man answered, "My wife is the only one who missed the bus."

I don't think this man had the love for his wife we are talking about, and I'm pretty sure his wife probably knows it too.

You Will Spend the Rest of Your Life
Preparing Her to Meet God

"That he might sanctify and cleanse it with the washing of water by the word, That he might present it to himself a glorious church, not having spot, or wrinkle, or any such thing; but that it should be holy and without blemish"(Eph. 5:26–27). Verses 26–27 reiterate the part about the husband being responsible for the sanctification of his wife just as Christ is the head of the church, and it is His job to sanctify the church. I want to point out that the church is the body of born-again believers. They have already been saved. Jesus isn't still trying to get the people in the church saved; that's already been done. What He is doing is trying to make the body become more like the head, and that is Christ. This is done by separating them from the world.

The husband has the same job with his wife. She is already saved, but his job is to separate her from the world and make her more Christ like so she will be perfect when Jesus comes back to take us home. Men should treat their wives like they care about them enough to spend their entire lives trying to prepare them for heaven. Notice it says this is accomplished by cleansing their wives with the Word of God. This means by teaching and training them in the Word of God. So yes, it is the husband's job to prepare their wives to meet God, but it isn't their job to arrange the meeting or make the appointment. Some men say God said divorce was wrong but I'm not certain about murder, yea that's wrong too.

You Will Dedicate Your Life to Guide,
Provide for, and Protect Her

"So ought men to love their wives as their own bodies. He that loveth his wife loveth himself. For no man ever yet hated his own flesh; but nourisheth and cherisheth it, even as the Lord the church" (Eph. 5:28–29). Men should love their wives as much as they love their own bodies or more because their wives are one with them. Therefore, he "that loves his wife loves himself." I'm sure most of you have heard that you need to learn to love yourself before you can truly love someone else. This verse seems to agree with that view. I think it is true, that you should love yourself first, and then you should love your wife even more than that. How much should you love her?

You should love her enough that you will spend your life nourishing her. To nourish means to bring her up to maturity or train her to maturity. This is talking about training her to be a mature Christian. It is the husband's job to train his wife or bring her up or guide her to be like Christ. Then the verse says the husband should love his wife enough to cherish her. To cherish her means to warm, brood, or foster her. These words carry with them the relationship between a mother hen and her baby chicks. She gathers them under her wings and protects them with her life. She keeps them warm, protects them with her life, and dedicates her life to fostering them (training them, bringing them up, developing them, encouraging them, and promoting their well-being).

Her Bone Is Your Bone, and Her Flesh Is Your Flesh

"For we are members of his body, of his flesh, and of his bones. For this cause shall a man leave his father and mother, and shall be joined unto his wife, and they two shall be one flesh" (Eph. 5:30–31).You should treat her like she is a part of you just like you are a part of Christ and Christ is a part of God. We are related to God, and that is why we are children of God, but it is even more significant than that. Jesus said you must be willing to put your relationship with God above all others like mother and father, sister and brother, and so forth. It is apparent then that this union we have with Jesus is more than just a relationship. We have become part of Him, and God is trying to tell us here that our union with our wives is more than just a relationship; she is part of us now. He says again here that you should leave father and mother and cleave unto your wife. I don't think this was incidental that He worded it this way. This is the leave-and-cleave principle that we talked about.

I think this is addressed to men because they seem to be the ones who have a problem with letting go of their parents. This is especially true with what is known as the "momma's boy." Don't get me wrong. It is important to have a good relationship with your parents, but it is more important to put your wife above that. Don't be the person who brags to your wife all the time about how good your momma's cooking was or how good a housekeeper she was. Your wife doesn't want to hear that. What you should be doing is complimenting her cooking and housekeeping skills instead. Okay, so maybe she isn't that good at it yet. Then brag on something she *is* good at. By the way, don't be one of those guys who is always talking about what he did with his girl friend or ex-wife either. She really doesn't want to hear about that, and she shouldn't have to.

She Is Your Equal

> And the LORD God said, It is not good that the man should be alone; I will make him an help meet for him. (Gen. 2:18)

> And out of the ground the LORD God formed every beast of the field, and every fowl of the air; and brought them unto Adam to see what he would call them: and whatsoever Adam called every living creature, that was the name thereof. (Gen. 2:19)

> And Adam gave names to all cattle, and to the fowl of the air, and to every beast of the field; but for Adam there was not found an help meet for him. (Gen. 2:20)

> And the LORD God caused a deep sleep to fall upon Adam, and he slept: and he took one of his ribs, and closed up the flesh instead thereof. (Gen. 2:21)

> And the rib, which the LORD God had taken from man, made he a woman, and brought her unto the man. (Gen. 2:22)

> And Adam said, This is now bone of my bones, and flesh of my flesh: she shall be called Woman, because she was taken out of Man. (Gen. 2:23)

> Therefore shall a man leave his father and his mother, and shall cleave unto his wife: and they shall be one flesh. (Gen. 2:24)

I find it interesting that God said He was going to make man a helpmeet in verse 18, and then He listed all the animals He had created. The words "help meet" come from the Hebrew words that translate to mean a worthy aide or assistant. The optimal word here is "worthy" to signify equality. This is verified by the fact that after God had created all the animals and birds and fish, He emphasized again that there still wasn't anything in creation that was equal to the man in verse 20. I think God decided that the only way He would be able to create someone else equal to the man was to take part of the man and make the woman. This is why the wife is equal; she is "bone of my bones, and flesh of my flesh." She is equal to me because she was created from me just as my children are equal to me because they too are created from me. This is what God says in verses 21–24. This is the same concept whereby we have become children of God and are therefore worthy to go to heaven. That is only because God gave us part of Himself so we could be one with Him, and that is through the Holy Spirit, who lives inside all born-again believers.

It Is Your Responsibility to Provide for Her

I think most Christians would be surprised how many men, even so-called religious ones, I have heard tell their wives, "This is my money. If you want something, you need to go get your own job and money." Look at this verse: "But if any provide not for his own, and specially for those of his own house, he hath denied the faith, and is worse than an infidel" (1 Tim. 5:8).

In this passage of scripture, the apostle Paul tells his convert Timothy, who is now a pastor, that the church should be accountable only to widows who are alone and have no family to take care of them. In doing so, however, he makes something else perfectly clear: any man who will not support his own family—wife, children, parents, grandparents, brothers, sisters, or anyone else who is part of his family—is worse than a nonbeliever. This is said only about men, not about women. The Bible also teaches that if a man won't work, he shouldn't eat (2 Thess. 3:10). A man should treat his wife like supporting her is his responsibility because it is.

The Marital Home Is Her Domain to Rule

"I will therefore that the younger women marry, bear children, guide the house, give none occasion to the adversary to speak reproachfully" (1 Tim. 5:14). If every person would only do what God designed him or her to do, this person would deprive the devil of any opportunity he might have to tempt him or her to do evil. Everybody knows that the Word of God teaches the husband is to be the head over the wife, and I'm not suggesting anything contradictory to that. What I am going to say is that this verse tells us that the wife should guide, control, direct, and rule her household.

Let's face it: there are some things (a lot of things actually) that women are better at than men. Keeping the house, taking care of the babies, making sure we all have nice clean clothes to wear, and planning and preparing meals are just a few of those things. I think this is because they simply care more about those around them than men do. This isn't limited to domestic items either; women are also great at multitasking and consequently generally make great pilots. Women are just naturally better at taking care of the home, and God essentially says to them, because I designed and created you to take care of your home, this is your job to do as you see fit.

If you, as a husband, are too hardheaded or stubborn to see this, then I can't help you. My wife takes care of all these areas for me, and she enjoys doing so. Personally, I wouldn't change places with her for all the money in the world. I love her, I respect her, I praise her, I adore her, and I trust her for what she does. A smart boss or manager doesn't know how to do everything. He knows how to find people who are good at what they do and leaves them alone to do it.

Now just because I said women are to be keepers at home doesn't mean they should never be allowed to leave the home or get a job outside the home. The home is her primary responsibility, but if she wants to do other things and they don't interfere with her responsibilities, then she should be free to do so. We already saw this message a while ago in Proverbs 31; we saw that the ideal wife takes care of her family's needs, but she also buys, sells, and makes things to sell. She trades with the local merchants. She buys property and grows crops. She helps take care of the poor and needy. A woman who isn't allowed to leave the house cannot do all these things, so don't use the Bible to tell your wife you have the right to make her housebound.

She Is Worth More to You Than a Bag of Rubies

If you treat your wife like she is special the way you should, then she will treat you the same way. My wife and I have a fun little saying at the house: "You are spoiled rotten, just like everyone else around here including me." We spoil each other, and I mean really bad. My wife has found out that she can't just casually mention to me that she would like to have something because she now knows that if she does, I will get it for her if there is any way possible.

A few months ago, she sent me a picture of a fishing boat she saw for sale on the side of the road. She sent a text with the picture that said, "I want this for my birthday." I replied that we had just paid off a bunch of bills, and I just didn't have the money to buy it for her at that time. She said, "I know. I'm just kidding." After I hung up the phone, I went to work, trying to find the boat in the picture and seeking to find a way to scrape up the money. Three hours later after I got off work, I came home with her boat behind my truck. I treat her like she is worth more than everything else I have because she is, and she knows it. But the fact is, she spoils me just as bad. Yeah, I love it. "Who can find a virtuous woman? for her price is far above rubies" (Prov. 31:10).

You Trust Her Totally

"The heart of her husband doth safely trust in her, so that he shall have no need of spoil" (Prov. 31:11). This verse simply says that if you trust your wife totally, she will provide everything you need in this life. You won't need anything else. If you won't let your wife leave the house or have her own transportation—or if you make her tell you her every move all day long—what kind of message are you giving her? This isn't trust; this is just the opposite.

She Satisfies You Completely

> Drink waters out of thine own cistern, and running waters out of thine own well. (Prov. 5:15)

> Live joyfully with the wife whom thou lovest all the days of the life of thy vanity, which he hath given thee under the sun, all the days of thy vanity: for that is thy portion in this life, and in thy labour which thou takest under the sun. (Eccl. 9:9)

> Let thy fountain be blessed: and rejoice with the wife of thy youth. Let her be as the loving hind and pleasant roe; let her breasts satisfy thee at all times; and be thou ravished always with her love. And why wilt thou, my son, be ravished with a strange woman, and embrace the bosom of a stranger? (Prov. 5:18–20)

To be "ravished always with her love" means to be intoxicated, reel from, be enraptured by, or be overtaken with intense joy or pleasure. This is how you should feel about the love you get from your wife. If you feel that way, you can't help but show it, and she will know it. What makes me the happiest is making her happy, and she feels the same way about me.

You Are Happy Being with Her

"Husbands, love your wives, and be not bitter against them" (Col. 3:19).The word translated "bitter" here means jealous, angry, resentful, or hurt due to the feeling of unjust treatment. I have seen many relationships destroyed because of this bitter feeling. Even if you had a jealousy problem at one time but you were able to defeat it, sometimes you have already created a significant amount of bitterness, and your partner isn't able to get past that. When people say things they don't mean, this creates bitterness. You must learn how to forgive and not hold a grudge. Bitterness will destroy your marriage. When your spouse cheats on you, even if you forgive him or her, the situation will create this bitterness. When enough bitterness builds up, it becomes impossible to overcome.

> For in many things we offend all. If any man offend not in word, the same is a perfect man, and able also to bridle the whole body. Behold, we put bits in the horses' mouths, that they may obey us; and we turn about their whole body. Behold also the ships, which though they be so great, and are driven of fierce winds, yet are they turned about with a very small helm, whithersoever the governor listeth. Even so the tongue is a little member, and boasteth great things. Behold, how great a matter a little fire kindleth! And the tongue is a fire, a world of iniquity: so is the tongue among our members, that it defileth the whole body, and setteth on fire the course of nature; and it is set on fire of hell. For every kind of beasts, and of birds, and of serpents, and of things in the sea, is tamed, and hath been tamed of mankind: But the tongue can no man tame; it is an unruly evil, full of deadly poison. Therewith bless we God, even the Father; and therewith curse we men, which are made after the similitude of God. Out of the same mouth proceedeth blessing and cursing. My brethren, these things ought not so to be. Doth a fountain send forth at the same place sweet water and bitter? Can the fig tree, my brethren, bear olive berries? either a vine, figs? so can no fountain both yield salt water and fresh. (James 3:2–12)

I like what the verse says here about setting on fire the course of nature—"and it is set on fire of hell." This is talking about the bitterness that begins to build when someone says things he or she shouldn't say, especially to his or her spouse. This little bitterness that starts is a fire that will continue to grow until it gets out of control. I'm talking about snide remarks, criticism, belittling, bringing up past mistakes, or saying mean or hurtful comments. For a Christian, these things ought not to be so.

Sometimes when you are trying to explain things to men like me, it's best just to say it straight up and not beat around the bush, so I have listed a few things men shouldn't do.

1. Don't leave your wife stranded at home.
2. Don't drive the new car and leave her a heap.
3. Don't make a big argument over small issues. (Choose what is worth fighting over.)
4. Don't ignore her when she is talking (or talk over her).
5. Don't pass off her concerns as insignificant.
6. Don't let discussions turn into arguments. (If you feel tension building, walk away.)
7. Don't get angry and lose control. (Be angry and sin not.)
8. Don't let jealousy control your actions. (Jealousy is not a sin; being out of control is.)
9. Don't try to control or intimidate with fear tactics. (Do you want your spouse to be scared of you?)
10. Don't try to scare her with weapons, even if just playing.
11. Don't be a bully or bossy. (My spouse and I are one.)
12. Don't try to manipulate her. (Controlling behavior is learned.)
13. Don't try to make her feel guilty.
14. Don't ever cheat on her or even consider it. (All actions start with a thought [Matt. 5:28].)
15. Don't abuse your God-given authority over her. (It should be used to provide, protect, and guide.)
16. Don't neglect to comfort her when she needs it.

17. Don't abandon her when she is sick or needs help. (When she doesn't feel good, you should stay with her. She may tell you that you don't have to, but your reply should be, "I know, but I want to.")
18. Don't criticize her family or friends.
19. Don't ever try to do anything for revenge. ("Vengeance is mine saith the Lord" [Rom. 12:19].)
20. Don't ever be physically abusive. (Get help.)
21. Don't ever be mentally abusive.
22. Don't ever be verbally abusive.
23. Don't ever force her to do any sexual acts. (They should be with consent.)
24. Don't say anything to hurt her feelings.
25. Don't cause her to feel remorseful.
26. Don't argue just for the sake of arguing (devil's advocate).
27. Don't keep her from walking away from an argument.
28. Don't curse her or call her names (this behavior causes bitterness).
29. Don't try to punish her; she is not your child.
30. Don't neglect to give her spiritual guidance.
31. Don't try to prove her wrong.
32. Don't try to make her do things you wouldn't do.
33. Don't ever tell her to do anything contrary to God's Word.
34. Don't expect her to be obedient to you if you're not obedient to God.
35. Don't neglect to lead by example.
36. Don't neglect to be kind and answer softly.
37. Don't treat her like she isn't trustworthy.
38. Don't commit acts of vandalism with her things.
39. Don't spend more time with other people than with her.
40. Don't neglect to show interest in things she is interested in.
41. Don't be rude or disrespectful to her friends.
42. Don't grope her in public. (This makes her feel cheap.)
43. Don't check out other women. (This results in jealousy.)

44. Don't ever do anything just because she asked you not to.
45. Don't try to make her angry on purpose. (Nothing good comes from anger.)
46. Don't pick fights.
47. Don't belittle her or her friends.
48. Don't make negative comments about her appearance.
49. Don't neglect to give her compliments.
50. Don't talk about experiences with ex-wives.
51. Don't brag on other women, even your mom.
52. Don't compare anything she does to another woman in a negative way.
53. Don't say or do anything to embarrass her.
54. Don't criticize her parents or other relatives.
55. Don't ever be rude to her family or friends.
56. Don't complain to her about how much she spends on necessary items.
57. Don't forget to take her out now and then.
58. Don't think she doesn't need your attention.
59. Don't neglect to do little things for her.
60. Don't ignore her.
61. Don't forget to compliment her every day.
62. Don't forget to be appreciative.
63. Don't forget to be grateful.
64. Don't neglect to pray for her every day.
65. Don't be quick to anger.
66. Don't forget to be forgiving.
67. Don't be deceitful.
68. Don't lie to her. ("Thou shalt not bear false witness" [Ex. 20:16].)
69. Don't be sneaky or deceitful.
70. Don't neglect to be trustworthy. (If you don't trust her, she won't trust you.)
71. Don't fail to keep your promises.
72. Don't make false promises.

73. Don't hide the truth (being deceitful).
74. Don't be disrespectful (looking at other women).
75. Don't ever give her a reason to doubt your word.
76. Don't forget she is the weaker vessel. (You can actually hurt her by trying to be cuddly.)
77. Don't neglect to tell her how much you love her daily.
78. Don't forget to tell her how much she means to you.
79. Don't forget to be helpful around the house.
80. Don't complain when she asks you for help ("honey dos").
81. Don't hold a grudge against her.
82. Don't store bitterness against her.
83. Don't be cruel to her animals.
84. Don't disrespect anything that belongs to her.
85. Don't ever threaten her with divorce.
86. Don't threaten her with things she is entitled to as your wife (provision, protection, guidance).
87. Don't speak to her harshly.
88. Don't threaten her with a lack of intimacy.
89. Don't forget to show her affection.
90. Don't forget to take out the trash (LOL).
91. Don't expect her to be able to do all the physical things you can.
92. Don't leave her vehicle broken down.
93. Don't put restrictions on her freedom.
94. Don't intentionally destroy anything of hers.
95. Don't take her presence for granted.
96. Don't force her to answer to you for every move she makes.
97. Don't stop her from getting a job, if she wants. (Providing a living is the man's job, but that doesn't mean she can't help if she wants to.)
98. Don't spy on her or have someone else do so.
99. Don't roll your eyes when she asks you to help her with something.
100. Don't act like she is too much trouble.

101. Don't lose the best thing that ever happened to you.

I want to point out one more thing before we move on. God considered it so important for a man to spend time with his wife that He made special rules just for this cause. The Bible says that when a man took a new wife, he wasn't allowed to go off to war or conduct any business that took him away from home for the entire first year of marriage. His task during that first year was to cheer up his wife (to make her happy). Happy wife, happy life. "When a man hath taken a new wife, he shall not go out to war, neither shall he be charged with any business: but he shall be free at home one year, and shall cheer up his wife which he hath taken" (Deut. 24:5).

As a husband, I would like to say here that I understand completely how unnatural it is for a man to continually tell his wife how much he loves her and how important she is to him. But I also know just how much she needs to hear it.

One wife asked her husband, "Why is it that you never tell me that you love me?"

The husband answered, "I told you that when I married you. If I ever change my mind, I will let you know."

Women are insecure creatures, and they need to know where they stand with their husbands all the time. Some are insecure because of the way other men have treated them in the past, and some are so just because God made them emotional creatures, but either way, they need to feel secure in their relationship with their husbands, and that is part of the husband's job.

CHAPTER 13

The Proper Way to Treat Your Husband

The Wife Should Be Submissive

I may as well start out with the elephant in the room. We all know women are instructed to be submissive to their husbands. According to this verse, they should do so as they would submit to the Lord. "Submitting yourselves one to another in the fear of God. Wives, submit yourselves unto your own husbands, as unto the Lord" (Eph. 5:21–22).

Because the Husband Is Held Accountable to God for Her

There are several points I believe should be made here. First, I think it is a lot easier for a wife to submit if she understands that the husband is held accountable to God for her spiritual guidance, as we have already seen. Ladies, if you want your husband to be held accountable to God for your actions, then you need to submit to his instructions just as you would to instructions from the Lord.

When you first read these verses, this seems to be the most obvious interpretation of what the verses say, but I tell you there is more being said here than just that. Verse 21 says that you should submit yourselves to one another in the fear of God. Too often this gets overlooked because it seems to be a contradiction. If the wife is always supposed to submit to her husband, then why does it say they should submit to one another? The qualifier is the second half of the verse: "in the fear of God." If the husband is the spiritual leader he should be, then you should follow him in the fear of God. If the woman is the spiritual leader in the home, then, husband, you should follow her in the fear of God. Paul told us the same thing in 1 Corinthians 7:12–16; there he said that the unsaved wife was sanctified by the saved husband and that the unsaved husband was sanctified by the saved wife.

In the book of Ephesians the Bible says, "Wives be subject to your husbands, as to the Lord." Eph 5:22. This doesn't just mean to obey your husband like you would obey the Lord. I believe it means to obey him in the way in which you obey the Lord. So how do you obey the Lord? Yes, with respect. Yes, without question, but the first thing you should do is make sure it is God who is telling you to do something. The devil is a master at deception and always trying to get you to do things contrary to God's will. After all, this is his job. So how do you know if it is God talking to you?

Every time you think God tells you to do something, you should put it through the test. Is it something that aligns with the Word of God? God won't tell you to do anything that contradicts the instructions He has already given you in His Word. Is it something that will cause you to get closer to God? God won't tell you to do anything that will draw you further away from Him. Is it something that will cause enmity between you and your neighbor? Your neighbor can be anyone. God says you should love your neighbor, so does it result in harm to your neighbor? Is it something that will grieve the Holy Spirit? The Spirit's job is to guide you into a closer relationship with God the Father. If He, the Spirit, lives in you, He will work in you through your conscience. If you can do this thing with a clear, innocent conscience, then it is probably part of God's will for you, but if your conscience tells you something isn't right, even if you can't really put a finger on the problem, you shouldn't do it.

This is called obeying God with discernment. So if you're going to obey your husband as unto God, you should obey him with discernment. The devil can try to deceive you through your husband as well. That being said, it brings up another question. A wife may think to herself, I know that the Lord would never ask me to do anything contrary to His Word, but I don't know that about my husband. After all, the best of men are still just men at best. This is a true statement, and that is precisely why you're not required to obey him if he is trying to make you do something contrary to God's will.

I'd like to point out that it says "your own husbands" and not just any man. God expects you to be submissive to your husband when you acknowledge that it is his job to help you grow spiritually and get closer to God. This doesn't in any way suggest that you should obey any man anytime or anywhere. Finally, to reiterate the previous point, it says "as unto the Lord." I believe this means to do what your husband says when you know God is speaking to you through him. I have already showed you that God generally leads the family through the husband,

Next, the Wife Should Be Submissive Because Her Husband Is the Savior of the Body

"For the husband is the head of the wife, even as Christ is the head of the church: and he is the saviour of the body" (Eph. 5:23). The husband is responsible for his wife's sanctification. We already saw this in 1 Corinthians. This is talking about sanctification, not salvation. The wife isn't saved because the husband is saved. Some religions teach that women can get to heaven only through their husbands; this isn't true. The husband is held accountable to God for keeping his family serving God and growing closer to Him, but he is not the source of their salvation. The last verse dealing with this topic here is saying that the wife should be subject to her husband in all things because he will be the one who has to answer to God for the spiritual state of his family. "Therefore as the church is subject unto Christ, so let the wives be to their own husbands in everything" (Eph. 5:24).

The Wife Should Respect Her Husband

"Nevertheless let every one of you in particular so love his wife even as himself; and the wife see that she reverence her husband" (Eph. 5:33). This verse alone is the key to a successful marriage. If the two partners will practice this behavior every day, they will be fine. They must learn to love and respect one another. At first, I thought *reverence* was a strong word. Back when I was preaching full-time, I didn't care for it when people called me "reverend." I believe only God deserves to receive reverence, but the word translated "reverence" here simply means to show great respect for or to hold in high regard. *Strong's Concordance* says this means, "to be in awe of." The word *awe* means amazement, admiration, mingled with fear. I don't believe a wife should fear her husband, but I do think she should show him respect because of the responsibilities God has put on his shoulders concerning the family. Check out the definition of the word *reverence* here in the 1828 *Webster's Dictionary.* "Fear mingled with respect and esteem; veneration." *Veneration* means "the highest degree of respect and reverence; respect mingled with some degree of awe; a feeling or sentiment excited by the dignity and superiority of a person, or by the sacredness of his character, and with regard to place, by its consecration to sacred services."

Again, I don't believe a husband is superior to his wife, but I believe this speaks to the position of authority God gave to the husband. The definition also includes the statement "by the sacredness of his character, and with regard to place, by its consecration to sacred services." I think the last part of this definition gets us closer to what God is trying to say. If a man is doing what God has told him to do in the family, then he should be treated with the highest form of respect because of the position God has placed him in. This is because of his sacred character and his consecration, which is God's ordination of someone to a sacred position. This term is often used to refer to someone God has ordained to serve in the sacred position of bishop or pastor. I believe that is a good way to see it.

If your husband is being the type of spiritual leader God expects him to be, then he is appointed by God to be the pastor of your home and deserves the same respect as the pastor of your church. I believe that is what Paul was trying to tell the women at the church in Corinth. "Let your women keep silence in the churches: for it is not permitted unto them to speak; but they are commanded to be under obedience as also saith the law. And if they will learn anything, let them ask their husbands at home: for it is a shame for women to speak in the church" (1 Cor. 14:34–35).

What Are Some Ways a Wife Can Show Her Husband Respect?

1. Say encouraging things to him.
2. Make him feel important to you and the family.
3. Say good things about him.
4. Tell him about the things he does that make you feel good.
5. Let him know how much you appreciate his hard work.
6. Tell him about the things you admire about him.
7. Tell him how much you love him.
8. Tell him you appreciate his spiritual guidance.
9. Tell him you admire his abilities and talents.
10. Tell him you are impressed with his interaction with the children.
11. Tell him he is a good husband, a good father, and a good person.

12. Tell him how much you appreciate his big heart and generosity.
13. Tell him you respect him for his character.
14. Tell him you respect him for the sacred position God has given him.
15. Tell him you appreciate him for the way he fills the position God gave him.
16. Support him in all he does.
17. Encourage him to be the leader in the home as God intended.
18. Let him know you support his position and authority.
19. Tell him you trust him for spiritual guidance, protection, and provision.
20. Support him in his spiritual decisions for the home and family.
21. Support all he does, especially in front of other people.
22. Support him in his decisions concerning raising the children.
23. Don't argue with him about the kids in front of the kids.
24. Respect his authority and teach the kids to do the same.
25. Always speak highly of him in public.
26. Be there for him even when he makes mistakes; he is still human.

Now, ladies, I understand that you may think, *My man has a big head already, and I don't want him to become proud and boastful.* I understand this, but I also trust God in his Word, and my personal experience has been a much different reaction. It has been one of humility and inadequacy. It has been an attitude of, "If I am going to be all that she needs me to be, then I need to become more spiritual and closer to God and try to be the man that she needs." This is the reaction of a godly man that wants to fulfill the roll that God intended for him.

The Wife Should Be Well Reported of for Her Good Works

"Well reported of for good works; if she have brought up children, if she have lodged strangers, if she have washed the saints' feet, if she have relieved the afflicted, if she have diligently followed every good work" (1 Tim. 5:10). I know you are wondering what this verse has to do with how a wife should treat her husband. The fact is, the way a man's wife acts in public reflects on the husband significantly. You will be treating your husband well if you have this kind of reputation, the kind of having brought up your children well, having provided shelter for strangers or even family members in need, having served the brothers and sisters in Christ with whatever needs they have, and having always helped those in need. If a man's wife is known for her good works, then so is he. When a woman behaves in a way that is contrary to what God wants for her, she brings shame or dishonor to her husband as well.

"But I would have you know, that the head of every man is Christ; and the head of the woman is the man; and the head of Christ is God. Every man praying or prophesying, having his head covered, dishonoureth his head. But every woman that prayeth or prophesieth with her head uncovered dishonoureth her head: for that is even all one as if she were shaven" (1 Cor. 11:3–5).

The Wife Will Have a Good Reputation of Godliness

> The aged women likewise, that they be in behaviour as becometh holiness, not false accusers, not given to much wine, teachers of good things; That they may teach the young women to be sober, to love their husbands, to love their children, To be discreet, chaste, keepers at home, good, obedient to their own husbands, that the word of God be not blasphemed. (Titus 2:3–5)

349

In like manner also, that women adorn themselves in modest apparel, with shamefacedness and sobriety; not with broided hair, or gold, or pearls, or costly array; But (which becometh women professing godliness) with good works. Let the woman learn in silence with all subjection. But I suffer not a woman to teach, nor to usurp authority over the man, but to be in silence. For Adam was first formed, then Eve. And Adam was not deceived, but the woman being deceived was in the transgression. Notwithstanding she shall be saved in childbearing, if they continue in faith and charity and holiness with sobriety. (1 Tim. 2:9–15)

1. She will behave with holiness (separated from the world).
2. She won't be a false accuser (busybody, gossiper, and so forth).
3. She won't be given to much wine. (In her right mind, she won't be controlled by alcohol, drugs, or anything else.)The Bible teaches, "And be not drunk with wine, wherein is excess; but be filled with the spirit" (Eph. 5:18).
4. She will be a teacher of good things. (Some women teach their daughters, "No man is going to tell me anything." This is not a good thing.)
5. She will teach her daughters to be sober (don't let anything control your mind [for example, alcohol, drugs]).
6. She will teach her daughters to love their husbands.
7. She will teach her daughters to love their children.

8. She will teach them to be discreet (keep personal things private).

9. She will teach them to be chaste (pure, clean, and faithful to their husbands).

10. She will teach them to be keepers at home (being a housewife and mother is the highest calling).

11. She will teach them to be good (just do right).

12. She will teach them to be obedient to their own husbands. (It's not hard to be obedient to someone who is looking out for your best interests. Obedience isn't a bad word. Do you try to be obedient to God or to the things your pastor tells you?) To disobey your husband is to blaspheme the Word of God. (To blaspheme means to speak irreverently of God or the things that pertain to God.)

13. She will dress modestly. (If my wife dressed in a manner that brought attention to her body seductively, it would be embarrassing to me.) She should be known for her inner being, not for her provocative appearance.

14. She will have shamefacedness. This means she is still innocent enough to blush when people talk dirty. She is easily embarrassed. Nowadays most women make me blush by the way they talk.

15. She will have sobriety (she will be sober, clearheaded, abstinent, moderate, and non-indulgent).

16. In church she should be listening and learning in all subjection. (The idea is that her husband is her pastor, as we have already discussed.)

17. She shouldn't exercise authority over men in the church. (This doesn't mean men can't learn

anything spiritual from their wives. It means God put the man in charge of spiritual leadership in the home.) In every organization, someone has to take the lead, or everyone would stray in his or her own direction. This also doesn't mean women shouldn't have positions of leadership in other situations, such as being the leader of a country or an organization. Because God the Father has authority over the Son, and the Son has authority over the church, the husband has authority over the wife. This husband-wife relationship pictures the relationship between the Father and the Son and the Son and the church. Women are also allowed to lead over children or other women even in the church, just not over men.

She is a good person, and everyone knows it. She is the kind of person her husband is proud to be seen with. Ladies, you know what I'm saying. If your behavior makes your husband ashamed to be seen with you in public, then this verse doesn't describe you. "That the Word of God be not blasphemed" means she is a Christian woman, and her behavior reflects this in the way she acts, dresses, deals with other people, and treats her husband. If she claims to be a Christian but her behavior causes people to speak irreverently about her, her husband, or her family, then she isn't acting properly. This makes her, her husband, and God look bad. I suppose we could go on and on about the way husbands and wives should treat each other, but I think you get the idea, so I'll sum it up with *love* and *respect*.

The Wife Will Understand Financial Responsibility

One of the main things couples argue about is money. Provided that the man is the main breadwinner in the home and has charge of the finances, then as I mentioned in the list of things that a man shouldn't do, he shouldn't give her a hard time about how much money it costs to take care of the home, buy food, and so forth. Of course, if she is spending more than the budget can support, then the husband might need to have a talk with her in a calm, polite way. He needs to realize that if he takes care of the bills, she is probably not even aware that she is spending too much with her card. She should have an allotted amount to spend on the household and on herself. If he hasn't given her a budget to follow, then if she overspends, it is his fault, not hers.

I am addressing this issue from the viewpoint that the husband is the main breadwinner in the household and that the wife is allotted what she needs to do what she needs to do, because this is how the situation traditionally works in most homes. Of course, if the wife is the main breadwinner in the home, then these roles would be reversed, but still it should be the same concerning a budget.

I believe every home should have a budget with clear limitations. When there is no budget, the result is always that one of the spouses spends inappropriately, resulting in arguments that could have been avoided. There are numerous resources to obtain a sample budget that can be modified to fit your needs. They are normally based on percentages of available income. Don't forget to take out the tithe. Some people, such as small business owners, have a high gross income, but after overhead is deducted, there is usually not nearly as much income left as most people think. I believe their tithe should be based on the net income after business expenses but before home expenses and taxes are deducted.

The Bible doesn't give a clear example to follow in this situation, but if someone's total business income is $200,000 per year but his or her net income after business expenses is $35,000, then it's reasonable to believe God doesn't expect him or her to pay $20,000 in tithes when your actual income would require only $3,500 in tithes for the entire year.

We shouldn't try to find ways to cheat God out of what is His, but we will have to use a little common sense. The IRS (Uncle Sam) usually makes most people pay around 30 percent of their adjusted gross income. I believe you should pay your Father ahead of your uncle; therefore, your tithe should be based on 10 percent of your adjusted gross income before taxes just like your taxes are. This is just my opinion, but I believe it is based on God's Word with a little common sense thrown in. The rest of your home budget should be set up using what is left of your income after the tithe is taken out. The following is a typical percentage scale for you to experiment with.

Tithe—10 percent
Saving—10 percent
Food—10 to 15 percent
Utilities—5 to 10 percent
Housing—25 percent
Transportation—10 percent
Health—5 to 10 percent
Insurance—10 to 25 percent
Recreation—5 to 10 percent
Personal spending—5 to 10 percent
Miscellaneous—5 to 10 percent

If your adjusted gross income before taxes is $40,000 per year, that comes out to be around $770 per week or $3,333 per month. Based on these figures, your budget would look something like this:

Tithe: $77per week
Savings: $77per week
Food: $77 to 115per week

Utilities: $38.50 to $77per week
Housing: $192.50 per week
Transportation: $77per week
Health: $38.50 to $77per week
Insurance: $77to $192per week
Recreation: $38.50 to $77 per week
Personal spending: $38.50 to $77per week
Miscellaneous: $38.50 to $77per week

Tithe: $330 per month
Savings: $330 per month
Food: $330 to $500 per month
Utilities: $170 to $330 per month
Housing: $833 per month
Transportation: $330 per month
Health: $170 to $330 per month
Insurance: $330 to $833 per month
Recreation: $170to $330 per month
Personal spending: $170to $330 per month
Miscellaneous: $170 to $330 per month

Obviously, these numbers won't work for everyone the same way, but this will give you a general idea. Once you know what your adjusted gross income is, use the percentages in the example above to determine an approximate amount normally spent in each area. The two of you should then sit down together and discuss what changes, if any, need to be worked on, and you should both come to an agreement on the final numbers. If both parties agree that, based on the numbers, this is what needs to be done, then everyone will know what he or she can and can't do without causing problems. Keep in mind that the amounts that are flexible may have to be adjusted to meet needs in areas that aren't.

It should also be pointed out that whatever money is left over after necessities should be split between the husband and wife equally. It doesn't really matter who the primary breadwinner is since the two of you are a team working toward the same goals. Some couples with both the husband and wife working use other methods such as splitting the household bills between the two and each partner having whatever is left of their own income to spend however he or she wants. Personally, I think putting all the money in a pot together and following a budget works best, but that is a preference, not a conviction.

One woman did all the household shopping with a credit card her husband gave her for that purpose. He never said anything to her about how much she was spending. One day her credit card was stolen, and she called her husband and told him right away. After a week or so, she still didn't have a replacement card, so she asked her husband if he had reported her card stolen and gotten a new card. He replied, "I never reported it."

She asked him, "Why not? Aren't you afraid someone is going to use it?"

He said, "They already are, but I didn't report it because they don't spend nearly as much every month as you did."

CHAPTER 14

Man's Divorce

Marriage Was Intended for Life

I titled this book *God's Marriage and Man's Divorce* because we know God intended marriage to be till death. Jesus stated the fact that God never approved of divorce, and it was Moses who allowed that to happen.

> The Pharisees also came unto him, tempting him, and saying unto him, Is it lawful for a man to put away his wife for every cause? And he answered and said unto them, Have ye not read, that he which made them at the beginning made them male and female, And said, For this cause shall a man leave father and mother, and shall cleave to his wife: and they twain shall be one flesh? Wherefore they are no more twain, but one flesh. *What therefore God hath joined together, let not man put asunder.* They say unto him, Why did Moses then command to give a writing of divorcement, and to put her away? He saith unto them, Moses because of the hardness of your hearts suffered you to put away your wives: but from the beginning it was not so.

And I say unto you, Whosoever shall put away his wife, except it be for fornication, and shall marry another, committeth adultery: and whoso marrieth her which is put away doth commit adultery. His disciples say unto him, If the case of the man be so with his wife, it is not good to marry. But he said unto them, All men cannot receive this saying, save they to whom it is given. For there are some eunuchs, which were so born from their mother's womb: and there are some eunuchs, which were made eunuchs of men: and there be eunuchs, which have made themselves eunuchs for the kingdom of heaven's sake. He that is able to receive it, let him receive it. (Matt. 19:3–12 emphasis added)

Jesus addressed several things in these few verses. Many of these we already discussed as we looked at the writings of the apostle Paul in several different places. This passage will serve as a verification concerning the things we already touched on and will also address some things we haven't talked about yet.

1. He made them male and female with the intent of a bond for life (Adam and Eve, not Adam and Steve or Eve and Ericka).
2. The man should leave his parents and cleave to his wife. You should never put your parents above your wife (remember the leave-and-cleave concept).
3. They become one flesh. This is a bond for life and pictures our relationship with God the Father and Jesus Christ and the relationship between Jesus and the church.
4. *What God hath joined together let not man put asunder.* This is where the book title came from. It is perfectly clear here that God put them together for life, but it is man who takes tears them back apart.

5. Moses allowed men to give their wives a bill of divorce and put them away because of the hardness of their hearts. The men were putting away their wives with only a verbal declaration, and this was leaving the women without any recourse. According to the law, they could be remarried if they had an official bill of divorce from their husbands, but if nothing was official, then they couldn't. Moses didn't command divorce. What he did was tell these men that if they were going to put their wives away, then they should put that in writing, which would give the women the right to remarry (Deut. 24:1–4).

6. The reiteration is that Moses allowed this, but from the beginning this was not so.

7. If a man divorces his wife for any reason other than fornication, he commits adultery; and if any man marries her who was divorced by her husband for any reason other than fornication, he also commits adultery. This is the same thing Paul told us already.

8. The disciples said to Jesus that it was better to stay single then. Jesus agreed that this would be true if they could stay single and chaste, also what Paul told us.

9. Jesus affirmed that yes, that is true. But not all men have the ability or gift to be able to stay single and pure. If you can't stay pure, then you can't stay single and be right with God.

Because of the Hardness of Their Hearts

I want to emphasize the fact that divorce was allowed because of the hardness of their hearts. *Hardness of the heart* is derived from the Greek word *sklerokardia*, which addresses the lack of spiritual discernment in their hearts. The word literally means to be destitute of spiritual perception. They simply didn't understand the spiritual significance of the institution of marriage. When a couple gets married, they literally become one ("flesh of my flesh and bone of my bone"). This depicts the joining that takes place between our spirit and the spirit of God at salvation and also the joining of Jesus with the church (born-again Christians) and with God the Father.

> And I will pray the Father, and he shall give you another Comforter, that he may abide with you for ever; Even the Spirit of truth; whom the world cannot receive, because it seeth him not, neither knoweth him: but ye know him; for he dwelleth with you, and shall be in you. I will not leave you comfortless: I will come to you. Yet a little while, and the world seeth me no more; but ye see me: because I live, ye shall live also. At that day ye shall know that I am in my Father, and ye in me, and I in you. He that hath my commandments, and keepeth them, he it is that loveth me: and he that loveth me shall be loved of my Father, and I will love him, and will manifest myself to him. Judas saith unto him, not Iscariot, Lord, how is it that thou wilt manifest thyself unto us, and not unto the world? Jesus answered and said unto him, If a man love me, he will keep my words: and my Father will love him, and we will come unto him, and make our abode with him. (John 14:16–23)

> And because ye are sons, God hath sent forth the Spirit of his Son into your hearts, crying, Abba, Father. Wherefore thou art no more a servant, but a son; and if a son, then an heir of God through Christ. (Gal. 4:6–7)

> Know ye not that your bodies are the members of Christ? shall I then take the members of Christ,

and make them the members of an harlot? God forbid. What? know ye not that he which is joined to an harlot is one body? for two, saith he, shall be one flesh. But he that is joined unto the Lord is one spirit. Flee fornication. Every sin that a man doeth is without the body; but he that committeth fornication sinneth against his own body. What? know ye not that your body is the temple of the Holy Ghost which is in you, which ye have of God, and ye are not your own? For ye are bought with a price: therefore glorify God in your body, and in your spirit, which are God's. (1 Cor. 6:15–20)

Neither pray I for these alone, but for them also which shall believe on me through their word; That they all may be one; as thou, Father, art in me, and I in thee, that they also may be one in us: that the world may believe that thou hast sent me. And the glory which thou gavest me I have given them; that they may be one, even as we are one. (John 17:20–22)

In John 14 we read where Jesus said the Spirit is with you and shall be in you. This is because during the Old Testament times the Spirit didn't indwell people. Instead, God allowed some of His chosen people to be filled with the Holy Spirit when they needed it. "To be filled again" means to be influenced by the Holy Spirit, not indwelled. When Christians get saved today, the Holy Spirit joins with their spirits, and they become one with God. This is what marriage is depicting. Just as marriage was intended to be for the remainder of your physical life, the joining of the Spirit of God with your spirit is intended for the remainder of your spiritual life, which is for eternity. You can be born physically only once, and you can be born spiritually only once. You cannot become unborn from the natural birth, and you cannot become unborn from the spiritual birth. You cannot be unborn, and you cannot be unborn again.

1. If a husband divorces his wife, this pictures Christ rejecting the church (which will never happen).
2. If a wife leaves her husband, this is like the church leaving Christ. (This is one reason our salvation is kept by God, not by us.)
3. Neither of these is even possible because Christ is the head of the church (the body), and the body can't live without the head.
4. It shouldn't be possible for the husband and wife to divorce because the husband is the head and the wife is the body, and the body cannot survive without the head.
5. This event would also indicate that it would be possible for Christ to be separated from the Father, but since Jesus and God are one, we know this is also impossible.
6. In addition, this would suggest that our spirits can be separated from God's Spirit after we are saved, and we know that isn't true either.

Now can you see how these men lacked spiritual understanding?

The Marital Relationship Is More Significant Than Blood Relations

The second thing I want to say in this chapter is that God hates divorce. I think, by what I have showed you already, that you are starting to understand why this is true, but you need to see why marriage is even more significant than blood relations. The following verses are some we already looked at earlier, but it's important to understand that God literally hates divorce because of what it causes as well as what it suggests is possible in the spiritual realm when it isn't true. We looked at these verses briefly in the chapter dealing with how a husband should treat his wife, but there is much more we can glean from these verses about marriage and divorce, so I want to go through them verse by verse.

"Judah hath dealt treacherously, and an abomination is committed in Israel and in Jerusalem; for Judah hath profaned the holiness of the LORD which he loved, and hath married the daughter of a strange god. The LORD will cut off the man that doeth this, the master and the scholar, out of the tabernacles of Jacob, and him that offereth an offering unto the LORD of hosts" (Mal. 2:11–12).Verses 11–12 provide the context for this conversation. The men of Israel were divorcing their godly wives and trading them in for women of the land of Canaan. These women were the daughters of men who worshipped false gods. Then they couldn't understand why God wouldn't accept their sacrifices or answer their prayers. God made it plain to them in the next few verses precisely why this was the case.

This reminds me of a story I heard years ago about a man who told his wife jokingly that since she had turned forty, he was going to trade her in on two twenties. She answered him by saying, "That's not going to happen because you're not wired for two twenty." If you didn't get that, ask an electrician.

"And this have ye done again, covering the altar of the LORD with tears, with weeping, and with crying out, insomuch that he regardeth not the offering any more, or receiveth it with good will at your hand" (Mal. 2:13). I believe the correct interpretation of this verse is that these were the tears of the men who had divorced their wives and gone after strange gods because of their new wives. The result was the betrayal or treacherous treatment of God and the ex-wives of these men. Because of this, God wouldn't listen to their words or answer their prayers. The bottom line is this: if your relationship isn't right with your wife or husband, it will cause God to refuse to listen to or answer your prayers.

"Likewise, ye husbands, dwell with them according to knowledge, giving honour unto the wife, as unto the weaker vessel, and as being heirs together of the grace of life; that your prayers be not hindered" (1 Peter3:7).There are two different offenses mentioned here. The first is the fact that these men had dealt treacherously with their wives by divorcing them. In this instance, "dealt treacherously" (Mal. 2:14) means being unfaithful to their real wives. God obviously didn't recognize these divorces or the new marriages and simply considered these men to be committing adultery against their real wives.

Second, they were committing an abomination against the Lord by marrying these heathen women. God had forbidden these marriages because He didn't want the Israelites to be corrupted by worshipping false gods. Here the word *abomination* refers to the practice of idolatry, which is abhorrent to God. As we mentioned before, this is God's definition of a mixed marriage.

"Yet ye say, Wherefore? Because the LORD hath been witness between thee and the wife of thy youth, against whom thou hast dealt treacherously: yet is she thy companion, and the wife of thy covenant" (Mal. 2:14). Herein lies the proof that God still considered these men to be married to their first wives. God says He was the witness between them and the wives of their youth. As I said before, one of the aspects of a marriage is a commitment, covenant, or promise the couple makes to each other before God as a witness. God continues by saying that the only thing that has happened here is that you have been unfaithful to her ("dealt treacherously"). Nothing has changed in the eyes of God; she is still the companion God made for him ("yet is she thy companion"). In other words, she is still the one you made the promise to, and I'm holding you to it ("and the wife of thy covenant").

One Wife for One Life

"And did not he make one? Yet had he the residue of the spirit. And wherefore one? That he might seek a godly seed. Therefore take heed to your spirit, and let none deal treacherously against the wife of his youth" (Mal. 2:15).

God continues to explain by saying, *And did not he make one* (Mal. 2:15). When Adam and Eve were created God only made one wife for Adam and Adam and Eve became one. *Yet had he the residue of the spirit.* If I had wanted Adam to have more than one wife, I still had the power of the Spirit to do so. I could have made as many wives as I wanted for Adam or for you, but My plan was and is, one wife for one life. *And wherefore one,* And so you ask, Why did I only want you to have one wife, just as I did Adam? *That he might seek a godly seed,* That is because it is more difficult to raise godly children in a home where there is or has been more than one wife or husband. *Therefore take heed to your spirit,* Therefore you should listen to your inner voice, which is giving you sensible or rational expression, or listen to your conscience. *And let none deal treacherously against the wife of his youth,* do not continue to be unfaithful to the wife you took first. God's design for the family has always been one wife for one life or for women, one man is God's plan. This union was intended for life and is a covenant to each other with God as your witness.

The main reason Malachi gives for this singular covenant (one man, one woman) is because it makes it easier to raise godly children. I believe this reaffirms the fact that we are getting further and further away from God in America because of the breakdown of the home and the family. Unfortunately you do not see a lot of preachers, or teachers of God's Word coming out of broken families. I'm not saying this is impossible or that it never happens but it certainly is true that it is harder to raise a godly seed in this type of environment.

God Hates Divorce

"For the LORD, the God of Israel, saith that he hateth putting away: for one covereth violence with his garment, saith the LORD of hosts:

therefore take heed to your spirit, that ye deal not treacherously" (Mal. 2:16).

Now that God has made it clear what His plan was concerning marriage and why, He is going to tell us why He hates divorce. Divorce is the one thing God plainly says in the Word of God that He hates. He says through Malachi in verse 16 that He alone is the LORD God of Israel and hates the "putting away" of the wife of your youth. "Putting away" is divorce, and the wife of your youth is your first marriage. Why, because "one covereth violence with his garment."

In the Hebrew days, they had a custom. When the future bride and groom became engaged, the man took his robe and draped it around his prospective bride as a symbol of protection and care that he was going to provide for her as her husband. Therefore, to cover one with the garment was a representation of marriage. To say that "one covereth violence with his garment" means that he is treating cruelly or treacherously the one he promised to protect. Then He concludes once again by saying, Do not "deal … treacherously" with your wife (commit adultery against her).This God hates.

Now I understand that for many, the one-wife or one-husband scenario is now water under the bridge, and there is nothing you can do about that. Unfortunately, it isn't an ideal world we live in, and divorce cannot always be prevented. For those of you who have already had a divorce that wasn't justifiable in the sight of God, all I can say is that you should ask God for forgiveness and move on. Just because you no longer have the opportunity to live under ideal circumstances doesn't mean you can't still be in God's will and have a good Christian life and relationship. God never stops forgiving, and you have a fresh start. Jesus said, "Neither do I condemn thee, now go and sin no more" (John 8:11).

Some Devastating Effects of Divorce in the USA

During a marriage most couples promise a love that will last a long time. But in the case of America, one out of two marriages ends in the courtroom. This shocking US divorce statistic is a reality. There are many causes and reasons behind it, and at times it is difficult to understand them. No matter, the impacts of it are both short termed and long termed. So before you decide to terminate your marriage, you must be aware of the effects. Most people aren't prepared for the changes they need to face in post-divorce life.

Effects on Children

Statistics show that each year, over one million American children suffer the decision made by their parents to end a relationship. The whole process can be a devastating experience for the children as well as the parents involved. It has physical, emotional, and financial effects on children. Children's reactions to the decision of their parents regarding dissolution of marriage depends on three factors: the quality of their relationship with each of their parents before the separation, the intensity and duration of the parental conflict, and the parents' ability to focus on the needs of children. Some of the broad impacts of divorce on children are the following:

Children become the victims of abuse because their parents have terminated their marriage. Also they are prone to more health, behavioral, and emotional problems that ultimately lead to drug abuse and even suicide.

The academic performances of such children are poor. Statistics show that such children are more likely to drop out of school than children from one-time-married couples.

Children from broken homes are much more likely to have a difficult time obtaining and maintaining steady employment.

The children of parents who have ended their marriage are more likely to become "teen parents," producing out-of-wedlock babies, than the children of lifelong married parents.

Such children are three times more likely to have emotional or behavioral problems than they will have if their biological parents stay together.

When parents end their marriage, there is a dramatic change in children's attitudes toward sexual behavior. Children's approval of premarital sex and cohabitation, and divorce rises dramatically, while their endorsement of marriage and childbearing is reduced.

Following a divorce, most mothers have to work full-time; this combination of divorced and full-time working mothers leads to the highest levels of sexual activity in teenagers.

Children of divorced parents move away from their families of origin more than children of intact marriages.

To a large degree, the marital instability of one generation is passed on to the next. This lowered quality of marriage for children of divorced couples is a big matter of concern.

Divorce gives birth to higher levels of jealousy, moodiness, infidelity, conflicts over money, and excessive drinking and drug use among children.

Daughters of divorced parents find it more difficult to value their femininity or to believe they are genuinely lovable.

Sons of divorced parents frequently demonstrate less confidence in their ability to relate with women, either at work or romantically.

Children in the age-group of three to five often face disturbances in sleeping patterns and become very attached to their parents due to fear of separation.

Children in the age-group of six to eight are more open about their grief to the departed parent and often have fantasies about their parents reuniting.

Children in the age-group of eight to eleven feel a lot of anger and powerlessness, and tend to favor and care for one parent over the other.

For children in the age-group of twelve to eighteen, the grief becomes more intense, and they tend to focus more on the moral issues causing them to judge their parents and become more fearful about relationships they will have in the future.

Such children also demonstrate an earlier loss of virginity, more cohabitation, higher expectations of divorce, higher divorce rates later in life, and less desire to have children.

Effects on Parent-Child Relationships

The relationship between children and separating parents often becomes less strong due to the emotions and negative feelings that come from the whole process.

It is hard for parents to recognize that their child is struggling because they get so caught up in their own feelings.

At times children can even feel responsible to look after their parents and make sure they are both mentally and physically okay.

If the parent doesn't make an effort to comfort his or her children, they often feel inadequate and abandoned.

Children can also become overwhelmed if one of the parents becomes involved with someone else.

The rate of bonding between stepparents and stepchildren is rather low. This is because there are fewer "parental feelings" toward their stepchildren.

Effects on Society

Family is the building block of society, and marriage is the foundation of the family. However, this foundation is growing weaker, with fewer adults entering marriage and more adults terminating it. The higher US divorce rate is having profound effects on society.

A recent US longitudinal study found that children without biological fathers in the home are roughly three times more likely to commit a crime leading to incarceration compared to children from intact families.

Also, children of divorced parents are significantly more likely to become delinquent by age fifteen compared to children living with their parents.

Often children of divorced parents don't marry and start families of their own, a phenomenon that can disturb social harmony.

Financial Effects

It's impossible to ignore the fact that divorce itself can be a financial hurdle. When you file a petition in court, you need to pay a lot of money. It's difficult to predict how much it will cost, but it ranges from $10,000 to $20,000 depending on the state where you reside and the complexity of your case. In the end, many families usually suffer financially.

For families that weren't poor before the divorce, the drop in income can be as much as 50 percent.

As the source of income becomes half and expenses are increasing, there is always a decline in the standard of living a couple enjoyed while married.

A drop in parents' income directly affects children over time in terms of proper nutrition, involvement in extracurricular activities, clothing, and school choices.

Sometimes a parent who stayed home with the children is forced into the workplace, and the children need to spend time in childcare.

The payment of child support to the custodial parent causes a severe reduction in household income.

As assets are divided in a divorce, this means assets acquired during the marriage by either spouse will generally be divided equally.

Other Important Facts

The overall effects differ by situation and personal circumstance and may be different for men and women.

Life expectancies for men and women who have ended their marriages are significantly lower than for married people.

Divorced men and women are more likely to suffer from health complications of some kind. This is mainly due to the emotional trauma of the whole legal process and its long-term impact on physical health.

Both men and women suffer a decline in mental health following the legal order. This is why there are more cases of depression and hostility among divorced men and women.

Alcoholism is much more likely to be a problem among those who have been divorced than among those who haven't.

The suicide rate is almost three times higher among the divorced than among lifelong spouses.

Divorced people are more likely to have problems with depression and other mental problems.

When divorce takes place, it often leads to disruption in religious practices. The diminished practice of religion, in turn, can have negative consequences.

Looking at the various impacts of divorce, it becomes essential for the US government to establish a goal to reduce the rate. This can be done by establishing pro-marriage education and mentoring programs to teach couples how to develop skills to handle conflict and enhance the marital relationship. Also, experts believe that by ending "no-fault" provision for parents with children under age eighteen, they can make a drastic change in the overall divorce rate in the USA. Also, states should organize innovative programs and classes to promote the idea that marriage is the best environment in which to raise healthy, happy children, who can achieve their potential, and that the family is the most important institution for social well-being.

David Boudreaux

To conclude, the decision to end a relationship can be traumatic, chaotic, and filled with contradictory emotions. So, before you make the final decision regarding divorce, always try to analyze the whole situation and then take a step only when you have exhausted all other possibilities of a resolution. [6]

Final Words from the Author

Perhaps the reason the Lord allowed me to go through so many bad relationship experiences in my life was so He could use me to help Him, to keep these same things from happening to other people. I'm not suggesting that God brought anything on me. I know that just like when you jump off a building you can expect to hit the ground, the difficult things I have experienced in my life are the results of my own actions. I only wish that I would have understood the warnings God had already told us about through His Word concerning these consequences. How I wish I would have known some of the things God has now taught me. My goal and prayers are that you will have clear, defined, and understood guidance in these areas that I didn't have. What I would have given to know some of the things I now know.

Personally, I believe going through a divorce is one of the most devastating things a person can go through on this earth. I know it is difficult to lose someone through death, but at least when this happens, you know that the person you loved and trusted above all others didn't betray your trust and abandon you on purpose. This is especially true when divorce involves children. I can tell you that when this happens, it feels like you are being ripped apart from the inside. For those of you who have experienced this, you know what

---

[6] Some Devastating Effects of Divorce in the USA
https://www.divorcestatistics.info/some-devastating-effects-of-divorce-in-the-usa.

I mean; and for those of you who have not, it is hard to express in comprehendible terms.

There are no words that can describe the emotional stress or unfathomable pain that is experienced. It is the kind of pain that will cause you to seek relief regardless of the cost. I have never felt this kind of pain physically, even though I have suffered physically in many ways. Cuts, tears, bruises, and broken bones don't even come close to the pain you can experience in the heart when you lose all those you have sworn to keep and hold most precious, with God as your witness. Those you love more than you do yourself. Those who are part of you. Those you vowed to God that you would spend your life providing for and protecting no matter the cost, even unto death.

I can vividly remember spending hours hurting, crying, and begging God and those around me in the emergency room to do something to help me end the pain. I pleaded with them to give me medication that would stop the hurt, put me to sleep, or even take my life if that was what it took to stop the pain. I can remember breaking down on the job and crying aloud in front of my coworkers for someone to help me. I can remember pulling over on the side of the road and crying my eyes out as I watched a happy family walk down the street hand in hand. I also know that the damage done between the parents and children can never be completely restored.

People will tell you that after your children get older you can restore your relationship with them. This is only partially true at best. You may have the opportunity to start a new relationship with them, but it won't be the relationship you had. You will be more like a friend of theirs and not the father or mother—or daughter or son— relationship you lost. Your children are the most impressionable when young, and if you don't get the chance to spend that time with them, you won't influence them in a good or bad way. Boys need their fathers, and girls need their mothers. This is what God intended. When a divorce takes place, no one wins, and the children suffer the most. I believe this is why families are falling apart and drugs have gone rampant in our country. This is why churches are empty and streets are full of crime. This is why jails and prisons are so full that criminals are being set free, and the government is doing dumb things like legalizing the poisonous drugs being handed out on the streets.

If you are in a marriage that is falling apart, please consider these things before throwing in the towel. The damage that will result cannot be repaired. I know that if your spouse has cheated on you that you believe there is no way you can stay with him or her. I'm telling you that the pain you have felt because of this betrayal is nowhere close to the pain that results from a divorce. I know God said that if your spouse commits adultery, then you have grounds for divorce, and I can't argue with this statement; but I can tell you that grounds for divorce doesn't necessarily always mean divorce is the only answer. God hates divorce, remember.

God also told us that when these men put away their wives and took in other women, they were dealing treacherously with their wives. In other words, even though they had taken new wives, God still considered them married and committing adultery on their previous wives (Mal. 2:16). It is difficult, but unfaithfulness can be forgiven, and what was wrong in the relationship that caused the unfaithfulness can be repaired. I can only imagine what it feels like to be cheated on, but I have witnessed this pain; and even though it is horrible and difficult to overcome, with proper counseling it is possible. Getting over the devastation caused by a divorce, especially with children involved, is a whole other thing.

If you are a spouse who has been cheated on, just consider the fact that whatever caused this situation can be fixed; and that should you decide to divorce because of it, your decision will have devastating consequences for everyone involved. If you are divorced, then both Paul and Jesus said it would probably be best if you stayed single and devoted all of yourself to serving God. But if you could do that, you probably wouldn't have been married to begin with. This may be possible if you are now older and more dedicated to God than when you married the first time, such as

Paul said about older widows, but if you are a young woman or man, it isn't likely you will be able to stay single and pure. If your husband or wife has died or has moved on and remarried or is living with another person (in a marriage-type relationship), then you are free to remarry.

If you have been through all of this and are remarried already, then this is all water under the bridge. Even if you are the one who committed adultery on your spouse and the situation ended up in divorce and that spouse has moved on and remarried someone else, then in my opinion, you are now free. Regardless of whether the circumstances give you freedom from an ex, there is still forgiveness. No matter where you have been concerning marriage and divorce, there is the forgiveness God offers to anyone who will repent and ask for forgiveness. When you are forgiven, the slate is wiped clean. You cannot change the road you have been down whether it was your fault or not. Don't sacrifice the peace of God you can have today because of mistakes you made in the past. As we have seen, in heaven there will be no marriages or genders, so all that happens on earth stays on earth if you have been saved and forgiven.

I have had people tell me that if you have been divorced and are remarried, even if your ex has moved on in another relationship, that if you get saved or decide you want to get right with God, then you will have to divorce your new spouse and go back to the first one or just stay single. I do not agree with that statement. If your ex has moved on then you are freed from them. If you just got saved then Paul told us to stay in whatever relationship you are in when it happens. Now if the new spouse is not saved and they decide they don't want to be with you anymore then you should let them go. After all this is accomplished and you still feel guilty in your conscience toward God just remember when you get saved the slate is wiped clean. If that still doesn't relieve your conscience then ask God to forgive you for the mistakes you have made and move on. You cannot back up and undo what has already been done. A second divorce will never undo the first one. Two wrongs never make a right.

I think the key here is "Go and sin no more" (John 8:11). The thing is, anything you have done in the past and have repented and asked for forgiveness for is in the past and should stay there, but it can't be in the past if you are still doing it. You can't tell God that you are sorry for living in a sinful situation and ask Him for forgiveness unless you are going to stop living in the sinful situation. If you know something is sinful and yet aren't willing to stop doing it to receive God's forgiveness, then you cannot be forgiven for that sin until you do. So now, if you have stopped doing the sin and asked God to forgive you, then you can't go back to it again. Thus Jesus said, "Now go and sin no more." Jesus knows you aren't capable of living without sin altogether, but He makes it clear here that you cannot be forgiven for a sin you intend to continue to commit or return to. The disciples asked Jesus how many times they should forgive someone. "Seven times?" Jesus replied, "Seventy times seven"(Matt. 18:22).This would suggest that you can be forgiven for committing the same sin over and over an unlimited amount of times provided that you truly were repentant when you asked for forgiveness each time.

Ask someone who is recovering from an addiction how many times he or she asked God to forgive him or her for the same mistake when the person was trying to stop using drugs. You can be sincere in asking God to forgive you with every intention of stopping the sin and then unintentionally return to the sin. If this has happened to you, then you can rest assured that God knows and understands the circumstances causing your failures and temptations, and He will forgive you as many times as it takes. I also understand that you can be caught up in a relationship that causes you to sin over and over in the same way, and He understands that as well; but you can't be forgiven unless you intend to stop the sinful behavior.

I have tried to cover as many areas as possible concerning

marriage, divorce, unfaithfulness, child-rearing, marital intimacy, Christian living, and on and on; but I know I have not covered every possible scenario. I do believe, however, that we have talked about enough different situations to give you a good idea of what God expects in a Christian marriage. Some of these areas, such as codependent relationships, drug and alcohol abuse, dissolution of marriage, and raising children, are very big topics I barely touched on. If you are having trouble in one of these areas, I hope I have given you enough information to at least identify the problem. I would encourage you to either find some Christian books that will help you more or seek out some good Christian counseling from your pastor or another Christian source.

This book's intent is to help you have the kind of marriage God wanted for all Christians who choose to marry. With one in every two marriages in the United States ending in divorce, it is obvious that someone needed to put out some information regarding this topic. I have heard many people say, "I'm sorry I made that mistake, but marriages, husbands, families, wives, and children don't come with instruction manuals." Well, now maybe they can.

My sincere prayer is that this book, which God told me to write with His guidance, will help you and your family be what God wants you to be and have the family and marriage God wants you to have. My suggestion is that both husband and wife, or potential husband and wife, should read this book either together or separately, then get together and discuss these issues. That would be the best way to possibly resolve any potential problems, even before they become problems. This is especially true for couples who are engaged and will be married soon. It is easier to let someone else help you get potential problems out in the open ahead of time and offer solutions than to do so after a problem develops. It is also better for most potential spouses to hear these solutions from a mutual party who has no invested interest in either person involved since this eliminates the possibility of any partiality or favoritism. If this book has helped you or your family in any way, please let me know so I can rejoice with you and pray for God to continually bless you in the future. Please send me an email at <u>tinbender dave@yahoo.com</u>.

May God bless you abundantly.
Your humble servant,
David Boudreaux

Printed in the United States
by Baker & Taylor Publisher Services